Pruitt and Fry
Kriesberg
Palmer
Birn

MW00649468

PEACE

PEACE

Meanings, Politics, Strategies

Edited by
LINDA RENNIE FORCEY

PRAEGER

New York
Westport, Connecticut
London

Copyright Acknowledgments

"Sex and Death in the Rational World of Defense Intellectuals" by Carol
Cohn is reprinted by permission of the University of Chicago Press,
Signs: Journal of Women in Culture and Society, Vol. 12, #4 (Summer
1987): 687–718.

"America's 'New Thinking' " by Daniel Yankelovich and Richard Smoke
is reprinted by permission of *Foreign Affairs*, Fall 1988. Copyright 1988
by the Council on Foreign Relations, Inc.

Library of Congress Cataloging-in-Publication Data

Peace : meanings, politics, strategies / edited by Linda Rennie
  Forcey.
       p. cm.
    Bibliography: p.
    Includes index.
    ISBN 0–275–92833–0 (alk. paper).—ISBN 0–275–92834–9
  (pbk. : alk. paper)
     1. Peace.   I. Forcey, Linda Rennie.
  JX1952.P338 1989
  327.1'72—dc19   89–3625

Library of Congress Catalog Card Number: 89–3625
ISBN: 0–275–92833–0
       0–275–92834–9 (pbk.)

First published in 1989

Praeger Publishers, One Madison Avenue, New York, NY 10010
A division of Greenwood Press, Inc.

Printed in the United States of America

The paper used in this book complies with the
Permanent Paper Standard issued by the National
Information Standards Organization (Z39.48–1984).

10 9 8 7 6 5 4 3 2 1

To My Mother and Father

Contents

Acknowledgments

I want to thank all the contributors to this volume. The genesis of this collection of essays was a conference at the State University of New York at Binghamton entitled "Toward a Paradigm for Peace: The Interrelationship Between Personal and Political Change," funded by the Conversations in the Disciplines Program of the State University of New York. Eight of these sixteen essays are revised papers from the conference—those from Betty Reardon, George Sackman, Christine Sylvester, Immanuel Wallerstein, Dean Pruitt, Louis Kriesberg, Donald Birn, and Warren Wagar. Five of the essays were solicited for this book by the editor—those from Hal Nieberg, Elise Boulding, Michael Klare, Glenn Palmer and Charles Hauss. Two of the essays, those by Carol Cohn, and Daniel Yankelovich and Richard Smoke, have been printed elsewhere. I also wish to thank my son and daughter-in-law, Peter and Annie Nash, for their helpful suggestions, my editor, Alison Bricken, for her encouragement along the way, and my husband for his patience.

I

Meanings

1

Introduction to Peace Studies

Linda Rennie Forcey

> The aim is to find (or create) an authentic public space, that is, one in which diverse human beings can appear before one another as, to quote Hannah Arendt, "the best they know how to be."
>
> —Maxine Greene, *The Dialectic of Freedom*

Something is happening. Peace studies is sweeping across the nation. There are currently more than 300 colleges and universities offering peace studies courses, with more than 150 having programs. The students and educators involved in peace studies recognize that both the material and spiritual survival of the human race demand education for peace. Many realize how much we have been educated to expect war, not peace. Although there is the threat of nuclear holocaust and an end to planetary life, most of use believe war inevitable—a part of the human condition, a necessary evil, a reality. "Live free or die," a slogan printed on New Hampshire license plates, reflects one of the most unquestioned values of citizenship. Electoral politics often focuses on men's war records. Our memories of war, nurtured by political propagandists, capture our fondest dreams, as well as our worst fears. We have unthinkingly and unquestioningly come to know, expect, love, and revere war.

Peace is a different story. Superpower summit talk aside, we have not been taught to think about peace. Although most of us seek some sort of meaningful peace in our personal lives, we see peace in the global sense as merely the absence of war, like the eye of some ever-lasting hurricane. Yet we also know that nuclear war would settle nothing and lead to a fiery end to all life on earth. We are aware that wars can no longer be a primary method for settling social, political, and economic differences. Virtually every "limited war" pushes us to-ward the brink of the final war. We must dare to think about global peace. More than forty years have passed since Albert Einstein pro-phesied unparalleled catastrophe were we not to change our thinking. Learning how we should change our thinking is peace studies.

The field of peace studies is relatively new, with broad parameters. It is, according to one useful guide:

an interdisciplinary academic field that analyzes the causes of war, violence, and systemic oppression, and explores processes by which conflict and change can be managed so as to maximize justice while minimizing violence. It en-compasses the study of economic, political, and social systems at the local, national and global levels, and of ideology, culture, and technology as they relate to conflict and change.[1]

Peace studies investigates these many dimensions of human life from a wide range of ideological and philosophical perspectives. As those of us involved are well aware, this broad definition mandates for its prac-titioners something more than we normally associate with traditional academic fields of study. It cannot be "taught" the traditional way—beginning with the assumption that the teacher is the only one who "knows." The Brazilian educator Paulo Freire describes traditional education as the "banking" method, whereby the teacher literally fills the student's "bank account" by "depositing" (or expounding) infor-mation that the student is expected to "store" (or memorize).[2] In peace studies, the teachers must dare to think aloud with students because the teachers also are unabashedly struggling to find answers. As a group, teachers are often deeply divided in their understandings of peace, their political ideologies or world views, and their approaches to the field. Few questions they pose can have "right" answers; nor can there be simple, unified approaches. Rather, there are as many strat-egies as there are paths to peace. This is the challenge of peace studies.

Peace studies attracts those who seek a more liberating education, one that demands a willingness of both teachers and students to assume personal and social responsibility for lifelong education. It is neither for the tender- nor tough-minded, but rather for those who are a mix-ture of both. The peace studies practitioner needs an appreciation of the role of personal values in the analysis of economic, political, and social structures that give shape to those issues. Ideally, she or he should have an enthusiasm for the Socratic approach to learning, self-consciousness in world view or ideological perspective, great tolerance for the human condition, and a global vision.

This volume thus seeks to challenge and to invite serious thinking about the study of peace. Thinking is reflecting on and examining the cliches and conventional codes of expression that govern our ordinary activities. It is detaching ourselves from our prejudices. Thinking about peace, like thinking about anything else, is difficult, sometimes exhausting. It has little to do with intelligence or stupidity or goodness or wickedness. It does not deal solely with abstract or impersonal mental processes, but includes intuitive and emotional mental processes that govern our personal relationships. Thinking about peace is a quest for meaning that does not necessarily lead to comforting answers, or answers suitable for all times and places.

There are certain moments in history when, as philosopher Hannah Arendt has written, thinking itself "ceases to be marginal . . . When everybody [at such moments] is swept away unthinkingly by what everybody else does and believes in, those who think are drawn out of hiding because their refusal to join is conspicuous and thereby becomes a kind of action."[3] This is such a moment. Peace studies students and educators are in the process of becoming thinkers in action. "Remember," Arendt counsels us, "Socrates called himself a gadfly: He knows how to arouse the citizens who, without him, will 'sleep on undisturbed for the rest of their lives,' unless somebody else comes along to wake them up again. And what does he arouse them to? To thinking, to examining matters, an activity without which life according to him, was not only not worth much but was not fully alive."[4] This volume aspires to gadfly status. Its chapters are meant to prickle, bite, or annoy us into thinking deeply about peace. It does this mainly by attempting to bring into focus the complex interrelationship of the personal and the structural dimensions of peace. From a wide variety of perspectives, it forces us to question and examine our own values in preparation for becoming peace thinkers in action.

Another objective is to present within a single volume a number of approaches to the study of peace, to better appreciate the total phenomenon of peace studies. In the fable of the elephant and the three blind men, the first man decides the elephant's prickly tail is a thick rope, the second mistakes its trunk for a rubber hose, while the third is certain the elephant's leg is a tree. Each arrives at a logical but false conclusion based on limited perspective. Each, with possibly fatal consequences, totally misses the complete picture. Peace Studies, like the elephant, is much more than it seems. This does not mean that all peace studies programs do, or should embrace all the components of the broad definition given above. The spectrum of courses under the rubric of peace studies ranges from arms control or security studies, international relations, and conflict resolution, to courses on nonviolence, hunger, human rights, civil rights, the environment, women's oppression, family violence and child abuse.[5] Some programs attempt many approaches; others focus either on such empirically oriented fields as political science, or the more visionary, social justice-oriented fields. Because none of us can hope to study peace in its entirety, we need to avoid becoming "a jack of all trades and master of none." We must make choices.

The third objective of this volume is to encourage active thought about the meanings we intuitively and consciously give to peace. It attempts to reveal the ways in which our politics might guide us to a committed approach to peace studies that suits us best. Students of peace must seek not only to avoid cynicism and apathy, but also the plain sloppy thinking that results from trying to do too much. This volume, therefore, invites clear choices as to the kind of education for peace that students and educators can best pursue together.

THE MEANINGS OF PEACE

How we find meanings for peace affects the way that we will think about it, and ultimately what we will have to say about it. Definitions of peace range from the absence of war among nations, to nonviolent resolution of strife within our communities, and to the serenity that follows resolution of internal conflicts. Correspondingly for war, the definitions range from violent conflict between nations or groups of nations, to crusades against such things as poverty, drugs or pornography, and to contention between the sexes.

Seeking greater clarity of discourse, many peace educators define peace as either negative or positive—with negative peace meaning only the absence of war, and positive peace incorporating the promotion of social justice issues as well. Any definition of positive peace must include an implicit set of normative assumptions about the nature of justice and priorities for a better world order. A set of normative assumptions is articulated by peace educator Betty Reardon in the chapter that follows this introduction. In the concluding chapter of Part I, sociologist Elise Boulding argues that a primary challenge facing "positive peace" proponents is to marshall sufficient social imagination about the meaning of peace to generate a vision for a better world order.

Most peace studies curricula embrace a broad definition of positive peace. The peace studies program at the State University of New York (SUNY) Binghamton, for example, seeks to maximize breadth. It purports to "explore organized nonviolence and violence; their relationship to society, behavior, and consciousness; and ways of working toward a just and harmonious world community." It also raises such cognate issues as "genetic and familial influence, male and female roles, the function of authority and coercion in domestic and business life, the structural violence implicit in unjust social relations, the role of ideologies in shaping national policy, the organization of science and technology, the place of religion in human culture, and visions of nonviolence and violence in literature and the arts."[6]

Such a broad definition of positive peace invites the charge of being so all-inclusive as to negate any legitimacy for this field of inquiry. Such is the theme of political scientist Hal Nieburg, who, in Part I, argues that human nature and the world of nation states being what they are, it is unrealistic and, therefore, meaningless to equate peace with social justice. To do so inevitably leads us into murky issues concerning ideal society. It is more expedient, he argues, to minimize the issues of equity while accepting the ways in which the term "peace" has normally been used in fields such as political science.

Nieburg's chapter well exemplifies what peace studies defines as the "negative" approach, whose adherents fall loosely into two schools: tough-minded realists who see the nation-state as the ultimate source of security and legitimacy, and tender-minded internationalists (sometimes called idealists) who find only international institutions the ultimate source of peace. Realists in the United States have, until very recently, focused on the post-World War II policy of nuclear deterrence in a bi-polar (two great powers) world as the only viable way to peace. According to this argument, we have peace (often called strategic stability) in the world because the United States has sufficient nuclear and long-range bomber capability to threaten the Soviet Union with unacceptable punishment if it should begin a war.

Because traditional nuclear deterrence policy is an extremely costly and dangerous psychological process, realists are increasingly talking about alternatives. For example, the principle of "minimum deterrence" was formally placed on the table by General Secretary Gorbachev in 1987. He said: "The Warsaw Treaty states have addressed NATO and all European countries with a proposal on reducing armed forces and armaments to a level of reasonable efficiency."[7] This message from Gorbachev is thought to mean, according to the *New York Times*, that he supports "an approach in which nuclear force would be reduced to a level that offered no threat to the U.S. but was sufficient to deter attack from abroad...," while yielding strategic nuclear arsenal re-

ductions "a good deal greater than 50%."[8] Some peace studies practitioners argue that the principle of "minimum deterrence" should be a
central component of contemporary peace studies definitions.

The distinction between negative and positive peace is somewhat
unfortunate in that negative implies something bad; however, few
would deny that this distinction contributes to peace thinking in essential ways. In Chapter 4, Carol Cohn, nevertheless, argues that the
language defense experts use to describe both peace and war helps to
determine perceptions of reality. Though we would be reluctant to
admit it, most of us gravitate unconsciously toward either the negative
or positive camps of thinking about peace. We do so because our definitions of peace reflect our core views toward truth and reality, and
our images of self as private and public. We define peace, therefore, as
part of our politics.

THE POLITICS OF PEACE

All of us, as William James reminds us, have a philosophy. In fact,
"the most interesting and important thing" about us is the way our
philosophy determines our perspectives. "It is only partly got from
books;" and he adds, "it is our individual way of just seeing and feeling
the total push and pressure of the cosmos."[9]

This sense of personal philosophy when systematized is often called
ideology or world view. Many social scientists, particularly those involved with peace studies, use the term "paradigm" to describe such
ways of patterning our view of reality. Our paradigms include a set of
beliefs about the nature of human beings and how they should behave,
about the nature of the universe and the way institutions should reg-
ulate society, and about the ways in which we define our security both
as individuals and as citizens. Paradigms are what politics is built
upon, at least in the broad Aristotelian sense used in this book. The
following captures that sense:

Politics is a social act that attempts to resolve the tension between human
needs and social facts. Human beings are born and die with needs. Needs are
food, security, love, self-esteem, and self-actualization. Social facts are conditions that limit or support the satisfaction of needs. The perception of tension
is political consciousness. Acting out of this consciousness is politics.[10]

Although some of us are more politically conscious than others, we are
all political in the sense that we all have a world view. If we didn't,
the information we assimilate about the world would be too chaotic to
think about at all. We cannot think about peace without thinking about
our own and others' world views.

Ideologies are usually related to economic and political systems; in the United States, Japan, and Western Europe, democratic capitalism, in the Soviet Union and its sphere, authoritarian socialism (Marxist-Leninism), and in China and much of the developing world, many variations of these forms. Since the late 1940s, the United States has escalated the ramifications of these ideological differences between itself and the Soviet Union into nothing less than a "Cold War." Yet, within these differing systems, there have always been tensions between a left and a right. In the United States, for example, some favor policies that promote a more equal distribution of wealth, while others favor policies that heavily reward those deemed most deserving. Peace and world security studies scholar Michael Klare argues in Part II that the political implications of these tensions are manifested in the United States' military policy of Low-Intensity Conflict (LIC). Clearly, similar tensions are currently being revealed under the Soviet leadership's *perestroika*.

Our ideologies are not unchanging, however. Recently, political analysts, such as Daniel Yankelovich and Richard Smoke, note a decided shift in Americans' attitudes toward national security issues, the first such shift since the start of the "Cold War." They conclude that although Americans are still suspicious of Soviet intentions, they, like Gorbachev, tend to place less importance on ideological differences between the superpowers and to increasingly view their country's economic power as important as its military. The trend was evident to the *Wall Street Journal* in late 1988 when it noted that the U.S. policy of containment of communism "doesn't fit an era in which the Soviet Union is struggling to restructure its ossified economy, communism is in decline as an ideology, and the American public worries more about economic competition from Japan or terrorist attacks against the U.S. than superpower confrontation."[11]

Our politics are not merely a reflection of where we stand on the global left, middle, and right ideological continuum. Politics arise whenever people engage in social relationships to fill human needs, thus creating the politics of the family, of religion, of business, of the environment, of education, and of the work place. What transpires in the peace studies classroom, for example, is political, from the selection of materials, to the organization of the course, to the revelations of its discourse. Engineering professor, George Sackman, opens Part II of this volume by describing how his political thinking ultimately led him to change his job and uproot his family. Politics, Sackman's chapter suggests, is about the personal as well as the political (to use the feminist slogan of the 1960s). Politics is about how we approach social relationships and identify human needs, and it depends upon many factors including our basic genetic makeup, familial backgrounds, race, class, ethnicity, and gender.

Gender is the factor that has particularly engaged both teachers and students. Many feminists argue that because of differences in the socialization of men and women, women think differently from men.[12] Women, they argue, tend to recognize the reality of interdependence and connectedness; they seem to be more concerned about caring for others. Women have a greater sensitivity than men to moral shadings, and to ambiguities and uncertainties in human life that cannot be reduced to a mathematical equation of rights and wrongs.

Feminist peace researchers argue that, on a personal level, women are more inclined toward an ethic of peaceful resolution.[13] My own experience with peace studies classes tends to confirm this observation. The women, by and large, express very different ideological perspectives from the men. These differences govern their choices of topics for term papers and classroom projects. Women tend to choose topics of an interpersonal nature, topics that involve themes centering around personal responsibility, nurturing relationships, and change within individuals. On the other hand, men tend to select topics that deal with broader, less personal themes of peace, and particularly themes of war. A growing number of feminist peace researchers (both women and men) regard the nurturing traits, so frequently associated with women, as strengths rather than weaknesses. They see an ethic of caring as an essential component of the peace studies curriculum.

Even so, the stereotypical image of the peaceable fairer sex, like all stereotypical images, is highly questionable in the realms of global politics. The record shows that women generally follow the leadership of their respective countries on issues of war versus peace. This might be explained by the fact that women, generally, have been absent from the public decision-making processes that place us where we are today. Their sphere of influence has largely been limited to the private, or interpersonal. They are less inclined, therefore, to think systematically and politically. Political scientist Christine Sylvester argues from a feminist perspective, that the arms race and other national security priorities have been major factors in the subordination of women. Future peace research may well show that other determining variables such as class, race, and ethnicity similarly affect women's thinking about peace.

The personal political implications of Immanuel Wallerstein's discussion of "Peace and War in the Modern World-System" in the concluding chapter of Part II are more problematic than those of other contributors. Representing the *Annales* school of historians,[14] Wallerstein argues that because we are living in a moment of historic social transformation, some fifty to one hundred years in length, during which the world will be transformed, the role that we play as political actors (peace activists, civil rights or human rights advocates, feminists, or whatever) is questionable indeed. This chapter well illustrates the interrelationship of the meanings we give peace, the political perspectives we hold, and the strategies we find most illuminating for understanding the world in which we live.

STRATEGIES FOR PEACE STUDIES

Understanding that people's perceptions about the world are dependent on their social and cultural milieu—where they are coming from—is called the sociology of knowledge. It affects our sense of control over our lives. It influences our view of learning and teaching. Although some of us may believe we merely have drifted into a particular field of study at college, there has been, in reality, a decision-making process at work. Depending on who we are, where we come from, and what avenues are open to us, we are inclined toward certain branches of learning—certain disciplines or fields.

These disciplines are governed by certain sets of assumptions or rules that determine their approaches to knowledge and acceptable methods they must use. Disciplinary assumptions are distinguished to a large extent by responses to the question: To what extent does "the system" control the people, or do the people control "the system"? Thus, disciplines vary most fundamentally by the degree of importance given to analysis of the political system as a whole versus that given to analysis of the individual self, which forms one of the basic contentions in social science.

Among the disciplines or fields involved in peace studies considered most respectable by traditional academics, grant-awarding foundations, and publishers are those that analyze issues of peace and war from a systematic perspective. Systems analysis is based on an assumption that the economic, social, political, cultural, and psychological interactions in human society are governed by certain basic laws, operating at all levels of social organization, that transcend the uniqueness of ordinary day-to-day life.

This kind of thinking focuses on social institutions as structures, rather than people as individuals. It is concerned with processes of structures that are patterned and regular over time. The war system, for example, is viewed as "an all-embracing structure of mutually interlocking organizational and behavioral variables, in which violence or force is accepted and legitimized as the ultimate arbitrator of social conflicts at all levels of human society."[15] As futurist historian Warren Wagar argues in Part III, war cannot be disentangled from the economic and political structures of society. A major conclusion from the structuralists' perspective is that war within the present world system is normal, inevitable, and may, in fact, serve the system. The elimination of the threat of war, therefore, would require nothing short of revolutionary efforts at systemic transformation.

The modus vivendi of other disciplines and fields of study that tend toward multidisciplinary, value, and advocacy-oriented approaches to peace studies, emphasizes the importance of people rather than systems. These are often referred to as the "softer," more "tender-minded" fields of inquiry. Advocates of this softer approach argue that systems theory fails to explain social change and the importance of specific individual actions. It, they contend, tends to reify concepts like the nation-state or collective security, thereby dehumanizing politics. They prefer to focus on the behavior and psychology of individuals rather than institutions.

As all of the contributors to Part III illustrate, however, the sets of assumptions underlying disciplines have become increasingly multidisciplinary. For example, the social psychology perspective of Dean Pruitt and William Rick Fry differs from traditional psychology in that it deals with the behavior of individuals and groups in all their complex social settings. History, normally not particularly reflective of the social sciences, now focuses less on the study of individual political actors and groups, and more on economies and institutions of societies as determined by such impersonal factors as demography, geography and climate. This multidisciplinary tendency of the social sciences toward an approach which integrates interpersonal and systemic/structural orientations to the issues of peace and war are exemplified in Part III by sociologist Louis Kriesberg's discussion of the application of conflict resolution ideas and practices to peacemaking. Pruitt and Fry review the variety of conditions under which conflict escalation is more or less likely in neighborhood disputes and among nations. Political scientist Glenn Palmer's description of game theory and Donald Birn's chapter on the lessons of history similarly reflect on an integration of these two orientations.

As political scientists Charles Hauss makes clear in the final chapter entitled "A Rational Basis for Hope," there is an urgent need to think anew about peace, due to the failure of our old ways of thinking. Yet, all of the contributors make clear, there is no one way to think about peace, but many. In order to think creatively about peace, we not only need to be aware of interpersonal-oriented perspectives on human needs, but also of systems-oriented approaches to the historical experience of the world.

The field of peace studies requires an integration of the interpersonal- and systems-oriented approaches through the contribution of a variety of disciplines or fields of study. Each approach has its areas of blindness and its areas of truth. To attempt to think about the peace process examining individual behavior and responsibility without reference to political and social collectivity is to neglect the realities of our historical situation. To stress the system to the point of eliminating individual behavior and responsibility may well mire us in cyclic determinism. Peace studies cannot afford an either/or approach. It is in the process of thinking and talking together about the meanings we give to peace, and the ways in which our politics affect our thinking about peace that we will find our own voices for strategies for peace.

OVERVIEW

As its title and the preceding discussion imply, this volume has been organized into three parts: Meanings, politics, and strategies. The contributors present a broad spectrum of personal, political, and disciplinary perspectives on the subject of peace, with themes that necessarily overlap. This is the very nature of peace studies: The meanings we give to the process of peace, the politics that govern the ways in which we view the world and our place in it, and the strategies for a better world we choose to pursue are so interrelated that they forestall neat compartmentalization.

Peace studies forces us to question and examine our own values in preparation for peace action. As peace studies practitioners, we need to think about the meanings we intuitively and consciously give to peace, as well as the ways in which our politics might guide us to a committed approach. A critical and reflective reading of the chapters in this volume should help to prepare us for making our personal choices about the kind of education needed for peace. To make our thinking active, educators and students alike need to ask ourselves:

1. What do I mean by peace?
2. In what ways does my politics (world view, ideology, paradigm) affect or impinge upon my thinking about peace?
3. Which strategy (approach, discipline) to peace studies best suits me?

Peace studies practitioners may take great comfort in Peter Elbow's call for educators to "embrace contraries." We, like most thinking educators and students, "have a hunger for coherence—yet a hunger to be true to the natural incoherence of experience."[16] That is the way it is, and that is what this volume is about. The challenge both for peace studies educators and students is to dare to think aloud as we together struggle for clarity and purpose.

NOTES

1. Daniel C. Thomas, ed. *Guide to Careers and Graduate Education in Peace Studies* (Amherst, Mass.: The Five College Program in Peace and World Security Studies, 1987), 5.

2. Paulo Freire, *Pedagogy of the Oppressed* (New York: Herder and Herder, 1970), 63.

3. Hannah Arendt, "Thinking and Moral Considerations: A Lecture." *Social Research* (October 1971): 417.

4. Ibid., 432.

5. As Ian Harris points out, peace studies courses throughout the world go under a variety of rubrics including "education for world citizenship," "disarmament education," "nuclear age education," "development education," and "human rights education." International relations can be included, but there is often a distinction made between international studies focusing on the existing world order and those that emphasize alternative paths to peace. "Security Studies," in so far as it focuses on how nations defend themselves, is considered a component of peace studies. Ian M. Harris, *Peace Education* (Jefferson, N.C.: McFarland, 1988), 44, 50, 56.

6. This definition of Peace Studies was developed by the Curriculum Committee of the Peace Studies Center at SUNY Binghamton.

7. *New York Times*, Nov. 2, 1987.

8. Ibid., Sept. 17, 1987.

9. William James, *Pragmatism: A New Name for Some Old Ways of Thinking* (New York: Longmans, Green and Co., 1947), 3, 4.

10. Robert A. Isaak and Ralph P. Hummel, *Politics for Human Beings* (North Scituate, Mass.: Duxbury, 1975), 14.

11. *Wall Street Journal*, Aug. 11, 1988.

12. A leading advocate of this view is Carol Gilligan, *In a Different Voice* (Cambridge, Mass.: Harvard University Press, 1982).

13. See, for example, Betty Reardon, *Sexism and the War System* (New York: Teachers College Press, 1985); and Brigit Brock-Utne, *Educating for Peace: A Feminist Perspective* (New York: Pergamon Press, 1985).

14. The *Annales* historians (originating with historians associated with the French journal *Annales*, whose sole editor from 1957 to 1968 was Fernand Braudel) represent a radical attempt to displace political actors and specific events from the center of historical analysis and replace them with analysis of broad social, cultural and geographical development over long periods of time. The most influential *Annales* work is Fernand Braudel, *Le Mediterranee et le monde mediterraneen a l'epoque de Philippe II*, 2nd rev. and aug. ed. 2 vols. (Paris, 1966); trans. by S. Reynolds, *The Mediterranean and the Mediterranean World in the Age of Philip II*, 2 vols. (London, 1972–1973).

15. Richard A. Falk and Samuel S. Kim, eds., *The War System: An Interdisciplinary Approach* (Boulder, Colo.: Westview Press, 1980), 2.

16. Peter Elbow, *Embracing Contraries* (New York: Oxford University Press, 1986), x.

2

Toward a Paradigm of Peace

Betty A. Reardon

PREFACE

There may be no more significant responsibility and challenge to peace
studies than the engagement of learners in the search for a new paradigm of peace to replace the present paradigm of war, which delimits
all thinking and determines our culture. That search is the great intellectual adventure of our time. This chapter is intended as an initial
inquiry into that search.

Three convictions are central to the assertions and arguments to be
made. First, there is the fundamental feminist conviction that there
is no essential separation between the personal and the political. Nor
is there a legitimate basis to separate means from ends. Second, there
is the conviction that processes and methods are equally as important
as, sometimes more important than, goals. The educational implications of the second conviction produce the third conviction that learning
modes must be organically, systematically, intentionally, and ethically
related to instructional goals. Both peace studies and peace education
will be used in this discussion of paradigm change. The former is used
to focus on the substance or subject matter of the field; the latter on
the learning and the educational methods.

TAMING THE LION WITHIN

The perspectives and parameters of my arguments, set forth by the
title Linda Forcey has assigned to this chapter, are totally congenial

to these convictions. As she points out in her introduction, paradigms are perhaps the most important conceptual tools we have and they not only constrain and influence the way we think but also the way we behave, the way we organize our societies, and conduct virtually all human affairs. As a feminist peace educator, I argue that the present paradigm is at once the source and the product of a war system that, for generations, has been transferred from our minds into our experience and from our experience back into our minds. We engage in war and violence because we think violently in images and metaphors of war. If we are to experience an authentic, fulsome peace, we must think peace. If we are to think peace, we need a paradigm of peace. We need not only a vision of peace but also the concepts, the language, the images, and the metaphors that will comprise a functioning and equally vigorous paradigm *of* peace, so that from it we can construct paradigms *for* peace, those explicit conceptual and political models around which we can organize a peaceful society in which we can conduct human affairs in a more humane manner. Searching for and speculating on such language, images, and metaphors is the stuff of which peace studies should be made. These concepts should be about transcending the war paradigm to enable us to think in terms of a peace system. Peace, then, of necessity, must be conceived in dynamic, active, challenging terms. It must provide for us all of that which we have sought in and through war. It must become the means by which human beings strive for the highest achievements, their most transcendent goals.

"Toward," the word with which Forcey began the title, is most important for the purposes of this chapter, for it is a word which connotes process and action as well as thought. It is the notion "toward" which helps to inform these reflections with the sense of dynamism that is so essential to bringing forth a vigorous peace paradigm that can instill vibrant peace images, images of new forms of power and accommodation that contrast sharply with the present concepts of peace and how it might be achieved.

The shapes and tones of such images are vividly expressed in a story by a naval chaplain and fellow peace educator about a Biblical zoo in Israel, in which the various animals mentioned in the Bible were arranged in tableaux, or Biblical images. The most problematic image was the lion lying down with the lamb. The zookeeper was working on this particular tableau during the time when Henry Kissinger was pursuing shuttle diplomacy for peace in the Middle East. "If anyone could give me the secret how this might be done," thought the zookeeper, "it will be Henry Kissinger." Sure enough, the very day after he had the good fortune to encounter Dr. Kissinger, the lion and lamb were lying down together. The next day, they were lying down together, and the next day and the next. One frequenter of the zoo was determined to discover the secret, and when pressed, the zookeeper did confess that the way to accomplish this was to put in a new lamb every morning. The zookeeper had considered a number of alternative structural arrangements to make this possible, but in the end, because the tableau depended on the behavior both of the lion and the lamb, he took a pragmatic political solution. The sacrificial lamb is very much a part of our politics and our paradigm, an image and symbol of peace through propitiation. It is suggested that the only way the lion and lamb image could be realized without continuing to incur a very high cost on the part of the lambs, would be a profound personal change and major paradigm shift, mainly on the part of the lion. In some respects, that is what we must be about in our attempts to construct a peace paradigm. We are about taming the lion in all of us.

Among the changes that have to be made for the achievement of such a shift, the most significant ones are within ourselves. The way in which we move toward these inner changes, the way in which we envision and struggle for peace and try to construct that new paradigm, is the most essential means through which we will be enabled to make the larger structural changes required for a peace system. Thus the journey is really more personally meaningful to us than the destination. What we are about, on a day-to-day basis, is actually how we change paradigms. We must change ourselves and our immediate realities and relationships if we are to change our social structures and our patterns of thought. We've known this for a long time. Shakespeare told us that the fault is not "in our stars, but in ourselves." St. Augustine reflecting on his own journey wrote, "I have sought thee outside and thou were within." His was a long and tortuous route to a new paradigm. A few decades ago, the Cunard Line tried to convince us that in traveling to Europe "getting there was half the fun." However, there are very few passenger ships that cross the Atlantic these days. We prefer to take the rapid route, by plane, to get to our destination, incurring jet lag and many other negative consequences. Paradigm changing is not only a difficult inner struggle, but also a time-consuming journey, so we had better be ready for a long voyage on turbulent waters.

Long voyages on turbulent waters require patience, steadiness, and strong stomachs. The journey toward a new peace paradigm is not likely to be undertaken by the faint of heart. Those who still fear sea monsters, and tremble at the possibility of sailing over the edge of the present paradigm, will certainly not board the good ship "Peace Studies" on its exploratory ventures. We know full well that few came to wave us off and wish us well in those early years when we first hoisted anchor with but a few courses, and only two programs; when we still purported to know our destination. Indeed, the queen did not pawn her jewelry, nor did foundations offer portions of their coffers to finance the earlier voyages to peacemaking knowledge. Yet, as the statistics indicate, the fleet has grown and we have the feeling that more are now following our route as we traverse the familiar waters of academe in search of a truly new world. If we are to entice even more educators and students into this search for new horizons of thought, the exploration of the terra incognita of a peace paradigm, we will need the equivalents of the maps of the Indies, the products of the imaginations of early global explorers who captured the minds of seamen and monarchs. For those we would have join us on the journey, we need to evoke images of what the new world might be like, and in which directions we should sail to reach it. World order scholars would say we need models of peace systems and transition strategies for the change from a war system to a peace system. We need an image which may well be as Utopian as the lamb lying with the lion, but we also need specific and particular approaches to the learnings, political movements, and personal behaviors which will take us toward our vision.

CHANGING LANGUAGE, TRANSFORMING IMAGES

Personal and political changes are very much interrelated and both will be the product of learning processes. It is for this reason that peace studies is central to the task, not only of paradigm change, but also in the achievement of structural and systems change in the global order. Peace studies must take on the task of nurturing new modes of thought. We cannot achieve a change unless we can think it. And we cannot rally others to support the changes if we cannot communicate our visions of change to them. Thus we need not only images and maps but also effective and appropriate language. If both the lion and the lamb are to undergo the personal changes that would make a new relationship possible, first they must be able to communicate the changes to each other.

Reflect for a moment on the language we tend to use most, on the shades of violence and combat which color so much of our discourse. Such language even creeps into the literature and discussions of peace studies and the peace movement. We speak of "fighting for peace" and "ammunition for peace makers." Feminist peace research is no exception. I received an interview questionnaire which included the following questions, "What has sustained you so long on the frontlines of the feminist battle?" We need only to monitor ourselves and others for less than a day to see how such language pervades so many of our exchanges, and includes not only the substance of the subject at hand, but also the standards of the war system which we salute constantly in our choice of words and metaphors. Our language and our metaphors reveal just how we think more clearly than our arguments and proposals.

Our thinking, thus, is frighteningly combative and antagonistic, a fact which has been at the core of much feminist criticism of our culture and scholarship. If we do wish to journey toward the peace paradigm, would it not at least be worth the attempt to change our language as a step toward changing our thinking? Many have conceded the significance of language as the reinforcement of racism and sexism. Can we not admit the same of militarism and the peace system? Would it not be more productive to try consciously to substitute alternatives for combative and militaristic terms? We might at least become more aware of the concepts that influence our thinking. For example, could we use "struggle" instead of "fight"? "Struggle" does not necessarily require an enemy or adversary, or even an opponent, as does "fight." It connotes vigorous effort to transcend an obstacle, resolve a problem, or bring forth a desired end, none of which calls for harm of others. Indeed, we need to think more in terms of avoidance of harm as a primary criterion for behaviors and policies. To do so is hardly a full commitment to nonviolence, but it can help us become aware of how violence evolves and how it might be limited, if not eliminated. In lieu of "ammunition," we can substitute "nourishment" or "food" or "fuel," something than can convey a source of energy for struggle without carrying along the concept of injury and death. I prefer to think of my involvement in the women's movement as tilling the fields of feminism, attempting to cultivate more humane attitudes and social structures. Can we not think in terms of tools and tasks instead of weapons and battles, nourishment and cultivation in lieu of artillery and victory? As we change our words, we will also begin to change our images, and our metaphors may be transformed as we move from the language of war and death toward one of peace and life. If we speak differently, we can become more intentional about changing how we think and teach.

Using images of cultivation in lieu of those of battle to connote energy concentrated toward the fulfillment of a purpose comes very close to common images of peace often articulated in drawings by children, or the pastoral paintings and poetry of some of the great artists of all cultures and languages. Serious peace people, educators, researchers, and activists, especially the "hard heads" among us, have often cited this type of imagery as evidence of our inability to think in as complex and concrete terms about peace, as about war. This assessment is questionable, although the fundamental assertion of this volume is that our education does not prepare us in any systematic way to think about peace. It is precisely for this reason that these types of images are so significant, for they do demonstrate our capacity to image peace. The thinking which rejects the pastoral as a practical or useful image of peace is the same kind of thinking which permits us, in a manifestation of the peace system, to abuse the environment, which is even more threatening to life on this planet than nuclear weapons and war. That is the same kind of thinking which has, in fact, produced weapons of mass destruction and reinforced the war system. This argument, too, has been a major assertion of feminist critiques of peace research and peace education.[1]

PEACE AS A DYNAMIC, ORGANIC PROCESS

There are several assumptions and assertions that point to peace as a dynamic, organized process. These assertions pertain to notions of peace, concepts of what peace education is and should do, and concerns about the way the present paradigm impedes the purposes of peace education, and is a virtually insurmountable barrier to peace. So long as this paradigm prevails there will be no authentic peace. We may cease to experience as much organized hostility and armed conflict as we presently do but at best, any peace we experience will be truly negative, for it will be nothing more than the kind of peace which oppresses not only women, as Christine Sylvester points out, but any who are vulnerable, less powerful or "lamblike." Such is indeed the case in areas of the world where there is no serious armed conflict, but structural violence is most evident. We might cite Brazil or Korea as examples of such peace.

There are perhaps as many reasonable and useful definitions of peace as there are approaches to peace studies. My own definitions have become more open, wider in scope—an organic concept of peace. As Warren Wagar asserts, "peace is life." If we define peace in its fullest, most varied sense, it reflects pastoral images. If we need to think of peace in structural or political terms, then we may say that peace results from social and economic structures, and public policies which sustain and enhance life; hence, the notion of harm and injury as primary policy making criteria. Admittedly, these are feminine notions, and to some degree "feminist." While such notions are, of course, repressed by patriarchy, they are in no way exclusively female. We need only look to some of the great religious and ethical traditions which were articulated to the world by such male prophets as Gautama Buddha, Jesus Christ, and Mohandas Gandhi to see that these notions are in fact human universals, only now beginning to be seen as new sources of actual as well as spiritual power, power in the positive life enhancing sense of the capacity to realize values and achieve goals. This is in essence the energy source which "inspires" (i.e., breathes life into nonviolence as social action and political mode, demonstrating quite clearly that authentic or "organic" peace is an active, dynamic state).

Organic peace is a source of energy for development, the breath of life which impels action. It does not exclude conflict, as is well argued by Dean Pruitt, but it governs and guides it to become a source of growth and change rather than harm and destruction. Organic peace is, above all else complex, as are life processes in general. It is not so easily modeled in static structural terms. While clearly we need the new structures, institutions, and systems emphasized by Warran Wagar, the structural is but one, quite limited dimension of organic peace, which comprises all those social processes and personal behaviors which facilitate change, growth, and fulfillment. Should we achieve peace by the twenty-first century, it will not be the same peace that prevails in the twenty-second century, else it will not be peace. As Tacitus instructed us, peace does not bloom in a desert. Deserts have limited forms of life, fewer varieties of flora and fauna than other natural environments, the richest being the rain forest which, literally, "is crawling with life." The most complex environments are the richest in diversity and are full of life. Yet we have confronted these natural phenomena as we have the questions of human social order. We reduce everything to its simplest, most manageable form. We seek to control and manage life rather than to live it. We have, in fact, not developed that far emotionally from our forebears who cowered in caves in fear of natural phenomena and other life forms. While the sophistication of our means of subjection has become greater with the evolution of modern science, human attempts to subdue, control, and simplify as a means to security may be as old as the species. It is no coincidence that in the process of seeking security through control, we have destroyed many life forms and are to the point of cutting off the very air we breathe through the destruction of the rain forest.

Critics of the present paradigm, such as Douglas Sloan and Jeremy Rifkin, attribute much of the reductionist character of contemporary thought to the initial intellectual separation of philosophy from the sciences.[2] Other critics, particularly of the sciences, see the drive for control of nature as patriarchal, and a primary cause of the evolution of a dehumanized technology which produces nuclear weapons and isolates genetic material.[3] However, this drive would seem to be far more deeply rooted in our history and our psyches than in Cartesian science or even patriarchy. It may be as much a cause as a consequence of patriarchy, other forms of repression, militarism and war itself.

The linear thinking which has been the dominant mode of thinking not only in the sciences but also in all of academe, is the most serious impediment to us who seek peace through education. Clearly, within the present paradigm, the primacy of a negative peace notion cannot be replaced with that of a positive one, much less one of organic peace. So long as this and the present forms of empiricism are our dominant intellectual values, we will not be effective learners about, or partners with, the complexity that is life. While some physicists and biologists are revealing startling notions about apparent randomness reflecting a beautifully choreographed pattern of interrelationships and repetitions from the smallest to the largest bits of creation,[4] and proposing through the Gaia hypothesis that the Earth itself is a living system, such concepts are by and large subjected to the rational, positivist version of the Galilean syndrome. If it is not revealed in our present scientific scriptures, nor pontificated by the highest authority, it is not true. This circumstance reflects the notion of fixed and limited truth, which cries for the kind of questioning advocated here, in order to open the windows of the frequently stifling ivory towers of academe to the air of new possibilities. The inquiry of peace studies should be based on queries mutually derived by instructor and student, each posing problems calling for various alternative responses, rather than predefined questions by the instructor, calling for predetermined answers from students.

PEACE EDUCATION AS LIFE ENHANCEMENT

What more comprehensive definition of peace education could we offer than learning to learn about, and functioning in and with complexity, so as to enhance the richness and diversity of life? Such a definition would apply to, and provide deeper purpose for cross-cultural education, conflict studies, world order modeling, human rights education, environmental studies, and most of the themes and subjects which comprise the broad and varied field of peace studies. Profound changes in present educational systems and methods are essential if we are to move toward a new paradigm. For starters, it would help us to comprehend more fully the significance of pastoral images of peace. We should see them as pictures of life in process, of cultivation, of intentional enhancement of life, and, hopefully, of diversity. The reductionist thinking which permits us to dismiss the importance of the loss of some species because they are, but rare insects for which we have no apparent use, is the same mode of thought that prevents us from seeing descriptions of peace in the drawings of children, whose imaginations have not yet been imprisoned by "fixed, demonstrable truth." With such a start, we might open and develop our capacities for imaging, which Elise Boulding sees as necessary to inspire us with viable concepts of peace. Imaging is a skill which can and should be developed through peace education.[5] To develop skill, however, is but a means of directing and giving communicable form to a fundamental capacity of the human imagination. These imaging capacities must be freed by a liberating form of education based on authentic inquiry, rather than the probe for predetermined answers. Only through such open authentic inquiry as described by Forcey, with students and teachers exploring the terra incognita of peace together, can education make a significant contribution to the formulation of a new paradigm.

Thus, a primary method of peace education should be authentic inquiry. Such a method would be derived from the posing of queries, which would perform three functions: Reveal apparent obstacles to peace, open avenues for exploring the causes of and alternative approaches to transcending the obstacles, and assess the alternatives according to criteria which would result in the most life-enhancing choice. The exploration would be conducted to maximize the possibilities for reflection, creativity, and full participation of all engaged in the study. It would reward rather than impede speculation, the most open form of inquiry, and the most encouraging form of creativity. It would preclude the premature narrowing of the broad creative process of speculation into the limitations of too few scientifically testable hypotheses. It would provide space for, and honor the need for, reticence and silence as a sometimes necessary environment for reflection—that deeper inner questioning that is essential to personal change and evolution on which the political and social changes of a new paradigm will depend. Without such reflection, learning cannot be fully integrated into the thinking and world views that condition our personal interpretations and assessments, from which we make the choices that lead us to action. An emphasis on integration reflects the notion of education and learning as part of the seeking of a wholeness that is the authentic meaning of integrity, and the essence of what has been most trampled upon by the reductionist nature of the present paradigm. Peace education, if not all education, should be intentionally designed to contribute to the search for integrity by individual learners and the whole society.

Integration of diversity in a mutually enhancing relationship is a fundamental process for maintaining life and for achieving peace. Our present emphasis on analysis has encouraged separation at the cost of integration. The reluctance to see things wholistically also may well contribute to the current alienation of individuals and to the disintegration of society. Rather than try to heal and reintegrate it, we have attempted to simplify it to better manage and control the conditions of separation and alienation, conditions largely responsible for the high degree of personal and social insecurity from which we suffer. This insecurity has, in fact, alienated us from life. We shun and fear difference, diversity, and complexity because we have not learned to live with them, and in the process we have shunned life itself. Peace requires the embracing of life in all its problematic fullness.

METAPHORS OF BIRTH AND LIFE

We need also to devise a life-affirming metaphor to replace the death-prone, war metaphor of destructive struggle that so conditions our language, our thought, and our learning. Since we want a set of images for positive struggle, the most likely new metaphor of life would be one centered on the origins, development, and maturation of living things—one based on conception, labor, birth, and parenting.

Were we to think in terms as all encompassing as conception, gestation, labor, birth, nurturing, parenting, education, and *caring*, we would have a whole new way of thinking about the human experience and social organization. We might think of the desired paradigm shift as one which moves us from a warring society to a parenting or caring society, in which all adults parent the young and care for the vulnerable. Care of the vulnerable, like avoidance of harm, is characteristic of both good parenting and a peaceful society. Our thinking would tend to focus on the long-range health and welfare of living beings, and on the enchancement of life. We might begin to organize intentionally planned learning toward development of the capacity to care, thus embracing one of the most fundamental purposes of peace education—an overarching concept for a comprehensive education for justice and peace, and for humane and fulfilling human relationships.

The concept and value of care as a core notion of peace education illuminates the inextricable interweaving of the personal and the political. As a primary learning goal, care brings into focus the essential significance of diversity and complexity. It makes it possible to sustain the struggle for integrity in the apparent chaos in which the emerging patterns and intricate order of actual relationships give us a glimpse of the multiple possibilities for a transformed reality and a paradigm of peace. In such a paradigm, peace and life would be perceived as the products of a diverse, dynamic, continuous set of processes of change in a magnitude of aesthetic quality we have only begun to grasp. If we can learn to become creative participants rather than destructive controllers of these life processes, we may yet reach a truly new world.

LEARNING: MERGER OF PERSONAL AND POLITICAL, MEANS AND ENDS

Learning is primarily personal, inward, and interactive. We learn as we use our paradigms (our world views, assumptions, and values) to assess and integrate our experiences. We learn in relationship to experience, to systems, and to persons. Mostly, we learn from and with each other. Authentic learning is a complex and sometimes chaotic process. Our notion of cognitive dissonance as a primary instigator of learning, is evidence to support the argument of authentic learning as far more varied than the linear processes on which most present instruction is based. Learning, like life, is an interrelational and wholistic process. Thus, methodology cannot be separated from purpose. If we seek truly new and transformed realities, we need to construct courses and learning experiences on genuine wholistic inquiry and speculation. Social and political processes, if they are to be viable and effective, must also be wholistic and integrative, recognizing that society, comprised of persons and politics is an aggregate of personal choices. If politics are to be altered to change the society, then people must also change. Personal change, if it is to be sustained over time, and not subject to repeated manipulation of outside forces, must be autonomously and intentionally embraced and integrated into the self. Just as a value consensus within a society is a necessary prerequisite to viable political and structural change, only change in people can change the culture which "cultivates" the values of the society.

Clearly, peace studies must begin to pursue wholism as the framework, process as the primary method, and peace in its widest sense as the goal, if it is to energize the intellectual transformation necessary to a paradigm of peace. The lion can lie down with the lamb in a nurturing rather than devouring relationship, only if each is able to transform its reality by transforming itself. These transformations are what peace studies should be about.

NOTES

1. Birgit Brock Utne, *A Feminist Perspective on Peace Education* (New York: Praeger, 1986).
2. Douglas Sloan, *Insight-Imagination: The Emancipation of Thought and the Modern World* (Westport, Conn.: Greenwood Press, 1983); Jeremy Rifkin, *Declaration of a Heretic* (Boston: Routledge & Kegan Paul, 1985).
3. Brian Easlea, *Fathering the Unthinkable: Masculinity, Scientists and the Nuclear Arms Race* (London: Pluto Press, 1983).
4. James Gleick, *Chaos: Making a New Science* (New York: Viking, 1987).
5. Betty A. Reardon, *Comprehensive Peace Education* (New York: Teachers College Press, 1988).

3

Problems of War and Peace Are Inseparable

Hal Nieburg

The problem with the field of peace studies is that it does not accept the offices of war. It deals extensively with conflict resolution and settlement of disputes by means short of violence. It fails to deal with the existence of evil in the very nature of things, and the role of violence in maintaining mutual incentives to limit violence. Simply put, like humans, nation-states are in a continual bargaining relationship with each other. If the behavior of some gives leverage to the intransigence of others, intransigence will be encouraged. Any nation that places too high a value on civility, encourages incivility by others. On the other hand, a decent and realistic prospect of mutual incivility may be the best means of containing conflict escalation at a reasonable cost.

CONVENTIONAL WISDOM

On the global level, assertions of right and wrong are relative. All nations perceive justice to be on their side in escalated international disputes. There is no rule of justice to be consulted and applied. Fundamentally, in each case, it is the discovery of such a rule that leads to escalation of the conflict. This means that the conventional wisdom of preparing for war as the best way to insure peace may still have something to offer. Yet, if peace studies were to seriously include such alternatives, its separation from the study of war and military strategy would be undermined. It would lose its purity and self-righteousness, along with its principal thrust, namely, an ideological attack against the "war system." In practical terms, this means that whomever particular pacifists oppose—generals, capitalists, munitions makers, liberals, Republicans, Methodists, or adults—could no longer be the enemy.

The essential impulse of peace studies is the advocacy of nonviolence as a way of life. Improbable as it may be, there is nothing wrong with it for individuals, but it may become mischievous as unilateral national policy. Thinking, to bring nations into lawful and municipal processes, similar to those within national boundaries, may be misguided. The number of civil wars is higher than international wars, and such conflicts, in terms of rational policy goals and outcomes, tend to be longer, more savage, and more irrational than international wars. Thinking, to bring nations into closer "family-like" relationships may be futile. Students of international peace must recognize that 50 percent of crimes of violence occur among members of the same family, and another 30 percent are perpetrated among people who know each other well in business, social, or romantic situations. Only approximately 20 percent of such crimes occur among strangers, or as side effects of other crimes. Bland repetition of phrases like "family love and consideration" testify to the affectional tensions of life, from which both joys and tragedies of the deepest kind arise. Indeed it can be said that the shrinking of the globe is itself a factor of increased instability and conflict. The irrational scale of violence in World Wars I and II, out of proportion to any rational war aims or policy goals, testifies to the affectional tensions of a shrinking world, the emerging unity of humankind. Blind destruction on such a scale is historically more characteristic of civil wars (or murder within a family) rather than international wars.

Pacifism, the guiding principle in one form or another of both the peace movement and peace studies, implies that moral disapproval of threats and acts of force can, in fact, deter their use by others. Unfortunately, it may have just the opposite effect. Further, it implies that those who refuse to join the fray bear no responsibility for what happens. First, the democracies failed to take timely and proportionate measures to contain fascism, and then acted as though Europe had to be destroyed in order to be saved. The refusal to apply limited measures of force ultimately led to unlimited force and unconditional surrender. In order to overcome the pacifist impulse, a dangerous absolutist approach dominated the war effort. That impulse must bear a share of responsibility for the great wars of this century, and the crimes of Adolf Hitler. To paraphrase what Jefferson said of revolution: Limited warfare, at shorter intervals may be the best means available to prevent major warfare at longer intervals. Efforts to prevent limited uses of violence, therefore, may insure catastrophic breakdowns, like those of this century, at predictable intervals.

Diplomacy is a bargaining continuum. The structure of the international arena, which may be straining to become a community, is still a congery of equal and sovereign states. In reality, sovereignty means that there is no appeal to higher authority, that the ultimate appeal for settlement will be to self-help and continued bargaining. "Power," in international affairs, means relative influence and leverage over the actions and premises of other actors in the system. All out warfare is a breakdown of the system, whereby the real power of the actors becomes uncertain, and must be reestablished by a test of arms. Under normal conditions, relative bargaining power is effective (without such a test) in bringing about the tentative and temporary adjustments that maintain peace. Cost and risk are intrinsic elements of the bargaining process, and under conditions of inevitable change, responsible statesmen must be attentive to these elements, conserving and maintaining their bargaining positions, without attempting radical revision that could lead to instability and an arms race. They must meet incipient revisions by others through build-ups of their own, in order to return the balance to stability.

In the final analysis, bargaining leverage is based on the perceived ability and will of nations to maintain their power rankings. For this reason, abstract calculations of potential military confrontations are not irrelevant. In the process of negotiating any current dispute, the negotiators of all sides must continuously demonstrate and rehearse possible scenarios of escalation. When two kids argue over a skate board, their relative belligerence and size are factors in the negotiation. The weaker kid may derive power from the knowledge that his older brother is near, and therefore run higher risks in order to win the argument. On the other hand, either kid may consider that the ultimate settlement will occur when an enraged parent enters the fray, thereby neutralizing the weight of the older brother in the negotiations. In the same way, every divisive issue in world politics is imbued with the perceptions that all parties (even innocent bystanders) have of the relative energy and military strengths of the great powers. The fantastic, abstract calculus of escalation inevitably plays a role. Actually, the older brother or the parent does not have to enter the fray. It is enough that the negotiators know what their next steps beckon, and how that may impact the costs and risks of continued conflict.

In a direct confrontation of super states, each must maintain a credible capability to meet and deny advantage to the other's military capabilities. If there is an obvious imbalance at some point during speculative escalation, one side will gain an immediate and real bargaining advantage. This may make a realistic settlement (at a low level of conflict) less likely, because it would impose an unacceptable regime for the disadvantaged party, or may begin a process of eroding the credibility of its bargaining position. It is such instability that usually leads to escalation or a dangerous showdown.

DINOSAUR IN A SWAMP

Writers such as George F. Kennan, John F. Kennedy, and others have argued convincingly that the pacifism of the democracies, before and between twentieth-century wars, contributed to their outbreaks; that if the democracies had been willing to take moderate and timely measures to maintain and use their international power, the absolutist war aims of the Axis powers might have been rendered ludicrous, and some balance could have maintained without the horrible costs eventually imposed on all. Kennan argues that democracies may be structurally incapable of dealing with the fine control and calculus of world politics. Sentimental pacifism, so popular in modern democracies, is one of the villains of twentieth-century history. In *American Diplomacy: 1900–1950*[1] Kennan uses the metaphor of America as a dinosaur in a swamp with a very large body and a very small brain; slow to react to provocation and, when finally aroused, prone to destroy not only the tormentor, but the swamp as well. "I see the most serious fault of our past policy formulation to lie in something that I might call the legalistic-moralistic approach to international problems." It arises from the belief, Kennan continues, that "it should be possible to suppress chaotic and dangerous aspirations of governments by the acceptance of some system of legal rules and restraints." This view seeks to discredit the motives and aspirations of disturbers of the peace, as though they were "not important and might justly be expected to take second place behind the desirability of an orderly world . . . " This view, he says, is unrealistic because it projects American values and interests as a universal code, binding on everyone else. "To the American mind, it is implausible that people should have positive aspirations, that they regard as legitimate, more important to them than the peacefulness and orderliness of international life."

Disputes and conflicting interests among states are the normal conditions of global structure. In this context, bargaining is meaningless if any powers are denied their full range of options, specifically including the right to appeal to violence. In practice, this right can have political effects, which, if credible, can preclude the test of arms. To maintain this credibility, states must maintain a war capability and, on occasion, push a confrontation to the brink. To the extent that a plurality of states recognizes and respects the viability of each other's

threats and ultimate options, "going to the brink" will likely be unnecessary.

It is not unlike the wild west before the arrival of the federal marshal.
Warfare is neither chronic nor inevitable. The universal presence of
the six-shooter is an equalizer. Most of the time, gunslingers maintain
a rough respect and civility for each other. Sometimes, an armed con-
sortium of ranchers may protect a community against intrusion or
attack. When Wyatt Earp arrives, he attempts to convince the community to abandon private settlement of disputes in favor of recourse
to legal processes. Even when the presence of a legitimate legal process
is manifest, people still maintain options for recourse to private measures. Disputants in real, often minor disputes do occasionally murder
each other and burn down each other's houses. The sense that there
is always danger of irrational escalation, in spite of police authority,
tends to temper positions in a dispute and enhance mutual desires to
refer the dispute to courts and attorneys. In such instances, the capability for self-help, specifically including violence, can have a very
positive effect, making recourse to legal process more, rather than less
probable. This makes clear the inseparability of violent and peaceful
means of conflict resolution. In an age of nuclear weapons, to say that
warfare is impossible is to paralyze nations that are unwilling to run
risks of diplomatic or conventional conflict, and gives the diplomatic
initiative to those leaders who want to take advantage of this paralysis.
In the course of events, unsatisfied nations will learn to escalate risks
as a method of testing the will of status quo powers.

Every student of Hans Morgenthau knows that ideologies of peace
are doctrines of the status quo, aiming to deny legitimacy to attempts
to effect change. Revisionist policies disturb the status quo, he argues
in his classic *Politics Among Nations*.[2] By expressing in pacifist terms
the objectives of his policy, "a statesman puts the stigma of warmon-
gering upon his opponents, clears his and his countrymens' conscience
of moral scruples, and can hope to win the support of all countries
interested in the maintenance of the status quo." The ideals of international law are part of an ideology of peace. Morganthau writes: "Law
in general, and especially international law...defines a certain distribution of power, and offers standards and processes to ascertain and
maintain it in concrete situations." In other words, interest in maintaining peaceful processes should be translated to interest in maintaining a particular power position.

Ideologies of peace attempt the utopian goal of arresting political
change. They seek to deter changes to the status quo by denying the
legitimacy and lawfulness of the ratio ultima of bargaining, threats of
self-help, and violent escalation of conflict. Thus they help create the
situation in which the weak may enhance their leverage by taking

dangerous risks and, eventually, the powerful may overreact. The desire for tranquility, without paying the costs of guarding it against latent threats, or acting to demonstrate power in small and timely ways, can ultimately force the great powers to act massively to reverse the tides of unsustainable change, exacting ultimate costs that are totally unrelated to the issues at stake. In this manner, the desire for cheap tranquility temporarily shifts power to the untranquil and the unsatisfied, achieving, in practice, effects that are opposite to those intended. It is this same syndrome that generates the problem of terrorism.

STRATEGIC DILEMMAS

Is there a way out of this paradox? This is where the problem of evil appears. Good reasons for conflict are never lacking. Whenever conflict arises, it can be rationalized in terms of morality and justice by all the parties. There is no flat principle or rule of law that can resolve the conflict of claims and values. In each case, it is the search for such a measure that underlies the dispute. In such a situation, there is no alternative except self-help and bargaining, whatever the levels to which the dispute, as a bargaining weapon, may be escalated. Being unreasonable and unrealistic tends to enhance the moral force of the otherwise weaker side that takes these positions. It is not inherently unreasonable for one side to refuse to negotiate, if that ploy causes the other to become more reasonable. The party that is divided, or unsure, is at a considerable disadvantage when the dispute is being played out for the national audiences of each side, or for world opinion. With contending political forces and unfinished arguments incessantly raging in all countries the attempt to dramatize issues of morality and justice can be an important factor to the eventual outcome.

Normally, even in the heat of warfare, bargaining continues. Incentives against further escalation may still operate, and mutual restraints may limit the means to be employed. Each side may avoid bombarding each other's undefended cities, may not use its bombers if each side's airfields are vulnerable, and so on. The possibility that escalation might zoom out of control acts to restrain all strategists, and normally serves to limit the war. This might, however, give leverage once again to the "irresponsible" party, who is willing to risk that escalation in order to get better terms at the bargaining table than can be won on the battlefield. To deny that leverage, the other side must also abandon reasonability, and thus the conflict widens and deepens. No one wants irrational and unlimited conflict. It might be said that "it just wants itself." The victim is restraint itself, and the escalation takes over like an irresistible force of nature, imposing grave and unacceptable costs on all participants, costs that are totally out of whack with the "war aims" and policy goals that are presumed to have been responsible for the original conflict.

The problem of evil in the world shows its ugly face. It is a genuine dilemma. No amount of good will or pacifistic moralizing removes it. The solution offered by the pacifists to these dilemmas is to stop the process at a much earlier point by eliminating escalated options and by offering fair means of settlement long before the situation gets out of hand. Unfortunately, perverse logic does its work at every point in a bargaining process. Fair and peaceful settlement of disputes is a face the parties wear now and then, in order to strike a moral pose to gain a temporary advantage. Or fair and peaceful settlement is post hoc— after the assessments of cost and risk are fully understood by leaders, and the case is already near solution. At this point, peacemakers and peace-loving noises save face for the participants, and provide a convenient way to enact the temporary suspension of hostilities that we call peace. The cases that cause serious war and travail are the ones in which at least one party (usually all are mirror images of each other) feels that violent action is necessary to test the assessments of cost and risk by all the parties, in order to assure that its own recognized bargaining power will be based upon realism. When matters reach an impasse, there is no way out except through directed means of force— to anticipate the enemy, to gain early advantage, to deny early advantage, to show determination, to deny the other side political advantage from its show of determination, and so on.

Let us now turn to the strategic dilemmas that fuel the arms race and threaten nuclear balance. We begin with the assumption that nuclear weapons tend to deter each other, and that their only purpose is to deny the other side a diplomatic edge based on possession and possibility of use. Thus, under stable conditions of finite deterrence, parity could mean "de facto outlawry" of nuclear weapons. Third parties would still require their own limited capabilities to balance their neighbors', or to avoid dependence on guaranteeing powers and loss of national control of their own options.

Diplomacy is not a game of Checkers, it is Chess. To play well, the players must always be looking hundreds of moves in advance. If one side makes a particular move, the other side can make a corresponding move. Such moves lead to perceived differences in options and bargaining power, and thus effect the intentions, planning, and actions of the parties. Capabilities, however hypothetical and far down the chain of possible/probable events, do effect the balance of power, and thus, the course of everyday real diplomacy. While we may have rough parity in nuclear weapons, we do not have symmetry. It is the nature of such things. We do not have symmetrical geopolitical conditions, resources, national interests, and strategic requirements. We do not have parity in all categories—manpower in readiness, proximity, technological skill, and productivity. We have competing strategic requirements, as well as obligations to Allies who have their own requirements. This imbalance is destabilizing. Two of the most asymmetrical relationships are those of the United States to Western Europe and the Soviet Union to China. It may be said that the Western European problem is at the heart of strategic dilemmas of the postwar decades. The United States is in the unenviable position of needing a credible nuclear capability more than the Soviet Union. Both need it equally to deter diplomatic threats based on the possession and deployment of nuclear weapons. But in other respects, the U.S. containment policy allows hostile conventional forces the early initiative, thus, in the areas continuous with Soviet boundaries, its ground forces probably have insurmountable advantages.

It is this asymmetry that the United States attempts to balance with its nuclear doctrines. It is also this asymmetry that leads to the interactive logic of the nuclear arms race. The Soviet Union's side, growing containment of China exhibits some of the same contradictions. The Soviet Union must maintain both conventional and nuclear capabilities as passive defense systems against China. It must have a two-war strategy. But the cumulative weight of such planning provides an invitation to a heightened arms race with the West. Missiles and armies are mobile, and the West feels threatened by Soviet numbers that seek to match both West and East. Add to these asymmetries the continuation of technological innovation and you have the basic sources of current strategic instability. Is the balance of nuclear terror in jeopardy? Nothing remains stable indefinitely, least of all the strategic stalemate. Security and danger are not absolutes and there is no alternative but to live in the real world. The disincentives for the use of nuclear weapons continue to outweigh the central role accorded them in strategic doctrines, a puzzling anomaly. There is a brazen contradiction between these disincentives and U.S. NATO guarantees, that creates divisions among Western governments and peoples, and undermines strategic credibility. In spite of changes in leadership, we can anticipate no important changes in the Soviet perspective, which will continue to be based on pervasive insecurity. Tight domestic political control will be combined with a cautious foreign policy. Soviet-U.S. negotiations on strategic weapons in the 1990s are promising, but will not be transforming.

The super states will not be comfortable without large and powerful strategic forces, which will make other nations uncomfortable. The asymmetrical nature of the Soviet threat to Europe, based on proximity and conventional force superiority, leads the West to maintain a first strike doctrine; and this underpins the web of counterforce logic that tends toward two results: (1) Soviet insistence on both theatre and strategic nuclear parity, to deny credibility to Western defense doctrine and retain the edge of conventional superiority; and (2) Spreading demand by other nations to escape the nuclear umbrellas of either side through banning the presence of all such weapons, or by insisting on their own arsenals and doctrines. The first result leads to a continuation of first strike doctrines and capabilities by both sides, which is inherently unstable and dangerous, and distorts budgets and resources. The second leads to agitation adroitly exploited by the Soviet Union against the predominant U.S. role in NATO to continued pressure for independent nuclear capabilities by other nations, and to conflict in the heart and soul of the West over credibility of the actions United States would actually take in the event of an escalated collision with the Soviet Union.

Technological progress leads to the higher accuracy that allows for more controlled and discriminating forces and doctrines, but at the same time increases the vulnerability of such systems as preemptive strikes, heightening, rather than allaying the incentives for such strikes. The response to declining credibility is not only reiterated declarations of doctrine, but also, more dangerously, deployments designed to deny options to the other side and thereby regaining credibility. This iron logic leads to arms reduction initiatives—as though each side were crying out to be saved from itself—while the logical engines of strategy grind on to make agreements ever more difficult to achieve. However, it is not a relentless and alarming picture: Both doves and hawks must be disappointed. Look for small incremental steps within the realm of the possible, steps which soften the risks and marginally reduce threats to security. The nuclear stalemate has served us well, despite its inherent dangers, and we should strive to preserve rather than undermine it. Of course, we should try to achieve this aim at a lower level of cost in all categories of weapons and troops.

We are living in the bi-polar legacy of World War II, a rigid and temporary condition. The period of reconstruction is over, and a variety of decentralizing pressures are building everywhere. The postwar dependencies cannot indefinitely be continued. In Europe, this would mean a withdrawal of U.S. unilateral guarantees to NATO and an independent nuclear deterrent with adequate matching of Warsaw Pact forces at every level, without U.S. participation. A loosening of Eastern Europe from the Soviet orbit could be expected to continue and hasten under these conditions. Eventual withdrawal of Soviet forward defenses could go hand-in-hand with the withdrawal of U.S. forces and generalship in Central Europe. Closer relations between Eastern and Western Europe, outside the content of the Soviet-American rivalry, would experience enormous growth. Strict second strike nuclear forces along with codified "no first use" treaties would reinforce the informal de facto outlawry that presently exists. We now begin to see the outlines of solutions to the threat of nuclear weapons, and the deep instability that we live with today.

At some point, the outlawry of nuclear weapons may even become feasible. In the Far East, it would mean bringing China into the equations of world politics, recognizing legitimate Soviet interests in balancing both East and West, including China in any major arms reduction treaties, and accepting with considerable equanimity the complex balancing acts that are likely to emerge from a five-polar balancing system. In such a world order, research on new weapons would continue as before, but hopefully, at a lower level, with fewer chances of instability, and with much less cost and risk to all parties.

TRAGIC AMBIGUITY

Peace advocates argue that the world may discover means to solve disputes that, in comparison with senseless violence, could require great and universal moral force. Moral force plays a great role in human affairs. An act of moral courage has great power over the imaginations of humans and nations. That is not to be gainsaid. However, it cannot be asserted with equal confidence that moral force is a factor for peace and tranquility among humans and nations. In fact, it is usually just the reverse. Moral force always occurs in a political context, and derives its essential meaning in terms that are relative to the disputants. The danger of escalated force would not be significant if the balance of morality were clear and objective in any sense. It is the clash of equally clear moral rights that constitutes the basis for disputes likely to lead to serious violence. It is usually the moral commitments of the parties that makes de-escalation so difficult. This is not to say that moral values and causes can be, or should be avoided. This is not possible. The moral thrusts of life are the processes of life itself, and give life its transcendental meaning. The laws of nature impose on us the dangers and miseries of our exaltations.

For both good and evil, the world is divided into moral entities that group humans together as well as apart, endowing everyone with the most essential and powerful values of their lives. Some of these values coincide with tribal, religious, ethnic or governmental boundaries, lending greater intensity to group aspirations, and making the problems of peacekeeping that much more ineffable. It must be said that the very things that make life worth living, and fill it with sweetness and meaning, can lead to group conflict with the opposite potential. Unfortunately, the reality of the former is inseparable from the reality of the latter. The most powerful fact of human existence is that people are capable of both good and evil, inescapably and forever. Attempts to separate them, as in the case of war and peace, can and do lead to mischief. How much better it would be for the world if peace studies changed its focus from trendy guilt trips, self-righteousness, and fund-raising gimmicks. It should set about arousing commitment to the traditional study of international politics, preserving the pluralism (including the views of moralizers and pacifists) of all the traditional and current approaches. Defining and defending the national interests, the nature of diplomacy, the status of nationalism, diplomatic history, military tactics and strategy, foreign language education, and so on, are far more deserving of enthusiasts who want to do more than blame someone else for the condition of the world.

It is true that the very things we must do to maintain peace can lead to war. But one of the least attractive aspects of peace studies is its self-righteousness, the tendency to blame someone else or policies with which it disagrees, for the problem of evil in the world. When, in fact, we are all involved and all guilty. More attractive is recognition of the inherent difficulty of the problem itself and a search for a ethic of shared responsibility. The problems of war arise from our common mortality. Violence in the world cannot be ascribed to certain violent people or institutions. It goes much deeper than that. The tragic plight of humankind is a heartrending spectacle. It is not helpful to attack with moral arguments those who are protecting us from the hard moral choices which someone must make. What is needed is respect for the inherent difficulty of the issues, and more charity toward the motives of others who are charged with dealing with them. It is true that simplistic and know-nothing slogans tend to give us the comfort of moral certainty, but they may not make a positive contribution. It is also true that there are insoluble problems and dilemmas, which force upon us the humility of our common humanity.

NOTES

1. George F. Kennan, *American Diplomacy 1900–1950* (Chicago: University of Chicago Press, 1951), 95.

2. Hans J. Morgenthau, *Politics Among Nations, The Struggle for Power and Peace.* 2nd Ed., (New York: Alfred A. Knopf, 1954), 83. He can be seen here to be an early advocate of the approach to law known as "Critical Legal Studies."

4

Sex and Death in the Rational World of Defense Intellectuals

Carol Cohn

> "I can't believe that," said Alice.
> "Can't you?" the Queen said in a pitying tone. "Try again: draw a long breath, and shut your eyes."
> Alice laughed. "There's no use trying," she said. "One can't believe impossible things."
> "I dare say you haven't had much practice," said the Queen. "When I was your age, I always did it for half-an-hour a day. Why, sometimes I've believed as many as six impossible things before breakfast."
>
> **Lewis Carroll, *Through the Looking Glass***

My close encounter with nuclear strategic analysis started in the summer of 1984. I was one of forty-eight college teachers (one of ten women) attending a summer workshop on nuclear weapons, nuclear strategic doctrine, and arms control, taught by distinguished defense intellectuals. Defense intellectuals are men (and indeed, they are virtually all men) "who use the concept of deterrence to explain why it is safe to have weapons of a kind and number it is not safe to use."[1] They are civilians who move in and out of government, working sometimes as administrative officials or consultants, sometimes at universities and think tanks. They formulate what they call "rational" systems for dealing with the problems created by nuclear weapons: how to manage the arms race, how to deter the use of nuclear weapons, and how to fight a nuclear war if deterrence fails. It is their calculations that are used to explain the necessity of having nuclear destructive capability at what George Kennan has called "levels of such grotesque dimensions as to defy rational understanding."[2] At the same time, it is their reasoning that is used to explain why it is not safe to live without nuclear weapons.[3] In short, they create the theory that informs and legitimizes U.S. nuclear strategic practices.

For two weeks, I listened to men engage in dispassionate discussion of nuclear war. I found myself aghast, but morbidly fascinated—not by nuclear weaponry, or by images of nuclear destruction, but by the extraordinary abstraction and removal from what I knew as reality that characterized the professional discourse. I became obsessed by the question: How can they think this way? At the end of the summer program, when I was offered the opportunity to stay on at the university's Center on Defense Technology and Arms Control (hereafter known as "the Center"), I jumped at the chance to find out how they could think the way they do.

I spent the next year of my life immersed in the world of defense intellectuals. As a participant observer, I attended lectures, listened to arguments, conversed with defense analysts, and interviewed graduate students at the beginning, middle, and end of their training. I learned their specialized language, and I tried to understand what they thought and how they thought. I sifted through their logic for its internal inconsistencies and its unspoken assumptions. But as I learned their language, as I became more and more engaged with their information and their arguments, I found that my own thinking was changing. Soon, I could no longer cling to the comfort of studying an external and objectified "them." I had to confront a new question: How can I think this way? How can any of us?

Throughout my time in the world of strategic analysis, it was hard not to notice the ubiquitous weight of gender, both in social relations and in the language itself; it is almost an entirely male world (with the exception of the secretaries), and the language contains many rather arresting metaphors. There is, of course, an important and growing body of feminist theory about gender and language.[4] In addition, there is a rich and increasingly vast body of theoretical work exploring the gendered aspects of war and militarism, that examines such issues as men's and women's different relations to militarism and pacifism, and the ways in which gender ideology is used in the service of militarization. Some of the feminist work on gender and war is also part of an emerging, powerful feminist critique of ideas of rationality as they have developed in Western culture.[5] While I am indebted to all of these bodies of work, my own project is most closely linked to the development of feminist critiques of dominant Western concepts of reason. My goal is to discuss the nature of nuclear strategic thinking; in particular, my emphasis is on the role of its specialized language, a language that I call "technostrategic."[6] I have come to believe that this language both reflects and shapes the nature of the American nuclear strategic project, that it plays a central role in allowing defense intellectuals to think and act as they do, and that feminists who are concerned about nuclear weaponry and nuclear war must give careful attention to the language we choose to use—whom it allows us to communicate with and what it allows us to think as well as say.

STAGE I: LISTENING

Clean Bombs and Clean Language

Entering the world of defense intellectuals was a bizarre experience—bizarre because it is a world where men spend their days calmly and matter-of-factly discussing nuclear weapons, nuclear strategy, and nuclear war. The discussions are carefully and intricately reasoned, occurring seemingly without any sense of horror, urgency, or moral outrage—in fact, there seems to be no graphic reality behind the words, as they speak of "first strikes," "counterforce exchanges," and "limited nuclear war," or as they debate the comparative values of a "minimum deterrent posture" versus a "nuclear war-fighting capability."

Yet what is striking about the men themselves is not, as the content of their conversations might suggest, their cold-bloodedness. Rather, it is that they are a group of men unusually endowed with charm, humor, intelligence, concern, and decency. I liked them. At least, I liked many of them. The attempt to understand how such men could contribute to an endeavor that I see as so fundamentally destructive became a continuing obsession for me, a lens through which I came to examine all of my experiences in their world. In this early stage, I was gripped by the extraordinary language used to discuss nuclear war. What hit me first was the elaborate use of abstraction and euphemism, of words so bland that they never forced the speaker or enabled the listener to touch the realities of nuclear holocaust that lay behind the words.

Anyone who has seen pictures of Hiroshima burn victims or tried to imagine the pain of hundreds of glass shards blasted into flesh may find it perverse beyond imagination to hear a class of nuclear devices matter-of-factly referred to as "clean bombs." "Clean bombs" are nuclear devices that are largely fusion rather than fission and they release a somewhat higher proportion of their energy as prompt radiation, but produce less radioactive fallout than fission bombs of the same yield.[7] "Clean bombs" may provide the perfect metaphor for the language of defense and arms controllers. This language has enormous destructive power, but without emotional fallout, without the emotional fallout that would result if it were clear one was talking about plans for mass murder, mangled bodies, and unspeakable human suffering. Defense analysts talk about "countervalue attacks" rather than about incinerating cities. Human death, in nuclear parlance, is most often referred to as "collateral damage," for, as one defense analyst said wryly, "The Air Force doesn't target people, it targets shoe factories."[8]

Some phrases carry this cleaning-up to the point of inverting meaning. The MX missile will carry ten warheads, each with the explosive power of 300–475 kilotons of TNT—*one* missile the bearer of destruction approximately 250–400 times that of the Hiroshima bombing.[9] Ronald Reagan dubbed the MX missile "the Peacekeeper." While this renaming was the object of considerable scorn in the community of defense analysts, these very same analysts refer to the MX as a "damage limitation weapon."[10] These phrases, only a few of the hundreds that could be discussed, exemplify the astounding chasm between image and reality that characterizes technostrategic language. They also hint at the terrifying way in which the existence of nuclear devices has distorted our perceptions and redefined the world. "Clean bombs" tells us that radioactivity is the only "dirty" part of killing people. To take this one step further, such phrases can even seem healthful/curative/corrective. So, we not only have "clean bombs" but also "surgically clean strikes"—"counterforce" attacks that can purportedly "take out" (accurately destroy) an opponent's weapons or command centers without causing significant injury to anything else. The image of excision by the offending weapon is unspeakably ludicrous when the surgical tool is not a delicately controlled scalpel but a nuclear warhead. And somehow it seems to be forgotten that even scalpels spill blood.[11]

White Men in Ties Discussing Missile Size

Feminists have often suggested that an important aspect of the arms race is phallic worship, that "missile envy" is a significant motivating force in the nuclear build-up.[12] I have always found this an uncomfortably reductionist explanation and have hoped that my research at the Center would yield a more complex analysis. But still, I was curious about the extent to which I might find a sexual subtext in the defense professionals' discourse. I was not prepared for what I found. I think I had naively imagined myself as a feminist spy in the house of death—that I would need to sneak around and eavesdrop on what men said in unguarded moments, using all my subtlety and cunning to unearth whatever sexual imagery might be underneath how they thought and spoke. I had naively believed that these men, at least in public, would appear to be aware of feminist critiques. If they had not changed their language, I thought that at least at some point in a long talk about "penetration aids," someone would suddenly look up, slightly embarrassed to be caught in such blatant confirmation of feminist analyses of "what's going on here."[13]

Of course, I was wrong. There was no evidence that any feminist critiques had ever reached the ears, much less the minds of these men. U.S. military dependence on nuclear weapons was explained "irresistible, because you get more bang for the buck." Another lecturer solemnly and scientifically announced "to disarm is to get rid of all your stuff." This may, in turn, explain why they see serious talk of nuclear disarmament as perfectly resistable, not to mention foolish. If disarmament is emasculation, how could any real man even consider it? A professor's explanation of why the MX missiles are to be placed in the silos of the newest Minuteman missiles, instead of replacing the older, less accurate ones, was "because they're in the nicest hole—you're not going to take the nicest missile you have and put it in a crummy hole." Other lectures were filled with discussion of vertical erector launchers, thrust-to-weight ratios, soft lay downs, deep penetration, and the comparative advantages of protracted versus spasm attacks—or what one military adviser to the National Security Council has called "releasing 70 to 80 percent of our megatonnage in one orgasmic whump."[14] There was serious concern about the need to harden our missiles and the need to "face it, the Russians are a little harder than we are." Disbelieving glances would occasionally pass between me and my one ally in the summer program, another woman, but no one else seemed to notice. If the imagery is transparent, its significance may be less so. The temptation is to draw some conclusions about the defense intellectuals themselves—about what they are *really* talking about, or their motivations, but the temptation is worth resisting. Individual motivations cannot necessarily be read directly from imagery because the imagery itself does not originate in these particular individuals, but in a broader cultural context.

Sexual imagery has, of course, been a part of the world of warfare since long before nuclear weapons were even a gleam in a physicists' eye. The history of the atomic bomb project itself is rife with overt images of competitive male sexuality, as is the discourse of the early nuclear physicists, strategists, and SAC commanders.[15] Both the military and the arms manufacturers are constantly exploiting the phallic imagery and promise of sexual domination that their weapons so conveniently suggest. A quick glance at the publications that constitute some of the research sources for defense intellectuals makes the depth and pervasiveness of the imagery evident. *Air Force Magazine*'s advertisements for the new weapons, for example, rival *Playboy* as a catalog of men's sexual anxieties and fantasies. Consider the following, from the June 1985 issue, emblazoned in bold letters across the top of a two-page advertisement for the AV–8B Harrier II: "Speak Softly and Carry a Big Stick." The copy below boasts "an exceptional thrust to weight ratio" and "vectored thrust capability that makes the . . . unique rapid response possible." Then, just in case we've failed to get the message, the last line reminds us, "Just the sort of 'Big Stick' Teddy Roosevelt had in mind way back in 1901."[16] An ad for the BKEP (BLU–106/B) reads:

The Only Way to Solve Some Problems is to Dig Deep.
THE BOMB, KINETIC ENERGY
PENETRATOR
Will provide the tactical air commander with efficient power to deny or significantly delay enemy airfield operations.
Designed to maximize runway cratering by optimizing penetration dynamics and utilizing the most efficient warhead yet designed.[17]

In case the symbolism of "cratering" seems far-fetched, I must point out that I am not the first to see it. The French use the Mururoa Atoll in the South Pacific for their nuclear tests and assign a woman's name to each of the craters they gouge out of the earth.

Another truly extraordinary source of phallic imagery can be found in descriptions of nuclear blasts themselves. Here, for example, is one by journalist William Laurence, who was brought to Nagasaki by the Air Force to witness the bombing. "Then, just when it appeared as though the thing had settled down in to a state of permanence, there came shooting out of the top a giant mushroom that increased the size of the pillar to a total of 45,000 feet. The mushroom top was even more alive than the pillar, seething and boiling in a white fury of creamy foam, sizzling upward and then descending earthward, a thousand geysers rolled into one. It kept struggling in an elemental fury, like a creature in the act of breaking the bonds that held it down."[18] Given the degree to which it suffuses their world, that defense intellectuals themselves use a lot of sexual imagery does not seem especially surprising. Nor does it, by itself, constitute grounds for imputing motivation. For me, the interesting issue is not so much the imagery's psychodynamic origins, as how it functions. How does sexual imagery serve to make it possible for strategic planners and other defense intellectuals to do their macabre work? How does it function in their construction of a work world that feels tenable? Several stories illustrate the complexity.

During the summer program, a group of us visited the New London Navy base where nuclear submarines are homeported, and the General Dynamics Electric Boat boatyards where a new Trident submarine was being constructed. At one point during the trip we took a tour of a nuclear submarine. When we reached the part of the sub where the missiles are housed, the officer accompanying us turned with a grin and asked if we wanted to stick our hands through a hole to "pat the missile." *Pat the missile?*

The image reappeared the next week, when a lecturer scornfully declared that the only real reason for deploying cruise and Pershing II missiles in Western Europe was "so that our allies can pat them." Some months later, another group of us went to be briefed at NORAD (North American Aerospace Defense Command). On the way back, our plane went to refuel at Offut Air Force Base, the Strategic Air Command headquarters near Omaha, Nebraska. When word leaked out that our landing would be delayed because the new B–1 bomber was in the area, the plane's passengers became charged with a tangible excitement that built as we flew in our holding pattern, people craning their necks to try to catch a glimpse of the B–1 in the skies, and climaxed as we touched down on the runway and hurtled past it. Later, when I returned to the Center I encountered a man who, unable to go on the trip, said to me enviously, "I hear you got to pat a B–1."

What is all this "patting"? What are men doing when they "pat" these high-tech phalluses? Patting is an assertion of intimacy, sexual possession, and affectionate domination. The thrill and pleasure of "patting the missile" is the proximity of all that phallic power, the possibility of vicariously appropriating it as one's own. But if the predilection for patting phallic objects indicates something of the homoerotic excitement suggested by the language, it also has another side. For patting is not only an act of sexual intimacy, it is also what one does to babies, small children, and the pet dog. One pats that which is small, cute, and harmless—not terrifyingly destructive. Pat it, and its lethality disappears.

Much of the sexual imagery I heard was rife with the sort of ambiguity suggested by "patting the missiles." Such imagery can be construed as a deadly serious display of the connections between masculine sexuality and the arms race. At the same time, it can also be used as a way of minimizing the seriousness of militarist endeavors, of denying their deadly consequences. A former Pentagon target analyst, in telling me why he thought plans for "limited nuclear war" were ridiculous, said, "Look, you gotta understand that it's a pissing contest—you gotta expect them to use everything they've got." What does this image convey? Most obviously, that this is all about competition for manhood, and thus there is tremendous danger. But at the same time, the image diminishes the contest and its outcome, by representing it as an act of boyish mischief.

FATHERS, SONS, AND VIRGINS

"Virginity" also made frequent, arresting, appearances in nuclear discourse. In the summer program, one professor spoke of India's explosion of a nuclear bomb as "losing her virginity"; the question of how the United States should react was posed as whether or not we should "throw her away." It is a complicated use of metaphor. Initiation into the nuclear world involves being deflowered, losing one's innocence, knowing sin, all wrapped up into one. Although the manly United States is no virgin, and proud of it, the double standard raises its head in the question of whether or not a woman is still worth anything to a man once she has lost her virginity.

New Zealand's refusal to allow nuclear-armed or nuclear-powered warships into its ports prompted similar reflections on virginity. A good example is provided by U.S. General Ross Milton's angry column in *Air Force Magazine*, entitled "Nuclear Virginity." His tone is that of a man whose advances have been spurned. He is contemptuous of the woman's protestation that she wants to remain pure, innocent of nuclear weapons—her moral reluctance is a quaint and ridiculous throwback. But beyond contempt, he also feels outraged—after all, this is a woman we have *paid* for, who *still* will not come across. He suggests that we withdraw our goods and services—and then we will see just how long she tries to hold onto her virtue.[19] The patriarchal bargain could not be laid out more clearly.

Another striking metaphor of patriarchal power came early in the summer program, while one of the faculty was giving a lecture on deterrence. To give us a concrete example from outside the world of military strategy, he described having a 17-year-old son, whose TV-watching habits he disapproves. He deals with the situation by threatening to break his son's arm if he turns on the TV again. "That's deterrence!" he said triumphantly. What is so striking about this analogy is that at first it seems so inappropriate. After all, we have been taught to believe that nuclear deterrence is a relation between two countries of more or less equal strength, in which one is only able to deter the other from doing it great harm by threatening to do the same in return. But in this case, the partners are unequal, and the stronger one is using his superior force not to protect himself or others from grave injury, but to coerce. But if the analogy seems to be a flawed expression of deterrence as we have been taught to view it, it is nonetheless extremely revealing about U.S. nuclear deterrence as an operational, rather than rhetorical or declaratory policy. What it suggests is the speciousness of the defensive rhetoric that surrounds deterrence—the idea that we face an implacable enemy and that we stockpile nuclear weapons only in an attempt to defend ourselves. Instead, what we see is the drive to superior power as a means to exercise one's will and a readiness to threaten the disproportionate use of force in order to achieve one's own ends. There is no question here of recognizing competing but legitimate needs, no desire to negotiate, discuss, or compromise, and most important, no necessity for that recognition or desire, since the father carries the bigger stick.[20]

The United States was frequently mentioned in discussions about international politics as "father," sometimes coercive, sometimes benevolent, but always knowing best. The single time that any mention was made of countries other than the United States, our NATO allies, or the Soviet Union was in a lecture on nuclear proliferation. The point was made that younger countries simply could not be trusted to know what was good for them, nor were they yet fully responsible, so nuclear weapons in their hands would be much more dangerous than in ours. The metaphor used was that of parents needing to set limits for their children.

Domestic Bliss

Sanitized abstraction, and sexual and patriarchal imagery, even if disturbing, seemed to fit easily into the masculinist world of nuclear war planning. What did not fit, what surprised and puzzled me most when I first heard it, was the set of metaphors that evoked images that can only be called domestic. Nuclear missiles are based in silos. On a Trident submarine, which carries twenty-four multiple warhead nuclear missiles, crew members call the part of the submarine where the missiles are lined up in their silos for launching "the Christmas tree farm." What could be more bucolic—farms, silos, Christmas trees?

In the ever-friendly, even romantic world of nuclear weaponry, enemies "exchange" warheads; one missile "takes out" another; weapons systems can "marry up"; "coupling" is sometimes used to refer to the wiring between mechanisms of warning and response, or to the psychopolitical links between strategic (intercontinental) and theater (European-based) weapons. The patterns in which a MIRVed missile's nuclear weapons land is known as a "footprint."[21] These nuclear explosives are not dropped, a "bus" "delivers" them. Additionally, nuclear bombs are not referred to as bombs or even warheads, they are referred to as "reentry vehicles," a term far more bland and benign, which is then shortened to "RVs," a term not only totally abstract and removed from the reality of a bomb, but also resonant with the image of recreational vehicles on the ideal family vacation.

These domestic images must be more than simply one more form of distancing, one more way to remove oneself from the grisly reality behind the words—ordinary abstraction is adequate to the task. Something else, something very peculiar, is going on here. Calling the pattern in which bombs fall a footprint almost seems a willful distorting process, a playful, perverse refusal of accountability—because to be accountable to reality is to be unable to do this work. These words may also serve to domesticate, to *tame* the wild and uncontrollable forces of nuclear destruction. The metaphors minimize; they are a way to make phenomena that are beyond what the mind can encompass smaller and safer, and thus they are a way of gaining mastery over the unmasterable. The fire-breathing dragon under the bed, the one who threatens to incinerate your family, your town, your planet, becomes a pet you can pat.

Using language evocative of everyday experiences also may simply serve to make the nuclear strategic community more comfortable with what they are doing. "PAL" (permissive action links) is the carefully constructed, friendly acronym for the electronic system designed to prevent the unauthorized firing of nuclear warheads. "BAMBI" (Ballistic Missile Boost Intercept) was the acronym developed for an early version of an antiballistic missile system. The President's Annual Nuclear Weapons Stockpile Memorandum, which outlines both short- and long-range plans for production of new nuclear weapons, is benignly referred to as "the shopping list." The National Command Authorities choose from a "menu of options" when deciding among different targeting plans. The "cookie cutter" is a phrase used to describe a particular model of nuclear attack. Apparently it is also used at the Department of Defense to refer to the neutron bomb.[22]

The imagery that domesticates, that humanizes insentient weapons, may also serve, paradoxically, to make it all right to ignore sentient human bodies, human lives.[23] Perhaps it is possible to spend one's time thinking about scenarios for the use of destructive technology and have human bodies remain invisible in that technological world precisely because that world itself now *includes* the domestic, the human, the warm, and playful—the Christmas trees, the RVs, the affectionate pats. It is a world that is in some sense complete unto itself, even including death and loss. But it is weapons, not humans, that get "killed." "Fraticide" occurs when one of your warheads "kills" another of your own warheads. There is much discussion of "vulnerability" and "survivability," but it is about the vulnerability and survivability of weapons systems, not people.

Male Birth and Creation

There is one set of domestic images that demands separate attention—images that suggest men's desire to appropriate from women the power of giving life and that conflate creation and destruction. The bomb project is rife with images of male birth.[24] In December 1942, Ernest Lawrence's telegram to the physicists at Chicago read, "Congratulations to the new parents. Can hardly wait to see the new arrival."[25] At Los Alamos, the atom bomb was referred to as "Oppenheimer's baby." One of the physicists working at Los Alamos, Richard Feynman, writes that when he was temporarily on leave following his wife's death, he received a telegram saying, "The baby is expected on such and such a day."[26] At Lawrence Livermore Laboratories, the hydrogen bomb was referred to as "Teller's baby," although those who wanted to disparage Edward Teller's contribution claimed he was not the bomb's father but its mother. They claimed that Stanislaw Ulam was the real father; he had the all important idea and inseminated Teller with it. Teller only "carried it" after that.[27]

Forty years later, this idea of male birth and its accompanying belittling of maternity—the denial of women's role in the process of creation and the reduction of "motherhood" to the provision of nurturance (apparently Teller did not need to provide an egg, only a womb)—seems thoroughly incorporated into the nuclear mentality, as I learned on a subsequent visit to the U.S. Space Command in Colorado Springs. One of the briefings I attended included discussion of a new satellite system, the not yet "on line" MILSTAR system.[28] The officer in charge of the briefing gave an excited recitation of its technical capabilities and then an explanation of the newly created Unified Space Command's role in the system. Self-effacingly he said, "We'll do the motherhood role—telemetry, tracking, and control—the maintenance."

In light of the imagery of male birth, the extraordinary names given to the bombs that reduced Hiroshima and Nagasaki to ash and rubble— "Little Boy" and "Fat Man"—at last become intelligible. These ultimate destroyers were the progeny of the atomic scientists, and emphatically not just any progeny but male progeny. In early tests, before they were certain that the bombs would work, the scientists expressed their concern by saying that they hoped the baby was a boy, not a girl—that is, not a dud.[29] General Grove's triumphant cable to Secretary of War, Henry Stimson, informing him that the first atomic bomb test was successful read, after decoding: "Doctor has just returned most enthusiastic and confident that the little boy is as husky as his big brother. The light in his eyes is discernible from here to Highhold and I could have heard his screams from here to my farm."[30] Stimson, in turn, informed Churchill by writing him a note that read, "Babies satisfactorily born."[31] In 1952, Teller's exultant telegram to Los Alamos announcing the successful test of the hydrogen bomb, "Mike," at Eniwetok Atoll in the Marshall Islands, read, "It's a boy."[32] The nuclear scientists gave birth to male progeny with the ultimate power of violent domination over female Nature. The defense intellectuals' project is the creation of abstract formulations to control the forces the scientists created, and to participate thereby in their world-creating/destroying power. The entire history of the bomb project, in fact, seems permeated with imagery that confounds man's overwhelming technological power to destroy nature with the power to create, imagery that inverts men's destruction and asserts in its place the power to create new life and a new world. It converts men's destruction into their rebirth.

William L. Laurence witnessed the Trinity test of the first atomic bomb and wrote: "The big boom came about a hundred seconds after the great flash—the first cry of a new-born world. . . . They clapped their hands as they leaped from the ground—earthbound man symbolizing the birth of a new force."[33] Watching "Fat Man" being assembled the day before it was dropped on Nagasaki, he described seeing the bomb as "being fashioned into a living thing."[34] Decades later, General Bruce K. Holloway, the commander in chief of the Strategic Air Command from 1968 to 1972, described a nuclear war as involving "a big bang, like the start of the universe."[35]

God and the Nuclear Priesthood

The possibility that language reveals an attempt to appropriate ultimate creative power is evident in another striking aspect of the language of nuclear weaponry and doctrine—the religious imagery. In a subculture of hard-nosed realism and hyper-rationality, in a world that claims as a sign of its superiority its vigilant purging of all nonrational elements, and in which people carefully excise from their discourse every possible trace of soft sentimentality, as though purging dangerous nonsterile elements from a lab, the last thing one might expect to find is religious imagery—imagery of the forces that science has been defined in *opposition to*. For surely, given that science's identity was forged by its separation from, by its struggle for freedom from, the constraints of religion, the only thing as unscientific as the female, the subjective, the emotional, would be the religious. And yet, religious imagery permeates the nuclear past and present. The first atomic bomb test was called Trinity—the unity of the Father, the Son, and the Holy Spirit, the male forces of Creation. The imagery is echoed in the language of the physicists who worked on the bomb and witnessed the test: "It was as though we stood at the first day of creation." Robert

Oppenheimer thought of Krishna's words to Arjuna in the *Bhagavad Gita*: "I am become Death, the Shatterer of Worlds."[36]

Perhaps most astonishing of all is the fact that the creators of strategic doctrine actually refer to members of their community as "the nuclear priesthood." It is hard to decide what is most extraordinary about this: The easy arrogance of their claim to the virtues and supernatural power of the priesthood; the tacit admissions (*never* spoken directly) that rather than being unflinching, hard-nosed, objective, empirically minded scientific describers of reality, they are really the creators of dogma; or the extraordinary implicit statement about who, or rather what, has become god. If this new priesthood attains its status through an inspired knowledge of nuclear weapons, it gives a whole new meaning to the phrase "a mighty fortress of God."

STAGE 2: LEARNING TO SPEAK THE LANGUAGE

Although I was startled by the combination of dry abstraction and counter-intuitive imagery that characterizes the language of defense intellectuals, my attention and energy were quickly focused on decoding and learning to speak it. The first task was training the tongue in the articulation of acronyms. Several years of reading the literature of nuclear weaponry and strategy had not prepared me for the degree to which acronyms littered all conversations, nor for the way in which they are used. Formerly, I had thought of them mainly as utilitarian. They allow you to write or speak faster. They act as a form of abstraction, removing you from the reality behind the words. They restrict communication to the initiated, leaving all others both uncomprehending and voiceless in the debate. But, being at the Center, hearing the defense analysts use the acronyms, and then watching as I and others in the group started to fling acronyms around in our conversation revealed some additional, unexpected dimensions.

First, in speaking and hearing, a lot of these terms can be very sexy. A small supersonic rocket designed to penetrate any Soviet air defense is called a SRAM (short-range attack missile). Submarine-launched cruise missiles are not referred to as SLCMs, but "slick 'ems." Ground-launched cruise missiles are "glick 'ems." Air-launched cruise missiles are not sexy but magical—"alchems" (ALCMs), replete with the illusion of turning base metals into gold. TACAMO, the acronym used to refer to the planes designed to provide communications links to submarines, stands for "take charge and move out." The image seems closely related to the nicknames given to the new guidance systems for "smart weapons," "shoot and scoot" or "fire and forget."

Other acronyms work in other ways. The plane in which the president supposedly will be flying around above a nuclear holocaust, receiving intelligence and issuing commands for the next bombing, is referred to as "kneecap" (NEACP—National Emergency Airborne Command Post). The edge of derision suggested in referring to the plane as "kneecap" mirrors the edge of derision implied when it is talked about at all, since few believe that the president really would have the time to get into it, or that the communications systems would be working if he managed to do so. Some might go so far as to question the usefulness of his being able to direct an extended nuclear war from his "kneecap" even if it were feasible. I never heard the morality of this idea addressed. But it seems to me that speaking about it with that edge of derision is *exactly* what allows it to be spoken about and seriously discussed at all. It is the very ability to make fun of a concept that makes it possible to work with it rather than reject it outright.

In other words, what I learned at the program is that talking about nuclear weapons is fun. I am serious. The words are fun to say; they are racy, sexy, snappy. You can throw them around in rapid-fire succession. They are quick, clean, light; they trip off the tongue. You can reel off just dozens of them in seconds, forgetting about how one might just interfere with the next, not to mention with the lives beneath them. I am not describing a phenomenon experienced only by the perverse, although the phenomenon itself may be perverse indeed. Nearly everyone I observed clearly took pleasure in using the words. It mattered little whether we were lecturers or students, hawks or doves, men or women, we all learned it, and we all spoke it. Some of us may have spoken with a self-consciously ironic edge, but the pleasure was there nonetheless. Part of the appeal was the thrill of being able to manipulate an arcane language, the power of entering the secret kingdom, being someone in the know. It is a glow that is a significant part of learning about nuclear weaponry. Few know, and those who do are powerful. You can rub elbows with them, perhaps even be one yourself.

That feeling, of course, does not come solely from the language. The whole set-up of the summer program itself, for example, communicated the allures of power and the benefits of white male privileges. We were provided with luxurious accommodations, complete with young black women who came in to clean up after us each day. Generous funding paid not only our transportation and food but also a large honorarium for attending. We met in lavishly appointed classrooms and lounges. Access to excellent athletic facilities was guaranteed by a "temporary privilege card," which seemed to me to sum up the essence of the experience. Perhaps most important of all were the endless allusions by our lecturers to "what I told John [Kennedy]" and "and then Henry [Kissinger] said," or the lunches where we could sit next to a prominent political figure and listen to Washington gossip.

A more subtle, but perhaps more important, element of learning the language is that, when you speak it, you feel in control. The experience of mastering the words infuses your relation to the material. You can get so good at manipulating the words that it almost feels as though the whole thing is under control. Learning the language gives a sense of what I would call cognitive mastery—the feeling of mastery of technology that is finally not controllable but is instead powerful beyond human comprehension, powerful in a way that stretches and even thrills the imagination. The more conversations I participated in using this language, the less frightened I was of nuclear war. How can learning to speak a language have such a powerful effect? One answer, I believe, is that the *process* of learning the language is itself a part of what removes you from the reality of nuclear war. I entered a world where people spoke what amounted to a foreign language, a language I had to learn if we were to communicate with one another. So I became engaged in the challenge of decoding the acronyms and figuring out which were the proper verbs to use. My focus was on the task of solving puzzles, developing language competency, not on the weapons and wars behind the words. Although my interest was in thinking about nuclear war and its prevention, my energy was elsewhere.

By the time I was through, I had learned far more than a set of abstract words that refers to grisly subjects, for even when the subjects of a standard English and nukespeak description seem to be the same, they are, in fact, about utterly different phenomena. Consider the following descriptions, in each of which the subject is the aftermath of a nuclear attack:

Everything was black, had vanished into the black dust, was destroyed. Only the flames that were beginning to lick their way up had any color. From the dust that was like a fog, figures began to loom up, black, hairless, faceless. They screamed with voices that were no longer human. Their screams drowned out the groans rising everywhere from the rubble, groans that seemed to rise from the very earth itself.[37]
[You have to have ways to maintain communications in a] nuclear environment, a situation bound to include EMP blackout, brute force damage to systems, a heavy jamming environment, and so on.[38]

There are no ways to describe the phenomena represented in the first description with the language of the second. Learning to speak the language of defense analysts is not a conscious, cold-blooded decision to ignore the effects of nuclear weapons on real live human beings— to ignore the sensory, the emotional experience, the human impact. It is simply learning a new language, but by the time you get through, the content of what you can talk about is monumentally different, as is the perspective from which you speak.

In the example above, the differences in the two descriptions of a "nuclear environment" stem partly from a difference in the vividness of the words themselves—the words of the first intensely immediate and evocative, the words of the second abstract and distancing. The passages also differ in their content; the first describes the effects of a nuclear blast on human beings, the second describes the impact of a nuclear blast on technical systems designed to assure the "command and control" of nuclear weapons. Both of these differences may stem from the difference of perspective. The speaker in the first description is a victim of nuclear weapons, the speaker in the second is a user. The speaker in the first is using words to try to name and contain the horror of human suffering all around her while the speaker in the second is using words to ensure the possibility of launching the next nuclear attack. Technostrategic language can be used only to articulate the perspective of the users of nuclear weapons, not that of the victims.[39]

Thus, speaking the expert language not only offers distance, a feeling of control, and an alternative focus for one's energies; it also offers escape from thinking of oneself as a victim of nuclear war. I do not mean this on the level of individual consciousness—it is not that defense analysts somehow convince themselves that they would not be among the victims of nuclear war, should it occur. But I do mean it in terms of the structural position the speakers of the language occupy, and the perspective they get from that position. *Structurally*, speaking technostrategic language removes them from the position of victim and puts them in the position of planner, the user, the actor. From that position, there is neither need nor way to see oneself as a victim. No matter what one deeply knows or believes about the likelihood of nuclear war, and no matter what sort of terror or despair the knowledge of nuclear war's reality might inspire, the speakers of technostrategic language are positionally allowed, even forced, to escape that awareness, to escape viewing nuclear war from the position of the victim, by virtue of their linguistic stance as users, rather than victims of nuclear weaponry.

Finally, then, I suspect that much of the reduced anxiety about nuclear war commonly experienced by both new speakers of the language and long-time experts comes from characteristics of the language itself—the distance afforded by its abstraction, the sense of control afforded by mastering it, and the fact that its content and concerns are that of the users rather than the victims of nuclear weapons. In learning the language, one goes from being the passive, powerless victim to the competent, wily, powerful purveyor of nuclear threats and nuclear explosive power. The enormous destructive effects of nuclear weapons systems become extensions of the self, rather than threats to it.

STAGE 3: DIALOGUE

It did not take very long to learn the language of nuclear war and much of the specialized information it contained. My focus quickly changed from mastering technical information and doctrinal arcana to attempting to understand more about how the dogma was rationalized. Instead of trying, for example, to find out why submarines are so hard to detect or why, prior to the Trident II, submarine-based ballistic missiles were not considered counterforce weapons, I now wanted to know why we really need a strategic triad, given submarines' "invulnerability."[40] I also wanted to know why it is considered reasonable to base U.S. military planning on the Soviet Union's military capabilities rather than seriously attempting to gauge what their intentions might be. This standard practice is one I found particularly troubling. Military analysts say that since we cannot know for certain what Soviet intentions are, we must plan our military forces and strategies as if we knew that the Soviets planned to use all of their weapons. While this might appear to have the benefit of prudence, it leads to a major problem. When we ask only what the Soviets *can* do, we quickly come to assume that this is what they *intend* to do. We base our planning on "worst-case scenarios" and then come to believe that we live in a world where vast resources must be committed to prevent them from happening.

Since underlying rationales are rarely discussed in the everyday business of defense planning, I had to start asking more questions. At first, although I was tempted to use my newly acquired proficiency in technostrategic jargon, I vowed to speak English. I had long believed that one of the most important functions of an expert language is exclusion—the denial of a voice to those outside the professional community.[41] I wanted to see whether a well-informed person could speak English and still carry on a knowledgeable conversation. What I found was that no matter how well-informed or complex my questions were, if I spoke English rather than expert jargon, the men responded to me as though I were ignorant, simpleminded, or both. It did not appear to occur to anyone that I might actually be choosing not to speak their language.

A strong distaste for being patronized and dismissed made my experiment in English short-lived. I adapted my everyday speech to the vocabulary of strategic analysis. I spoke of "escalation dominance," "preemptive strikes," and, one of my favorites, "subholocaust engagements." Using the right phrases opened my way into long, elaborate discussions that taught me a lot about technostrategic reasoning and how to manipulate it. I found, however, that the better I got at engaging in this discourse, the more impossible it became for me to express my own ideas, my own values. I could adopt the language and gain a wealth of new concepts and reasoning strategies, but while the language gave me access to things I had been unable to speak about before, it radically excluded others. I could not use the language to express my concerns because it was physically impossible. This language does not allow certain questions to be asked or certain values to be expressed. To pick a bald example: The word "peace" is not a part of this discourse. As close as one can come is "strategic stability," a term that refers to a balance of numbers and types of weapons systems, and not the political, social, economic, and psychological conditions implied by the word "peace." Not only is there no word signifying peace in this discourse, the word "peace" itself cannot be used. To speak it is immediately to brand oneself as a soft-hearted activist instead of an expert, a professional to be taken seriously.

If I was unable to speak my concerns in this language, more disturbing still was that I found it difficult even to keep them in my own head. I had begun my research expecting abstract and sanitized discussions of nuclear war and had readied myself to replace my words for theirs, to be ever vigilant against slipping into the never-never land of abstraction. But no matter how prepared I was, no matter how firm my commitment to staying aware of the reality behind the words, over and over I found that I could not stay connected, could not keep human lives as my reference point. I found I could go for days speaking about nuclear weapons without once thinking about the people who would be incinerated by them. It is tempting to attribute this problem to qualities of the language, the words themselves—the abstractions, the euphemisms, the sanitized, friendly, sexy acronyms. Then all we would need to do is change the words, make them more vivid; get the military planners to say "mass murder" instead of "collateral damage" and their thinking would change. The problem, however, is not only that defense intellectuals use abstract terminology that removes them from the realities of which they speak. There *is* no reality of which they speak. Or, rather, the "reality" of which they speak is itself a world of abstractions. Deterrence theory, and much of strategic doctrine altogether, was invented largely by mathematicians, economists, and a few political scientists. It was invented to hold together abstractly, its validity judged by its internal logic. Questions of the correspondence to observable reality were not the issue. These abstract systems were developed as a way to make it possible to "think about the unthinkable," not as a way to describe or codify relations on the ground.[42]

So the greatest problem with the idea of "limited nuclear war," for example, is not that it is grotesque to refer to the death and suffering caused by *any* use of nuclear weapons as "limited" or that "limited nuclear war" is an abstraction that is disconnected from human reality but, rather, that "limited nuclear war" is itself an abstract conceptual system, designed, embodied, and achieved by computer modeling. It is an abstract world in which hypothetical, calm, rational actors have sufficient information to know exactly what size nuclear weapon the opponent has used against which targets, and in which, they have adequate command and control to make sure that their response is precisely equilibrated to the attack. In this scenario, no field commander would use the tactical "mini-nukes" at his disposal in the height of a losing battle; no EMP-generated electronic failures, or direct attacks on command, and control centers, or human errors would destroy communications networks. Our rational actors would be free of emotional response to being attacked, free of political pressures from the populace, free from madness or despair or any of the myriad other factors that regularly affect human actions and decision making. They would act solely on the basis of a perfectly informed mathematical calculus of megatonnage.

So to refer to "limited nuclear war" is already to enter into a system that is de facto abstract and removed from reality. To use more descriptive language would not, by itself, change that. In fact, I am tempted to say that the abstractness of the entire conceptual system makes descriptive language nearly beside the point. In a discussion of "limited nuclear war," for example, it might make some difference if in place of saying "In a counter-force attack against hard targets collateral damage could be limited," a strategic analyst had to use words that were less abstract—if he had to say, for instance, "If we launch the missiles we have aimed at their missile silos, the explosions would cause the immediate mass murder of 10 million women, men, and children, as well as the extended illness, suffering, and eventual death of many millions more." It is true that the second sentence does not roll off the tongue or slide across one's consciousness quite as easily. But it is also true, I believe, that the ability to speak about "limited nuclear war" stems as much, if not more, from the fact that the term "limited nuclear war" refers to an abstract conceptual system rather than to events that might take place in the real world. As such, there is no need to think about the concrete human realities behind the model; what counts is the internal logic of the system.[43]

This realization that the abstraction was not just in the words but also characterized the entire conceptual system itself helped me make sense of my difficulty in staying connected to human lives. But there was still a piece missing. How is it possible, for example, to make sense of the following paragraph? It is taken from a discussion of a scenario ("regime A") in which the United States and the Soviet Union have revised their offensive weaponry, banned MIRVs, and gone to a regime of single warhead (Midgetman) missiles, with no "defensive shield" (what is familiarly known as "Star Wars" or SDI):

The strategic stability of regime A is based on the fact that both sides are deprived of any incentive ever to strike first. Since it takes roughly two warheads to destroy one enemy silo, an attacker must expend two of his missiles to destroy one of the enemy's. A first strike disarms the attacker. The aggressor ends up worse off than the aggressed.[44]

"The aggressor ends up worse off than the aggressed"? The homeland of the aggressed has just been devastated by the explosions of, say, a thousand nuclear bombs, each likely to be ten to one hundred times more powerful than the bomb dropped on Hiroshima, and the aggressor, whose homeland is still untouched, "ends up worse off"? How is it possible to think this? Even abstract language and abstract thinking do not seem to be a sufficient explanation. I was only able to make sense of it when I finally asked myself the question that feminists have been asking about theories in every discipline: What is the reference point? Who (or what) is the *subject* here?

In other disciplines, we have frequently found that the reference point for theories about "universal human phenomena" has actually been white men. In technostrategic discourse, the reference point is not white men, it is not human beings at all; it is the weapons themselves. The aggressor thus ends up worse off than the aggressed because he has fewer weapons left; human factors are irrelevant to the calculus of gain and loss.

In "regime A" and throughout strategic discourse, the concept of "incentive" is similarly distorted by the fact that weapons are the subjects of strategic paradigms. Incentive to strike first is present or absent according to a mathematical calculus of numbers of surviving weapons. That is, incentive to start a nuclear war is discussed not in terms of what possible military or political ends it might serve but, instead, in terms of numbers of weapons, with the goal being to make sure that you are the guy who still has the most left at the end. Hence, it is frequently stated that MIRVed missiles create strategic instability because they give you the incentive to strike first. Calculating that two warheads must be targeted on each enemy missile, one MIRVed missile with ten warheads would, in theory, be able to destroy five enemy missiles in their silos; you destroy more of theirs than you have expended of your own. You win the numbers game. In addition, if you do not strike first, it would theoretically take relatively few of their MIRVed missiles to destroy a larger number of your own—so you must, as they say in the business, "use 'em or lose 'em." Many strategic analysts fear that in a period of escalating political tensions, when it begins to look as though war may be inevitable, this combination makes the incentive to settle first well nigh irresistible. Incentive to launch a nuclear war arises from a particular configuration of weapons and their hypothetical mathematical interactions. Incentive can only be so narrowly defined because the referents of technostrategic paradigms are weapons, not human lives, not even states and state power.

The fact that the subjects of strategic paradigms are weapons has several important implications. First, and perhaps most critically, there simply is no way to talk about human death or human societies when you are using a language designed to talk about weapons. Human death *is* simply "collateral damage"—collateral to the real subject, which is the weapons themselves.

Second, if human lives are not the reference point, then it is not only impossible to talk about humans in this language, it also becomes, in some sense, illegitimate to ask the paradigm to reflect human concerns. Hence, questions that break through the numbing language of strategic analysis and raise issues in human terms can be dismissed easily. No one will claim that the questions are unimportant, but they are inexpert, unprofessional, and irrelevant to the business at hand. The discourse among the experts remains hermetically sealed.

The problem, then, is not only that the language is narrow, but also that it is seen by its speakers as complete or whole unto itself, as representing a body of truths that exist independently of any other truth or knowledge. The isolation of this technical knowledge from social or psychological or moral thought, or feelings, is all seen as legitimate and necessary. The outcome is that defense intellectuals can talk about the weapons that are supposed to protect particular political entities, particular peoples and their way of life, without actually asking if weapons *can* do it, or if they are the best *way* to do it, or whether they may even damage the entities you are supposedly protecting. It is not that the men I spoke with would say that these are invalid questions. They would, however, simply say that they are separate questions, questions that are outside what they do, outside their realm of expertise. So their deliberations go on quite independently, as though with a life of their own, disconnected from the functions and values they are supposedly to serve.

Finally, the third problem is that this discourse has become virtually the only legitimate form of response to the question of how to achieve security. If the language of weaponry was one of competing voices in the discussion, or one that was integrated with others, the fact that the referents of strategic paradigms are only weapons would be of little note. But when we realize that the only language and expertise offered to those interested in pursuing peace refers to nothing but weapons, it limits become staggering, and its entrapping qualities (the way in which, once you adopt it, it becomes so hard to stay connected to human concerns) become more comprehensible.

STAGE 4: THE TERROR

As a newcomer to the world of defense analysts, I was continually startled by likeable and admirable men, by their gallows humor, by the bloodcurdling casualness with which they regularly blew up the world while standing and chatting over the coffee pot. I also *heard* the language they spoke—heard the acronyms and euphemisms, and abstractions, heard the imagery, heard the pleasure with which they used it. Within a few weeks, what had once been remarkable became unnoticeable. As I learned to speak, my perspective changed. I no longer stood outside the impermeable wall of technostrategic language and, once inside, I could no longer really hear it. And once inside its protective walls, I began to find it difficult to get out. The impermeability worked both ways.

I had not only learned to speak a language, I had started to think in it. Its questions became my questions, its concepts shaped my responses to new ideas. Its definitions of the parameters of reality became mine. Like a white queen, I began to believe six impossible things before breakfast. Not because I consciously believed, for instance, that a "surgically clean counterforce strike" was really possible, but instead because some elaborate piece of doctrinal reasoning I used was already predicated on the possibility of those strikes, as well as on a host of other impossible things.[45]

My grasp on what I knew as reality seemed to slip. I might get very excited, for example, about a new strategic jusification for a "no first use" policy and spend time discussing the ways in which its implications for our force structure in Western Europe were superior to the older version.[46] And after a day or two I would suddenly step back, aghast that I was so involved with the military jusitifications for not using nuclear weapons—as though the moral ones were not enough. What I was actually talking about (the mass incineration caused by a nuclear attack) was no longer in my head. Or I might hear some proposals that seemed to me infinitely superior to the usual arms control fare. First, I would work out how and why these proposals were better and then work out all the ways to counter the arguments against them. But then, it might dawn on me that even though these two proposals sounded so different, they still shared a host of assumptions that I was not willing to make (e.g., about the inevitable, eternal conflict of interests between the United States and the Soviet Union, or the desirability of having some form of nuclear deterrent, or the goal of

"managing," rather than ending, the nuclear arms race). After struggling to this point of seeing what united both positions, I would first
feel as though I had really accomplished something. And then all of a
sudden, I would realize that these new insights were things I actually
knew *before I ever entered* this community. Apparently, I had since
forgotten them, at least functionally, if not absolutely. I began to feel
that I had fallen down the rabbit hole, and it was a struggle to climb
back out.

CONCLUSIONS

Suffice it to say that the issues about language do not disappear after
you have mastered technostrategic discourse. The seductions remain
great. You can find all sorts of ways to seemingly beat the boys at their
own game. You can show how even within their own definitions of
rationality, most of what is happening in the development and deployment of nuclear forces is wildly irrational. You can also impress
your friends and colleagues with sickly humorous stories about the
way things really happen on the inside. There is tremendous pleasure
in it, especially for those of us who have been closed out, who have
been told that it is really all beyond us and we should just leave it to
the benevolently paternal men in charge. But as the pleasures deepen,
so do the dangers. The activity of trying to out-reason defense intellectuals in their own games gets you thinking inside their rules, tacitly
accepting all the unspoken assumptions of their paradigms. You become subject to the tyranny of concepts. The language shapes your
categories of thought, "good nukes" or "bad nukes," not, nukes or no
nukes, and defines the boundaries of thought (as you try to imagine a
"minimally destabilizing basing mode" rather than a way to prevent
the weapon from being deployed at all).

Yet, the issues of language have now been somewhat less vivid and
central to me. Some of the questions raised by these experiences remain
important but others have faded and been superseded by new questions.
While still not precisely the questions of an "insider," these are questions I could not have had without being inside, without having access
to the knowledge and perspective the inside position affords. Many of
my questions now are more practical, such as, which individuals and
institutions are actually responsible for the endless modernization and
proliferation of nuclear weaponry? What role does technostrategic rationality actually play in their thinking? What would a reasonable,
genuinely defensive "defense" policy look like? Others are more philosophical. What is the nature of the rationality and realism claimed
by defense intellectuals for their mode of thinking? What are the many

different grounds on which their claims to rationality can be shown to be spurious?

My own move away from a focus on the language is quite typical. Other recent entrants into this world have commented to me that, while it is the cold-blooded, abstract discussions that are most striking at first, within a short time "you get past it, you stop hearing it, it stops bothering you, it becomes normal, and you come to see that the language itself is not the problem." However, I think it would be a mistake to dismiss these early impressions. They can help us learn something about the militarization of the mind, and they have, I believe, important implications for feminist scholars and activists who seek to create a more just and peaceful world.

Mechanisms of the mind's militarization are revealed through both listening to the language and learning to speak it. *Listening*, it becomes clear that participation in the world of nuclear strategic analysis does not necessarily require confrontation with the central fact about military activity—that the purpose of all weaponry and all strategy is to injure human bodies.[47] In fact, as Elaine Scarry points out, participation in military thinking does not require confrontation with, and actually demands the elision of, this reality.[48] Listening to the discussion of nuclear experts reveals a series of culturally grounded and culturally acceptable mechanisms that serve this purpose and that make it possible to "think about the unthinkable," to work in institutions that foster the proliferation of nuclear weapons, and to plan mass incinerations of millions of human beings for a living. Language that is abstract, sanitized, full of euphemisms; language that is sexy and fun to use; paradigms whose referent is weapons; imagery that domesticates and deflates the forces of mass destruction; imagery that reverses sentient and nonsentient matter, that conflates birth and death, destruction and creation; all are part of what makes it possible to be radically removed from the reality of what one is talking about and from the realities one is creating through the discourse.[49]

Learning to speak the language reveals something about how thinking can become more abstract, more focused on parts disembodied from their context, and more attentive to the survival of weapons than the survival of human beings. That is, it reveals something about the process of militarization, and the way in which that process may be undergone by man or woman, hawk or dove. Most often, the act of learning technostrategic language is conceived of as an additive process: you add a new set of vocabulary words; you add the reflex ability to decode and use endless numbers of acronyms; you add some new information that the specialized language contains; you add the conceptual tools that will allow you to "think strategically." This additive view appears to be held by defense intellectuals themselves; as one said to me, "Much of the debate is in technical terms—learn it, and decide whether it's relevant later." This view also appears to be held by many who think of themselves as antinuclear, be they scholars and professionals attempting to change the field from within, or public interest lobbyists and educational organizations, or some feminist antimilitarists.[50] Some believe that our nuclear policies are so riddled with irrationality that there is a lot of room for well-reasoned, well-informed arguments to make a difference. Others, even if they do not believe that the technical information is very important, see it as necessary to master the language simply because it is too difficult to attain public legitimacy without it. In either case, the idea is that you add the expert language and information, and proceed from there.

However, I have been arguing throughout this paper that learning the language is a transformative, rather than additive process. When you choose to learn it you enter a new mode of thinking—a mode of thinking not only about nuclear weapons but also, de facto, about military and political power and about the relationship between human needs and technological means. Thus, those of us who find U.S. nuclear policy desperately misguided appear to face a serious quandary. If we refuse to learn the language, we are virtually guaranteed that our voices will remain outside the "'politically relevant" spectrum of opinion. Yet, if we do learn and speak it, we not only severely limit what we can say but we also invite the transformation, the militarization, of our own thinking.

I have no solutions to this dilemma, but I would like to offer a few thoughts in an effort to reformulate its terms. First, it is important to recognize an assumption implicit in adopting the strategy of learning the language. When we assume that learning and speaking the language will give us a voice recognized as legitimate and will give us greater political influence, *we are assuming that the language itself actually articulates the criteria and reasoning strategies upon which nuclear weapons development and deployment decisions are made.* I believe that this is largely an illusion. Instead, I want to suggest that technostrategic discourse functions more as a gloss, as an ideological curtain behind which the actual reasons for these decisions hide. That rather than informing and shaping decisions, it far more often functions as a legitimation for political outcomes that have occurred for utterly different reasons. If this is true, it raises some serious questions about the extent of the political returns we might get from using technostrategic discourse, and whether they can ever balance out the potential problems and inherent costs.

I do not, however, want to suggest that none of us should learn the language. I do not believe that this language is well suited to achieving the goals desired by antimilitarists, yet at the same time, I, for one, have found the experience of learning the language useful and worthwhile (even if at times traumatic). The questions for those of us who do choose to learn it, is what use are we going to make of that knowledge? One of the most intriguing options opened by learning the language is that it suggests a basis upon which to challenge the legitimacy of the defense intellectuals' dominance of the discourse on nuclear issues. When defense intellectuals are criticized for the cold-blooded inhumanity of the scenarios they plan, their response is to claim the high ground of rationality; they are the only ones whose response to the existence of nuclear weapons is objective and realistic. They portray those who are radically opposed to the nuclear status quo as irrational, unrealistic, and too emotional. "Idealistic activists" is the pejorative they set against their own hard-nosed professionalism.

Much of their claim to legitimacy, then, is a claim to objectivity born of technical expertise and to the disciplined purging of the emotional valences that might threaten their objectivity. But if the surface of their discourse (its abstraction and technical jargon) appears at first to support these claims, a look just below the surface does not. There we find currents of homoerotic excitement, heterosexual domination, the drive toward competency and mastery, the pleasures of membership in an elite and privileged group, the ultimate importance and meaning of membership in the priesthood, and the thrilling power of becoming Death, shatterer of worlds. How is it possible to hold this up as a paragon of cool-headed objectivity?

I do not wish here to discuss or judge the holding of "objectivity" as an epistemological goal. I would simply point out that, as defense intellectuals rest their claims to legitimacy on the untainted rationality of their discourse, their project fails according to its own criteria. Deconstructing strategic discourse's claims to rationality is, then, in and of itself, an important way to challenge its hegemony as the sole legitimate language for public debate about nuclear policy.

I believe that feminists, and others who seek a more just and peaceful world, have a dual task before us—a deconstructive project and a reconstructive project that are intimately linked.[51] Our deconstructive task requires close attention to, and the dismantling of, technostrategic discourse. The dominant voice of militarized masculinity and decontextualized rationality speaks so loudly in our culture, it will remain difficult for any other voices to be heard until that voice loses some of its power to define what we hear and how we name the world—until that voice is delegitimated. Our reconstructive task is a task of creating compelling alternative visions of possible futures, a task of recognizing and developing alternative conceptions of rationality, and a task of creating rich and imaginative alternative voices—diverse voices whose conversations with each other will invent those futures.

NOTES

1. Thomas Powers, "How Nuclear War Could Start," *New York Review of Books* (January 17, 1985), 33.

2. George Kennan, "A Modest Proposal," *New York Review of Books* (July 16, 1981), 14.

3. It is unusual for defense intellectuals to write for the public, rather than for their colleagues, but a recent, interesting exception has been made by a group of defense analysts from Harvard. Their two books provide a clear expression of the stance that living with nuclear weapons is not so much a problem to be solved but a condition to be managed rationally. Albert Carnesale and the Harvard Nuclear Study Group, *Living with Nuclear Weapons* (Cambridge, Mass.: Harvard University Press, 1984); and Graham T. Allison, Albert Carnesale, and Joseph Nye, Jr., eds. *Hawks, Doves, and Owls: An Agenda for Avoiding Nucelar War* (New York: W. W. Norton & Co., 1985).

4. For useful introductions to feminist work on gender and language, see Barrie Thorne, Cheris Kramarae, and Nancy Henley, eds., *Language, Gender, and Society* (Rowley, Mass.: Newbury Publishing House, 1983); and Elizabeth Abel, ed., *Writing and Sexual Difference* (Chicago: University of Chicago Press, 1982).

5. For feminist critiques of dominant Western conceptions of rationality, see Nancy Hartsock, *Money, Sex, and Power* (New York: Longman, 1983); Sandra Harding and Merrill Hintikka, eds., *Discovering Reality: Feminist Perspectives on Epistemology, Metaphysics, Methodology and the Philosophy of Science* (Dordrecht: D. Reidel Publishing Co., 1983); Evelyn Fox Keller, *Reflections on Gender and Science* (New Haven, Conn.: Yale University Press, 1985); Jean Bethke Elshtain, *Public Man, Private Woman: Woman in Social and Political Thought* (Princeton, N.J.: Princeton University Press, 1981); Genevieve Lloyd, *The Man of Reason: "Male" and "Female" in Western Philosophy* (Minneapolis: University of Minnesota Press, 1984), which contains a particularly useful bibliographic essay; Sara Ruddick, "Remarks on the Sexual Politics of Reason," in *Women and Moral Theory*, ed. by Eva Kittay and Diana Meyers (Totowa, N.J.: Rowman & Allanheld, in press). Some of the growing feminist work on gender and war is explicitly connected to critiques of rationality. See Virginia Woolf, *Three Guineas*, (New York: Harcourt, Brace, Jovanovich, 1966); Nancy C. M. Hartsock, "The Feminist Historical Materialism," in Harding and Hintikka, eds., *Discovering Reality*, 283–310; "The Barracks Community in Western Political Thought: Prolegomena to a Feminist Critique of War and Politics," in *Women's and Men's Wars*, ed. by Judith Hicks Stiehm (Oxford: Pergamon Press, 1983); Jean Bethke Elshtain, "Reflections on War and Political Discourse: Realism, Just War and Feminism in a Nuclear Age," *Political Theory* 13, no. 1 (February 1985): 39–57; Sara Ruddick, "Preservative Love and Military Destruction: Some Reflections on Mothering and Peace," in *Mothering: Essays in Feminist Theory*, ed. by Joyce Trebilcot (Totowa, N.J.: Rowman & Allenheld, 1984), 231–62; Genevieve Lloyd, "Selfhood, War, and Masculinity," in *Feminist Challenges*, ed. by E. Gross and C. Pateman (Boston: Northeastern University Press, 1986), There is a vast and valuable literature

on gender and war that indirectly informs my work. See, for example, Cynthia Enloe, *Does Khaki Become You? The Militarization of Women's Lives* (Boston: South End Press, 1983); Jean Bethke Elshtain, "On Beautiful Souls, Just Warriors, and Feminist Consciousness," in Stiehm, ed. *Women and Men's Wars*, 341–48; Sara Ruddick. "Pacifying the Forces: Drafting Women in the Interests of Peace," *Signs: Journal of Women in Culture and Society*, 8, no. 3 (Spring 1983): 471–89; "Drafting Women: Pieces of a Puzzle," in *Conscripts and Volunteers: Military Requirements, Social Values, and the All-Volunteer Force*, ed. by Robert K. Fullinwider (Totowa, N.J.: Rowman & Allanheld, 1983); Amy Swerdlow, "Women's Strike for Peace versus HUAC," *Feminist Studies*, 8, no. 3 (Fall 1982): 493–520; Mary C. Segers, "The Catholic Bishops' Pastoral Letter on War and Peace: A Feminist Perspective," *Feminist Studies*, 11, no. 3 (Fall 1985): 619–47.

6. I have coined the term "technostrategic" to represent the intertwined, inextricable nature of technological and nuclear strategic thinking. The first reason is that strategic thinking seems to change in direct response to technological changes, rather than political thinking, or some independent paradigms that might be isolated as "strategic." (On this point see Lord Solly Zuckerman, *Nuclear Illusions and Reality* [New York: Viking Press, 1982]). Even more important, strategic theory not only depends on, and changes in, response to technological objects, it is also based on a kind of thinking, a way of looking at problems (formal, mathematical modeling, systems analysis, game theory, linear programming) that are part of technology itself. So I use the term "technostrategic" to indicate the degree to which nuclear strategic language and thinking are imbued with, indeed constructed out of, modes of thinking that are associated with technology.

7. Fusion weapons' proportionally smaller yield of radioactive fallout led Atomic Energy Commission Chairman Lewis Strauss to announce in 1956 that hydrogen bomb tests were important "not only from a military point of view but from a humanitarian aspect." Although the bombs being tested were 1,000 times more powerful than those that devastated Hiroshima and Nagasaki, the proportional reduction of fallout apparently qualified them as not only clean but also humanitarian. Lewis Strauss is quoted in Ralph Lapp, "The Humanitarian H-Bomb," *Bulletin of Atomic Scientists*, 12, no. 7 (September 1956): 263.

8. I must point out that we cannot know whether to take this particular example literally: America's list of nuclear targets is, of course, classified. The defense analyst quoted, however, is a man who has had access to that list for at least two decades. He is also a man whose thinking and speaking is careful and precise, so I think it is reasonable to assume that his statement is not a distortion, that "shoe factories," even if not themselves literally targeted, accurately represent a category of target. Shoe factories would be one among many "military targets" other than weapons systems themselves. They would be military targets because an army needs boots. The likelihood of a nuclear war lasting long enough for foot soldiers to wear out their boots might seem to stretch the limits of credibility, but that is an insufficient reason to assume that they are not nuclear targets. Nuclear targeting and nuclear strategic planning in general frequently suffer from "conventionalization—the tendency

of planners to think in the old, familiar terms of "conventional" warfare rather than fully assimilating the ways which nuclear weaponry has changed warfare. In avoiding talking about murder, the defense community has long been ahead of the State Department. It was not until 1984 that the State Department announced it will no longer use the word "killing," much less "murder," in official reports on the status of human rights in allied countries. The new term is "unlawful or arbitrary deprivation of life" (*New York Times*, February 15, 1984, as cited in *Quarterly Review of Doublespeak*, 11, no. 1 [October 1984]: 3).

9. "Kiloton" (or kt) is a measure of explosive power, measured by the number of thousands of tons of TNT required to release an equivalent amount of energy. The atomic bomb dropped on Hiroshima is estimated to have been approximately 12 kt. An MX missile is designed to carry up to ten Mk 21 reentry vehicles, each with a W–87 warhead. The yield of W–87 warheads is 300 kt, but they are "upgradable" to 475 kt.

10. Since the MX would theoretically be able to "take out" Soviet land-based ICBMs in a "disarming first strike," the Soviets would have few ICBMs left for a retaliatory attack, and thus damage to the United States theoretically would be limited. However, to consider the damage than could be inflicted on the United States by the remaining ICBMs, not to mention Soviet bombers and submarine-based missiles as "limited" is to act as though words have no meaning.

11. Conservative government assessments of the number of deaths resulting from a "surgically clean" counterforce attack vary widely. The Office of Technology Assessment projects 2 million to 20 million immediate deaths. (See James Fallows, *National Defense* [New York: Random House, 1981], 159.) A 1975 Defense Department study estimated 18.3 million fatalities, while the U.S. Arms Control and Disarmament Agency, using different assumptions, arrived at a figure of 50 million (cited by Desmond Ball, "Can Nuclear War Be Controlled?" *Adelphi Paper* no. 169 [London: International Institute for Strategic Studies, 1981]).

12. The phrase is Helen Caldicott's in Helen Caldicott, *Missile Envy: The Arms Race and Nuclear War* (Toronto: Bantam Books, 1986).

13. For the uninitiated, "penetration aids" refers to devices that help bombers or missiles get past the enemy's defensive systems, for example, stealth technology, chaff, or decoys. Within the defense intellectual community, they are also familiarly known as "penaids."

14. General William Odom, "C³I and Telecommunications at the Policy Level," Incidental Paper, *Seminar on C³I: Command, Control, Communications and Intelligence* (Cambridge, Mass.: Harvard University, Center for Information Policy Research Spring 1980), 5.

15. This point has been amply documented by Brian Easlea, *Fathering the Unthinkable: Masculinity, Scientists and the Nuclear Arms Race* (London: Pluto Press, 1983).

16. *Air Force Magazine* 68, no. 6 (June 1985): 77–78.

17. Ibid.

18. William L. Laurence, *Dawn over Zero: The study of the Atomic Bomb* (London: Museum Press, 1974), 198–99.

19. U.S.A.F. Retired General T. R. Milton, "Nuclear Virginity," *Air Force Magazine*, 68, no. 5 (May 1985): 44.

20. I am grateful to Margaret Cerullo, a participant in the first summer program, for reporting the use of this analogy to me and sharing her thoughts about this and other events in the program. The interpretation I give here draws strongly on hers.

21. MIRV stands for "multiple independently targetable re-entry vehicles." A MIRVed missile not only carries more than one warhead, its warheads can be aimed at different targets.

22. Henry T. Nash, "The Bureaucratization of Homicide," *Bulletin of Atomic Scientists* (April 1980), reprinted in E. P. Thompson and Dan Smith, eds., *Protest and Survive* (New York: Monthly News Review Press, 1981), 159. The neutron bomb is notable for the active political contention that has occurred over its use and naming. It is a small warhead that produces six times the prompt radiation but slightly less blast and heat than typical fission warheads of the same yield. Pentagon planners see neutron bombs as useful in killing Soviet tank crews while theoretically leaving the buildings near the tanks intact. Of course, the civilians in the nearby buildings, however, would be killed by the same "enhanced radiation" as the tank crews. It is this design for protecting property while killing civilians along with soldiers that has led people in the antinuclear movement to call the neutron bomb "the ultimate capitalist weapon." However, in official parlance the neutron bomb is not called a weapon at all, it is an "enhanced radiation device." It is worth noting, however, that the designer of the neutron bomb did not conceive of it as an anti-tank personnel weapon to be used against the Soviets. Instead, he thought it would be useful in an area where the enemy *did not have* nuclear weapons to use. (Samuel T. Cohen, in an interview on National Public Radio, as reported in Fred Kaplan, "The Neutron Bomb: What It Is, the Way It Works," *Bulletin of Atomic Scientists* [October 1981], 6.).

23. For a discussion of the functions of imagery that reverses sentient and insentient matter, that "exchange[s] ... idioms between weapons and bodies," see Elaine Scarry, *The Body in Pain: The Making and Unmaking of the World* (New York: Oxford University Press, 1985), 60–157, esp. 67.

24. For further discussion of men's desire to appropriate from women the power of giving life and death, and its implications for men's war-making activities, see Dorothy Dinnerstein, *The Mermaid and the Minotaur* (New York: Harper & Row, 1976). For further analysis of male birth imagery in the atomic bomb project, see Evelyn Fox Keller, "From Secrets of Life to Secrets of Death" (paper delivered at the *Kansas Seminar*, Yale University, New Haven, Conn., November 1986); and Easlea, *Fathering the Unthinkable*, 81–116.

25. Lawrence is quoted in Herbert Childs, *An American Genius: The Life of Ernest Orlando Lawrence* (New York: E. P. Dutton, 1968), 340.

26. Feynman writes about the telegram in Richard P. Feynman, "Los Alamos from Below," in *Reminiscences of Los Alamos, 1943–1945*, ed. by Lawrence Badash, Joseph O. Hirschfelder, and Herbert P. Broida (Dordrecht: D. Reidel Publishing Co., 1980), 130.

27. Hans Bethe is quoted as saying that "Ulam was the father of the hydrogen bomb and Edward was the mother, because he carried the baby for

quite a while" (J. Bernstein, *Hans Bethe: Prophet of Energy* [New York: Basic Books, 1980], 95).

28. The MILSTAR system is a communications satellite system that is jam resistant, as well as having an "EMP-hardened capability." This means that the electromagnetic pulse set off by a nuclear explosion would theoretically not destroy the missiles' electronic systems. There are, of course, many things to say about the sanity and morality of the idea of the MILSTAR system and of spending the millions of dollars necessary to EMP-harden it. The most obvious point is that this is a system designed to enable the United States to fight a "protracted" nuclear war (the EMP-hardening is to allow it to act as a conduit for command and control of successive nuclear shots, long after the initial exchange). The practicality of the idea would also appear to merit some discussion—who and what is going to be communicating to and from after the initial exchange? And why bother to harden it against EMP when all an opponent has to do to prevent the system from functioning is to blow it up, a feat certain to become technologically feasible in a short time? But, needless to say, exploration of these questions was not part of the briefing.

29. The concern about having a boy, not a girl, is written about by Robert Jungk, *Brighter Than a Thousand Suns*, trans. by James Cleugh (New York: Harcourt, Brace & Co., 1956), 197.

30. Richard E. Hewlett and Oscar E. Anderson, *The New World, 1939/46: A History of the United States Atomic Energy Commission*, 2 vols. (University Park: Pennsylvania State University Press, 1962), 1:386.

31. Winston Churchill, *The Second World War*, vol. 6., *Triumph and Tragedy* (London: Cassell, 1954), 551.

32. Quoted by Easlea, *Fathering the Unthinkable*, 130.

33. Laurence, *Dawn over Zero*, 10.

34. Ibid., 188.

35. From a 1985 interview in which Holloway was explaining the logic of a "decapitating" strike against the Soviet leadership and command and control systems—and thus how nuclear war would be different from World War II, which was a "war of attrition," in which transportation, supply depots, and other targets were hit, rather than being a "big bang" (Daniel Ford, "The Button," *New Yorker Magazine*, V. 61, no. 7 [April 8, 1985]:49).

36. Jungk, *Brighter Than a Thousand Suns*, 201.

37. Hisako Matsubara, *Cranes at Dusk* (Garden City, N.Y.: Dial Press, 1985). The author was a child in Kyoto at the time the atomic bomb was dropped. Her description is based on the memories of survivors.

38. General Robert Rosenberg (formerly on the National Security Council staff during the Carter Administration), "The Influence of Policymaking on C^3I," Incidental Paper, *Seminar on C^3I* (Cambridge, Mass.: Harvard University, Center for Information Policy Research, Spring 1980), 59.

39. Two other writers who have remarked on this division of languages between the victims and the professionals (variously named) are Freeman Dyson and Glenn D. Hook. Dyson, in *Weapons and Hope* (New York: Harper & Row, 1984), notes that there are two languages in the current discussion of nuclear weapons, which he calls the language of "the victims" and the language of "the warriors." He sees the resulting problem as being the difficulty the two

groups have in communicating with each other and, thus, in appreciating each other's valid concerns. His project, then, is the search for a common language, and a good portion of the rest of the book is directed toward that end. Hook, in "Making Nuclear Weapons Easier to Live With: The Political Role of Language in Nuclearization," *Journal of Peace Research*, v. 22, no. 1 (1985): 67–77, follows Camus in naming the two groups "the victims" and "the executioners." He is more explicit than Dyson about naming these as perspectives, as coming from the positions of greater or lesser power, and points out that those with the most power are able to dominate and define the terms in which we speak about nuclear issues, so that no matter who we are, we find ourselves speaking as though we were the users, rather than the victims of nuclear weapons. Although my analysis of perspectives and the ways in which language inscribes relations of power is similar to his, I differ from Hook in finding in this fact one of the sources of the experts' relative lack of fear of nuclear war.

40. The "strategic triad" refers to the three different modes of basing nuclear warheads: at land, on intercontinental ballistic missiles; at sea, on missiles in submarines; and "in the air," on the Strategic Air Command's bombers. Given that nuclear weapons based on submarines are "invulnerable" (not subject to attack) since there is not now nor likely to be in the future any reliable way to find and target submarines, many commentators (mostly from outside the community of defense intellectuals) have suggested that the Navy's leg of the triad is all we need to ensure a capacity to retaliate against a nuclear attack. This suggestion that submarine-based missiles are an adequate deterrent becomes especially appealing when it is remembered that the other basing modes (ICBMs and bombers) act as targets that would draw thousands of nuclear attacks to the American mainland in time of war.

41. For an interesting recent discussion of the role of language in the creation of professional power, see JoAnne Brown, "Professional Language: Words That Succeed," *Radical History Review*, no. 34 (1986):33–51.

42. For fascinating, detailed accounts of the development of strategic doctrine, see Fred Kaplan, *The Wizards of Armageddon* (New York: Simon & Schuster, 1983); and Gregg F. Herken, *Counsels of War*, (New York: Alfred A. Knopf, 1985).

43. Steven Kull's interviews with nuclear strategists can be read to show that on some level, some of the time, some of these men are aware that there is a serious disjunction between their models and the real world. Their justification for continuing to use these models is that the "other people" (unnamed, and on asking, unnameable) believe in them and that they therefore have an important reality ("Nuclear Nonsense," *Foreign Policy*, no. 58 [Spring 1985]:28–52).

44. Charles Krauthammer, "Will Star Wars Kill Arms Control?" *New Republic*, no. 3,653 (January 21, 1985): 12–16.

45. For an excellent discussion of the myriad uncertainties that make it ludicrous to assume the targeting accuracies posited in the notion of "surgically clean counterforce strikes," see Fallows, *National Defense*, chap. 6.

46. "No first use," refers to the commitment not to be the first side to introduce nuclear weapons into a "conventional" war. The Soviet Union has a "no first use" policy, but the United States does not. In fact, it is NATO doctrine

to use nuclear weapons in a conventional war in Western Europe, as a way of overcoming the Warsaw Pact's supposed superiority in conventional weaponry and troop strength.

47. For an eloquent and graphic exploration of this point, see Scarry, *The Body in Pain*, 73.

48. Scarry catalogs a variety of mechanisms that serve this purpose (Ibid., 60–157). The point is further developed by Sara Ruddick, "The Rationality of Care," in *Thinking about Women, War, and the Military*, ed. by Jean Bethke Elshtain and Sheila Tobias (Totowa, N.J.: Rowan & Allanheld, in press).

49. My discussion of the specific ways in which this discourse creates new realities is in the next part of this project, entitled, "The Emperor's New Armor." I, like many other social scientists, have been influenced by post-structuralist literary theory's discussion of deconstructing texts, point of view, and narrative authority within texts, and I take the language and social practice of the defense intellectuals as a text to be read in this way. For a classic introduction to this literature, see Josue Harari, ed., *Textual Strategies: Perspectives in Post-structuralist Criticism* (Ithaca, N.Y.: Cornell University Press, 1979); and Jacques Derrida, *Of Grammatology* (Baltimore: Johns Hopkins University Press, 1976).

50. Perhaps the most prominent proponent of this strategy is Sheila Tobias. See "Demystifying Defense: Closing the Knowledge Gap," *Social Policy*, v. 13, no. 3 (1983): 29–32; and Sheila Tobias, Peter Goudinoff, Stefan Leader, and Shelah Leader, *What Kinds of Guns Are They Buying for Your Butter?* (New York: William Morrow & Co., 1982).

51. Harding and Hintikka, *Discovering Reality*, ix–xix, esp. x.

5

Can Peace Be Imagined?

Elise Boulding

It was over thirty years ago that Fred Polak wrote his *Image of the Future*[1] to lament the decline in the ability of the western world to picture a peaceful and better future after the crushing experiences of World War II. It was his contrasting of the immobilizing pessimism of this postwar era with the extraordinarily creative futures-imaging that had been going on from the Renaissance to the Enlightenment, and which had in fact produced the industrial society and the welfare state, which led me to the study of futurism and its relationship to peace in our times.

THE SIGNIFICANCE OF UTOPIAN IMAGERY

In my first survey of futurism in the 1960s, I divided futurists into (1) social planners/systems designers, brainstormers, and technocratic futurists on the one hand and (2) humanist, participatory, evolutionist, ecological/revolutionary futurists on the other.[2] I dismissed the technocratic futurists as operating within too narrow a frame, both temporally and spatially; the technocrats were projecting western-style development step by step into the global future with no account taken of other civilizational traditions. By contrast I saw signs of thinking in a wider planetary frame of reference among the evolutionary/ecological/revolutionary futurists, with hints of transcendance and societal transformation here and there. Optimism, I noted, rode high in both camps.

Now we are on the verge of the 1990s, on a militarized planet with a life-destroying nuclear holocaust on everyone's mind. The social terrain is strewn with failed liberation movements, domestically and internationally, and the gap between the rich and the poor is wider than ever. The facile optimism of both the technocratic and the evolutionary futurists rings a bit hollow. As my own work has come to focus more and more on possible alternative social orders, I find that the *act* of generating imagery about alternatives, which I took for granted in the 1960s, is now in itself problematic. Why, with all the energy that has gone into peace and social change movements over the past few decades, do we edge steadily closer to the nuclear abyss? I am not exactly sure when it began to dawn on me that most of the peace movement activists I knew, from arms controllers to out-and-out disarmers, did not in their hearts believe that a world without armies was possible. They were working for goals they did not believe were achievable, but they were working for them anyway, because the situation was too dangerous for inaction. Something had to be *done,* but that something was unaccompanied by any mental images of what a successful outcome might be like. Having, in the meantime, satisfied myself through a brief investigation of utopian imagery in other civilizational traditions that an inclination to visualize one's own society in a future peaceable state was testified to in the literary and oral traditions of every major culture,[3] I had to ask why that kind of mental picturing was not going on in our own time. I discovered through intergenerational interviewing,[4] that people born in the first two decades of this century were still doing that kind of picturing, but that it became progressively rarer for more recent generations.

There is of course no simple causal explanation for this state of affairs. Many different strands of culture, science, and technology have helped weaken the social imagination. I have become increasingly convinced, however, that we suffer from an experience deprivation which leads to image deprivation. We who live in the privileged sectors of the industrialized world, both East and West, inhabit a technological shell that intervenes between us and the actual experience of the physico-social environment in which we live. We interpret the social order in terms of Comtean[5] and Spencerian[6] concepts of successive stages in human development, from tribal to military to industrial, in the largely unquestioned conviction that our particular industrial developmental sequence represents the leading edge, in the Teilhardian sense, of the next development in the species.[7] A fascination with technological mastery of the environment has led many to equate technological mastery with human development. This has produced ways of life insulated from the cycles, ebbs, and flows of the organic surround and the organic within. It is because all social problems are seen as having technological solutions, that industrial societies, East and West, have come to depend on high-tech weapons systems to protect them from having to interact in problem-solving ways with adversaries.

THE CENTRALIZATION OF DECISION-MAKING

Nowhere has the effect of the technological-fix approach been felt more pervasively than in the educational systems of industrial societies. The same numeracy, letter, and design literacy which provided the tools for the develoment of the industrial revolution have gradually been harnessed to a kind of product-oriented mental activity, which has left little room for the mental playfulness that has characterized all great civilizational flowerings. Children don't even have to be scolded for daydreaming any more. They move between the two worlds of ready-made imagery—the TV at home, and the computer at school. All reality is on the screens. In front of the TV, one simply absorbs it. In front of the computer, one *makes* it, omnipotently, by manipulating figures and numbers. War games assure us that this kind of training for young children will ensure rational thinking (presumably the kind of rational thinking of which the wargamers themselves are masters). Very little information is stored in the mind, to be played within a process well known to oral tradition societies. Why bother, when it can be so easily accessed on the computer?

As decision making becomes increasingly centralized for efficiency, we are moving toward more and more decision making based on highly schematic computer-screen representations of reality, more and more divorced from the on-the-ground reality of human life in specific local environments. Thus, what began as a movement to free the human mind from the negative constraints of hunger and excessive physical labor has ended by equipping the mind with ever more abstracted representations of reality, and emptying it of concrete local experience outside the office and the laboratory. In short, young people grow up with fewer and fewer opportunities to *exercise* their imaginations on their own. The situation is compounded by a pervasive social fear of the threat of violence, which affects the behavior of adults and children alike. There is violence not only in urban areas, but also in small communities and within households. Behind all other fears lurks the fear of nuclear winter and an end to all life. One indisputable finding of behavioral science is that fear produces behavioral rigidity and freezes the imagination.

To talk of cultivating the social imagination in a society which relies on technological solutions, and is cramped by fear, may sound wildly unrealistic. Nevertheless, Polak's formulation boiled down to its simplest version, that people are empowered to action by their own sense of the possible and desired other, carries even more weight today than when he first proposed it in the early 1950s. It has been empirically demonstrated in all sorts of experiments that people with the same capacities, but with different aspiration levels, perform according to their aspiration levels, not according to their capacities. While there are plenty of successful individual achievers in the "me" generation, the absence of aspiration for the society as a whole, for the planet as a whole, condemns humanity to a sorry performance in terms of human welfare. Polak assumed that if people were told of the importance of imaging the social future, they would do it. He correctly predicted that technological futurists would not be much help because they were not able to make the mental leaps necessary to make what he called a breach in time, into a sense of the other, so powerful that it could act on the present. Why have not the evolutionary futurists (the contemporaries he was really addressing) been able to generate the kind of vibrant, liberating imagery that makes for sustained society-wide action in a new direction over time?

Of course, we are looking at a very short time span, from the 1960s to the 1980s, and social change needs time. However, it is also true that many major social changes have taken place within twenty-year spans. The twenty-year period from 1945 to 1965 saw the addition of about fifty new independent nations to the international system, forever changing its character. The almost fifty additional nations added over the next twenty years has only increased the momentum of international change begun in 1945. I will return to this subject again, because embedded in that phenomenon lie many of the raw materials for futures imaging neglected by the countries of the North. For the moment, it is enough to point out that during this change-rich period, the United States has moved away from the early twentieth-century American Dream of economic and social well-being for all, to fears of armageddon. One of the most determined efforts to avert armageddon, the nuclear freeze movement, is charcterized by an absence of imagery about what a post-freeze world could be like.

Who could now turn the tide? Not the aquarians, because they counted on a kind of inevitable social transformationism, sparked by key individual transformers networking with one another. Not the revolutionaries either, because they counted on an equally inevitable political kind of transformationism. The environmentalists have probably provided the strongest impulse for turnaround and social change, because they have the kind of on-the-ground knowledge of the world as it is, and mental pictures of how it could be, that can fire social action. The fact that environmentalists have now joined forces with the peace movement based on a common reaction against the threat of nuclear winter is one of hope to the futurist field. The social evolutionists continue to be front-line imagers, keeping the concept of the future alive. While they cheer up people with their macrohistorical views (no small thing in bleak times) it is hard to translate evolutionary concepts into action-inspiring, concrete social imagery for the public at large.

Surveying the present scene, I see futurists facing a primary challenge of cultivating the social imagination of the post-World War II generations, so individuals can experience hitherto longed-for but not-believed-in possibilities in their own minds, and, thus, be empowered to actions on behalf of those imaged possibilities. Because our own social and educational environment works against this kind of imagery, it has to be taught as a kind of literacy—image literacy.

IMAGE LITERACY

The person who invented the concept of image literacy is Warren Ziegler,[8] of Futures Invention Associates. Ziegler and I got together several years ago to try to apply his workshop technique of community problem-solving to the macroproblem of the global arms race through imagining what things would be like if a given problem were solved. Since the problem was so much larger in scale than the local problems Ziegler usually dealt with, and visualizing a weapon-free world within the short time span (two decades) required for an appropriate sense of immediacy seemed to require such an overwhelming suspension of disbelief, we were not sure the process could work for imaging within whole social order. While there has been no lack of problems connected with effective workshop development, we were both taken by surprise by the powerful emotional reactions of the majority of people who went through the workshop experience. Even though their imagery of a world without weapons was fragmentary at best, what they saw "with the inward eye" was so compellingly real to them, that they developed convictions about the viability of successful arms reduction that changed their attitudes toward their activity in the present. Some saw new activity directions they had not thought of before, others saw increasing relevance to what they were already doing. With very few exceptions, participants were galvanized by a new sense of the possible in a venture that earlier had looked hopeless.

What is the imaging process that can galvanize people in this way? For many people, it is very difficult to begin imagining in a fantasy mode that is at the same time guided by a certain level of intentionality within the imager. They can daydream and they can use their intellects to make rational scenarios, but they can't easily step into a future world and *see* something. That is precisely what image literacy is about. It is *not* precognition or prediction, and it is *not* simple personal wish-fulfillment. The individual draws on the entire coded store of what has been heard, read, seen, felt, smelled, tasted, and thought, from the womb to the present, in a relaxed free-floating manner, on the other side of a breach in time, to discover what a world would look like with no weapons in it. Getting through the breach in time, liberating the store of impressions in the subconscious, so imagery can form, and letting the *intention* to see that world act as monitor over the imagery, is not easy.[9] For a few, despair prevents the liberation of imagery, or will let only demonic imagery through. These workshops are not for them. However, workshops designed precisely to deal with despair, such as Joanna Macy's Despair and Empowerment workshops,[10] can bring the despairing to the point where they can recover their own capacity to image the good. Most people can find a way through the breach in time to a world, but they need a little help to get started. Every time I conduct a workshop, I learn something new about how to help people into the process. I have also learned humility through the helping role, because, often, would-be imagers can help each other better than a workshop leader can help them.

Of course, the images are of special settings, people doing specific things. The social order, as such, cannot be visualized because it is an abstraction. The important thing is that participants experience in their imaginations some fragments of social life unrelated to anything they now know (though, of course, all imagery is a mosaic of their own store of past impressions), and perceive clues as to how things might be. These image fragments, developed in the fantasy mode, are the raw materials for the more intellectual task of constructing a coherent social order into which the fragments can fit. Since any one individual's image fragments may be too few for the entire construction process, the pooling of individual imagery is very important. Image fragments from different people may contradict each other, so the pooling process is a complex one. I always point out that contradictions and conflicts are at the core of human experience in society, and that a world without weapons would continue to contain contradictions and conflicts. Over time (a serious workshop needs several days to work this out properly), a group is able to work out the implications of their image fragments by constructing a social order that appears to be viable, sustainable, and weapon-free. The most important thing is that it is a world they would like to work toward, and one they would like to live in.

The point of imaging the future is, of course, action in the present. So an important part of these workshops involves returning to the fantasy mode, going back through the breach in time, and remembering from that future world "how it all happened". This is accomplished in five year periods, working from the future back to the present. In the course of these "rememberings", categories of events and actors emerge that one would not necessarily think of while working forward in a planning mode. The final part of the workshop is an analysis of one's own life spaces in the present, in order to determine options for actions in those spaces in the light of the recently visualized future. Obviously, very few people are ever going to participate in imaging workshops. What is interesting is that the very concept of the process of imaging a world without weapons seems to empower people. They may go ahead and do it on their own, which is precisely the way imaging the future has worked over the millennia. What people need today is encouragement for this type of activity, and a removal of opprobrium from the word *utopian*.

So far we have been considering the imaging capacity of the West. If I had written the 1960s assessment in today's language, it would have been entitled the imaging capacity of the North. Although East-West confrontation in the North is so serious that the threat of nuclear winter comes almost entirely from it, both parties to that confrontation are northern industrial societies. Marx and Keynes are both thinkers from the North. In fact, within the working structures of the United Nations, an East-West division does not exist. The ECE (Economic Commission for Europe), established in 1946, includes *all* of Europe and North America in one administrative structure. Both superpower blocs are heirs to the same Greek-Roman-Byzantine traditions. Except for China's role, the major ideological struggles in this century have been among the sister-nations of the North.

All the oldest civilizational traditions on the planet come from the South. All the newly independent nations, from 1946 to the present, are in the South. Most of the new thinking about a new international order, in its many dimensions of economic order, information, culture and security, has been initiated from the South, from ancient cultures progressively impoverished by the "old economic order"—the industrial order created in the North. The first public articulation of the new order came in 1974, when the "Group of 77" (now comprising 118 nations) gained adoption in the United Nations General Assembly under the Program of Action on the Establishment of a New International Economic Order. Since that time there has been a series of international commissions consisting of scholars and leaders from the North (both Eastern and Western blocs), and from the South, to spell out the meaning of each dimension of the new order, to set goals, and to propose mechanisms.[11] Instead of welcoming this opportunity for dialogue with the South to draw on fresh sources of insight and new cultural resources to deal with increasingly pressing world problems, the North has retreated into an aggressive, hostile posture towards anything that hints of new orders. Most of my colleagues in the United States do not understand, for example, what the new information order is all about. They are convinced that it has to do with a plot to curtail freedom of the press. They have not read the United Nations documents, and writings from the South, about this order.[12] If they had, they would have learned that it has to do with a free information flow concept, applied to the South as well as to the North. It provides for many different source points for information around the globe to replace an information order controlled by the superior communication resources of the North (with source points chiefly in the North).

It is no longer appropriate to treat the imaging capacity of the North (read old West) as a separate resource for human development on the planet, any more than it is appropriate to treat the interests of the North as a set of interests worthy of priority attention in the world. It is true that futurists of the North use the language of globalism a lot more frequently, but it is globalism with a strong northern accent. The emergence of a viable concept of world interest to replace the national or regional interests of Northern countries can come about only through dialogue with the South. Futurists who romanticize the wisdom of the East are not contributing to this dialogue because they are responding to stereotypes, instead of listening to what is being said by the "Group of 77," or by the growing group of nonaligned nations (100 now), who cry to the North, "a plague on both your houses."[13] The images of the future now being generated in the South need to be studied, discussed, and worked over, in a situation of equal dialogue rather than one of condescending interest. Bioregionalism, one of the most promising concepts to come out of ecological futurism, draws heavily on the so-called traditional knowledge of the South in its approach to interdependent self-sufficiency.[14] Because bioregionalism (though not by that name) emerged so often in the imagery of middle-class Americans visualizing a demilitarized world in imaging workshops, it would seem to be a particularly useful bridging concept for North-South dialogue.

When I think back to the 1960s and its can-do optimism, I realize that I vastly underestimated the power of the warrior culture over the human mind, and how this would affect our capacity to image peace in the twentieth century. It is true that every traditional civilization had images of peace in the background, while nations fought their wars. The vision of Zion, where the lion lay down with the lamb and a little child could walk unafraid between them, coexisted with the concept of the holy war, fought with the deity at one's side. In eras of hand-to-hand combat, neither image destroyed the other. In an era when battles are fought on computer screens, Zion fades, because it depends on the experience of *relationship*. War thrives because it depends on non-relationship. In the media, battle imagery has replaced the imagery of peace. Battle imagery is used to make and sell children's toys, to sell clothes (look at a Sears Roebuck catalogue), to sell lifestyles, and to make points in debates. We use battle imagery frequently in ordinary conversations. The man on horseback, who down through the centuries has brandished his sword to defend his people, is now deep in the minds of every man, woman and child, even though we have developed social know-how which should have made him obsolete.

Reconstructing the imagery of societies at peace, at a time when that imagery is disappearing from our culture, will be a very difficult thing to do. Polak thought in the 1950s that it was only necessary to remind people for them to begin to image again. It is now clear that we have some serious work to do with the archetypes within, with the deep structures of the mind that give insidious permission for domination and conquest, if we are to be able to produce imagery that corresponds to our own conscious intentionality, and our wishes for a continued flowering of the human species. I am not proposing a primary focus on an inward journey. Within and without are one. The inward potential, and the outward act, are the two faces of humanity, and they both come to fruition in relationship with other humans, and in relationship with the state of being. I take great comfort from the fact that "mediation" is presently the fastest growing profession in the United States. Mediation is a highly intentional, listening form of relationship that enhances the well-being of all who participate in it, and it thrives on imagery of the "other", the new solution, that which did not exist before. It may seem like an odd source for the reconstruction of imaging capacity, but it is in odd places that we must look. We will not find it on TV screens.

It is clear to me that the human capacity for imaging the good society is not lost, only weakened. It can be nurtured back to vigorousness, liveliness. Vigor in imagery leads to vigor in social action. All human beings have known times of individual despair, times during which they have had to "walk through to the other side" to begin life again. This is a time in human society when we must all help each other walk through the social despair. Retrieving and reiterating messages about the more humane social order we see on the other side is one of the most important things any of us can do.

IMAGING A WORLD WITHOUT WEAPONS:WORKSHOP PROCEDURES[15]

The Goal Statement

Because the individual's hopes, wishes, and intentions for the future are so important in directing the imaging, the first task in the workshop is to write out a goal statement about what you would like to see achieved in the social order three decades from now—not goals for your personal life, but for society. The goal statement should, by workshop definition, be compatible with an arms-free world. Note that the future moment chosen is 30 years hence. This is far enough into the future for substantial changes to have taken place. Yet it is close enough to the present that many of you will still be alive and, thus, can feel a personal stake in this future.

Giving yourself permission to state what you would like to see achieved in the future rather than what can realistically be expected is generally very difficult. We have all been taught to set a high premium on being realistic. This exercise requires a deliberate setting aside of ordinary notions of the possible, and focusing primarily on hopes and wishes. The effort can be treated as a conscious act of disciplining the mind to ignore what it "knows" about reality constraints in the social order.

Childhood Memories

This exercise is intended to free up your imaging capacity by having you step into remembered images of the past, in order to experience the type of imaging you will be doing when you move into the future.

Moving into the Future

It is the responsibility of the workshop leader to help participants move through the barrier separating the present-present from the future-present. Some can do it easily, for others, it takes longer. An exploratory trip then a brief return to the present to discuss how it is working is provided for, followed by a twenty-minute to half-hour stay in the future, observing and recording.

Clarification

The experienced imagery becomes clarified through explaining it to others. At this point, more can be added to the imagery as each of you checks forward mentally to the future, in response to questions from within the small group in which the clarification takes place.

Consequence Mapping and World Construction

Given what you have seen in your explorations of the future-present moment, what kind of world is it? How is it ordered, what institutions function and how? Particularly, how is conflict managed? What has been seen in the imaged visit to the future must now be treated as a set of indicators of the condition of that world. These indicators must now be treated analytically to construct the social order they point toward. This is first an individual exercise, although carried out in 2- or 3-person groups. Once each group has *their* individual images clear, then larger groups are formed based on common themes. Contrasting or conflicting imagery among participants is a problem that must be dealt with just as it is in the real world of conflicting perceptions—by negotiation. This world construction is transferred to newsprint, using pictures and/or diagrams, and schematic representations, to indicate how the social order functions. Since the whole social order can not realistically be accounted for in the time available, each group will choose themes based on its own initial input of image fragments, and develop them more fully on the newsprint.

Futures History

Standing in the future-present moment and looking into the past, you will individually remember how the world got to its future-present state. You will work back from the future to the past of 30 years ago in five-year periods. For some of you, watershed events will appear, others will remember a gradual change. This exercise should also be repeated within the "World Construction" teams, going through the process of negotiating conflicting historical "memories."

Action Planning in the Present

The pictured future and the remembered events leading up to it now become the basis for short-term action planning in the present, and long-term strategizing about the future. The difference between the planning and strategizing we normally do, and the same activities in this context, is that we now have in a certain sense experienced the future reality of what is being planned. This gives the wished-for future a quality of thereness, of authenticity in relation to the human possibility, which adds new dimensions to practical reality-testing in the present.

NOTES

1. Fred Polak, *Image of the Future,* vols. trans. by Elise Boulding (New York: Oceana Press, 1961); Trans. from *Toekomst is Verleden Tyd* (Utrecht, 1955); also one-vol. abr. by Elise Boulding (San Francisco: Jossey-Bass, Elsevier, 1972).

2. Elise Boulding, "Futuristics and the Imaging Capacity of the West," in

Human Futuristics, ed. by Magorah Maruyama and James A. Dator (Honolulu: University of Hawaii, Social Science Research Institute, 1971); Repr. in *World Futures Society. Bulletin,* v. 3, no. 12 (December, 1970); also in *Cultures of the Future,* ed. by Majorah Maruyama (Germany: Mouton, 1978).

3. Elise Boulding, "A Disarmed World: Problems in Imaging the Future," *Journal of Sociology and Social Welfare,* v. 4, no. 3/4 (1977): 656–658.

4. Elise Boulding, Evolutionary Visions, Sociology and the Human Life Span," in *The Evolutionary Vision,* ed. by Erich Jantsch (Boulder, Colo.: Westview Press, 1981).

5. Auguste Comte, *Cours de philosophie positive,* tome VI (Paris: Schlacher, 1908).

6. Herbert Spencer, *Principles of Sociology* (New York: Appleton, 1986).

7. Pierre Teilhard de Chardin, *The Future of Man,* tr. by Norman Deumy (New York: Harper & Row, 1964).

8. Warren Ziegler, "Planning as Action: Techniques of Inventive Planning Workshops," in *Participatory Planning in Education* (Paris: OECD, 1974).

9. It should be pointed out that imaging itself is a neutral process and can be used to image the "bad" as well as the "good." That is why intentionality is stressed.

10. Joanna Macy, *Despair and Personal Power in the Nuclear Age* (Philadelphia: New Society Publishers, 1983).

11. The following are examples: *North-South: A Programme for Survival,* Willy Brandt, Commission Chair (London: Pan Books, 1980); *Common Crises North-South: Cooperation for World Recovery,* Willy Brandt, Commission Chair (London: Pan Books, 1983); *Many Voices, One World,* Sean McBridge, Commission Chair (Paris: UNESCO, 1980); *Common Security: A Blueprint for Survival,* Olof Palme, Commission Chair (New York: Simon and Schuster, 1982); and Herbert Shore, *Cultural Policy: UNESCO's First Cultural Development Decade* (Washington, D.C.: U.S. National Commission for UNESCO, 1981). Also note the national *Cultural Policies Studies* (Paris: UNESCO, 1975).

12. See, for example, the Development Dialogue issue on *Towards a New World Information and Communication Order* (Paris: UNESCO, 1981:2).

13. Rikhi Jaipal, *Non-Alignment: Origins, Growth and Potential for Peace* (New Delhi: Allied Publishers, n.d.).

14. *Coevolution Quarterly,* special issue on "Bioregions," no. 32 (Winter, 1981).

15. This workshop draws on procedures developed by Warren Ziegler, *Mindbook for Imaging a World Without Weapons* (Denver, Colo.: Ziegler's Futures Invention Associates, 1982), address at 2260 Fairfax, Denver, Colorado, 80207. For information about future workshops and workshop leadership training opportunities, contact Mary Link, Coordinator, World Without Weapons Project, 4722 Baltimore Ave., Philadelphia, PA, 19143. A full version of the workbook will be found in Elise Boulding, *Building a Global Civic Culture: Education for an Interdependent World* (New York: Columbia University, Teachers College Press, 1988).

II

Politics

6

Changing My Mind: Reflections of an Engineering Professor

George L. Sackman

How is it that an engineer should be writing a chapter in this volume on thinking about peace, especially a professor of electrical engineering? The answer is, of course, that an engineer is a person like anyone else, and as such has personal thoughts and experiences which might be relevant to the subject. Traditionally, engineers have a long-standing association with warfare. In fact, the term "civil engineer" was first used to make the distinction from the ancient profession of engineer (essentially, military engineer), responsible for the design of fortifications. If there is to be a fundamental change in the way people think about peace, it might be instructive to examine the process through which a person, whose profession is closely associated with war, goes about changing his life to support the cause of peace.

CHANGE IS POSSIBLE

This is a narrative of my own conscientious sword-into-plowshare transformation. It is a demonstration that significant change is possible, that changing the way we think can lead to action in spite of risk and fear of unknown results.

I was born and raised in the Deep South, where the Civil War tradition of honor and respect for the military remains a part of the culture. As a child during World War II, I was conventionally patriotic, later joined the Army Reserves while in college during the Korean

War, and served two years on active duty in Europe after the truce. I accepted army life, but didn't glorify the military. I just took it for granted that war was an occasionally necessary evil, and looked upon military service as my duty to that component of society charged with protecting the rest of us from enemies. After going to graduate school (partially supported by the G.I. bill), and working in industry for a while, I decided that a career as a college professor was the most appealing. When an opportunity appeared to teach electrical engineering at a military graduate school, I accepted eagerly. For almost twenty years, I enjoyed teaching engineering to young officers, did research in military electronics, and became something of a specialist in several applications of electrical engineering to warfare.

When I first joined the faculty I taught more-or-less standard courses typical of any technical graduate school such as MIT or Cal Tech. My specialty was microwaves, but as an outgrowth of my industry experience, I also initiated research into ultrasonic image systems for underwater "television" applications in murky water—hunting for mines, sunken ships or crashed airplanes. At that time there were only two or three research groups in the world experimenting with the same technique (primarily for medical applications similar to X-ray—the medical equipment has now become commonplace, but the underwater systems are still not perfected). This research continued for several years, during which I was adviser for several dozen graduate students writing masters theses. My interest in underwater sound expanded into teaching courses on sonar, and conducting research related to anti-submarine warfare and mine sweeping. It was also very flattering to be welcomed as an expert during visits to government laboratories and administrative offices in Washington. Some of my students served on nuclear ballistic missile submarines. It was impressive that just one of these subs would have enough firepower to destroy dozens of major cities with one salvo. The result of this involvement with primarily military technology was a fascination with the engineering aspects of the applications, with scarcely a moment's reflection on the implications of the work in a wider context. I never discussed the military aspects of my work with my family or anyone else other than my professional colleagues. My home life was devoted to activities with my wife and children, my hobbies of keyboard and choral music, and tinkering with old, exotic cars. I sang in a church choir, and was active in a conservationist organization.

About five years or so before the end of this period of teaching at a military graduate school, I attended some seminars sponsored by a non-profit educational foundation concerned with the development of the human potential. These seminars were held once or twice a year at a beautiful conference center in a forested mountain area. Each seminar lasted several days, with morning, afternoon, and evening sessions meeting in one of several comfortable, rustic lodges. The majority of the attendees were young professional and business people, usually married couples. The subjects under discussion were the most basic kinds of questions imaginable: Who am I? Am I here for a reason? Is there a God? What is worthwhile? In the interim months between the intensive seminars, local meetings were held in the homes of participants to continue the process of introspection, dialogue, and debate, followed by planning meetings especially directed toward converting ideas into action in everyday life, both public and private. The goal was the stimulation of creativity and initiative—working together to look for positive aproaches to the most serious problems of personal relationships, society, and civilization, then, going out and doing something concrete with our talents, time, and money. These periods of activity would then be followed by study of lessons learned, more introspection, dialogue, and debate. In this dynamic environment, a lot of personal development took place in a relatively short time.

After all this study and reflection, it gradually became apparent to me that the day-to-day reality I was living (my paradigm) had some serious implications. In particular, the acceptance of war, in its traditional role as the ultimate arbiter of conflict, was a way of thinking which could only lead to "unparalled catastrophe" in the words of Einstein. This realization was further reinforced after viewing the film, *The Last Epidemic,* which shows the medical effects of a nuclear missile attack, presented at a conference of the Physicians for Social Responsibility.[1] I became active in a grass roots educational movement called "Beyond War"[2] The movement began in the early 1980s, as a growing awareness of the threat of nuclear war spread throughout the nation, articulated, for example, in the series of articles by Jonathan Schell entitled, "The Fate of the Earth," published in the *New Yorker* magazine (later collected in a book).[3]

"Beyond War" workers make presentations to groups in homes, and to church and civic groups in a lecture/discussion format called "An Orientation to a World Beyond War." The key concept is based on the quote from Einstein that identified the root cause of the threat of war as being in the *way we think* about war, about ourselves, and about others. The solution to the problem of war requires, therefore, nothing less than changing the way people think all over the world. A corollary, however, is the necessity to first change our own way of thinking. We cannot force others to change at such a fundamental level. People change from within, as a result of gaining a new appreciation of the implications of not changing. The first task of the "Beyond War" movement is to inform and stimulate people to educate themselves. When our thinking truly changes, then our actions will reflect it. "Beyond

War" workers distilled the new way of thinking into two phrases: "War is obsolete," and "We are One." The first phrase implies that war no longer can accomplish its traditional purpose, since any war could escalate into a catastrophic end to civilization, with no possible winner. The second phrase implies that we are all in this together, united by a common air, water, and food supply at the ecological level, so, to threaten an enemy is to threaten ourselves. In fact, the very concept of "enemy" is called into question by the enormity of the danger posed by any war to all life on the planet, no matter how seemingly remote or insignificant.

In the process of studying these concepts in preparation for presentations, my thinking began to change as my knowledge increased. The effect on me was extremely disturbing, causing what psychologists call a "cognitive dissonance"[4] (known colloquially as being between a rock and a hard place). The term "cognitive dissonance" means a sort of paradox of consciousness, in which contradictory views of "reality" demand our simultaneous acceptance. For example, I was in a secure, respected profession, committed to my responsibility toward my country and my family—how could I reconcile the certain knowledge that continued reliance on war was suicidal with the fact that I was teaching electrical engineering to students whose profession was warfare?

THE CHALLENGE OF CHANGING

At this point in my life I was 50 years old, so any significant change had far-reaching implications beyond my individual self. To minimize the disruption, I first considered simply restricting my teaching and research activities to fundamental scientific and engineering principles, with the rationalization that their application by my students would be of no concern to me. This rationalization did not satisfy my conscience. I then considered returning to industry with a local company, a choice that would have allowed me and my family to remain at the same residence. However, after interviewing for such a job, it was clear to me that industry lifestyle was not appealing. I felt my best talent and strongest interest were really in teaching, and I would never be satisfied in industry. Finally, I came to the conclusion that I would have to resign from the faculty of the military school and look for a position at a university. This was a major change. Many people would be affected—family, colleagues, and friends. There would be the problem of even finding another job at my age, and, most certainly, moving to another city would be a problem. Was I willing to risk these changes, or would I rationalize with my conscience? How could I have been so deeply involved with military technology all these years without consciously recognizing the direction in which it was heading? I realized that I had become a divided person. I had adapted to my environment as humans adapt to cigarette smoking, to pollution, and to acceptance of world poverty and starvation.

To change would require an unknown price. The human psyche can separate itself into compartments, within each everything fits together nicely—engineering professor with officer students and military research; father with family, hobbies, friends, church and choir. However, at the boundaries of the compartments, there is tension. To the extent that these compartments communicate with each other, the personality is well integrated. To the extent that they are isolated, the psyche suffers at an unconscious level. I knew for a long time that something was wrong, but I didn't know what. This condition is sometimes called "psychic numbing." The unconscious knows that there is a risk in raising the boundaries of the compartments to consciousness. Serious problems will have to be solved with unforeseeable consequences.

THINKING ABOUT PEACE: A DECISION

The process of thinking about peace also involves thinking about changing one's way of life. Within recorded history, people of the world have never lived without thoughts of war. The very idea that we must change our minds, about *all* war, and seriously recognize peace as the *only* way to survive, is psychologically threatening. First we want to know the answer to the question: "What will peace be like?" However, we cannot have it that way. First we must make the decision forever to reject war as an option in our personal lives. Only then can we begin to solve the inevitable problems. In my professional life, it first was necessary for me to make the decision to cease teaching directly for the military. I had to convince myself that this decision was a deliberate move, not based on just an emotional reaction to my conscience. Fortunately, I had the opportunity to go away for a year on a visiting professorship to a state university, and then return to my old job to see if I still wanted to make a permanent change.

The experience at the state university was like a breath of fresh air after being in a smoke-filled room. The variety of ways of thinking, the free and creative search for alternatives, and the broad spectrum of political and sociological viewpoints expressed in open forum were refreshing and stimulating. And it was also just plain fun to teach enthusiastic undergraduates in engineering. Returning to the military school was anticlimatic, and felt like a step backward. I attempted to incorporate some thinking about peace in my classes, but the reactions of most of the officer students was decidedly negative, and I soon realized that anything I said on the subject of peace was discounted as being just idiosyncratic behavior. This was a valuable experience, because it served to reinforce my original decision, and yet gave me the freedom of choice without the immediate necessity of "burning bridges behind me." I eventually was able to secure a challenging new job at a university in another state.

It is important to realize when faced with a decision, that we do not have to solve all the attendant problems alone, or at once. We can seek help and, in fact, we are all in it together, whether we realize it or not. In my decision to seek another job, I was assisted by emotional support from my wife and family, by the good will of friends and colleagues, and by professional psychological counseling. In spite of the serious difficulties, I am confident that society has the resources to support itself in evolving a new paradigm of peace. We are afraid mostly of the unknown, which can best be overcome by education. This chapter will be my contribution to that effort.

AFTER CHANGE: WHAT DIFFERENCE DOES IT MAKE?

Because they have very few other options, most of my present electrical engineering students will take jobs supported directly or indirectly by preparation for war. Furthermore, the most technically sophisticated and highest paying jobs are military-related. Therefore, the only difference between my present students and the young officers I was teaching before, is that the university students have not already made the choice to work for the military. I also realize that my place teaching electrical engineering to military officers has long since been filled. My former colleagues kindly say that they miss me and that my replacement does not relate as well to the students. What difference, after all, has it made to have disrupted my life by changing jobs and moving to a different place? The change came at an opportune time for my children. The youngest had just gone away to college. However, the new job is in a city thousands of miles away from them. It is hard to assess the impact of the change on our children, since they were at a period in their lives when change is expected. Certainly, the realization that "home" was no longer the same place came as a certain amount of shock. After visiting us, one of the children said that she could accept our new residence as equivalent to "home" since we were there, and there were still a few familiar things in the new house.

To begin a new life without the benefit of the ready-made acquaintances I acquired along with the job required a great deal of adjustment by my wife. She had to start from scratch in making friends and becoming involved in the community, even though she had, in fact, lived in that same city many years ago. The change has made a great deal of difference to me personally. I feel that I had a choice and exercised it. Most of my present students still have a choice of jobs, without having to be concerned about the welfare of wife and family, job security, or other extensive commitments. I am fortunate to have come to a campus where thinking about peace has academic respectability (at least among *some* of the faculty and students), and finally to have the opportunity of expressing my thoughts on the subject of peace in such a forum as this.

THE MILITARY: AN ORGAN OF SOCIETY

In contrast to the account of my personal reactions to teaching in a military environment, it is necessary to put the role of the military into a larger perspective. It is a mistake to blame the military for society's reliance on war as a way of resolving conflict. The people in military service have chosen that profession because they sincerely believe that preparation for war is the best way to preserve peace, or at least to protect us from enemies. The military is an organ of society, and to the extent that the common paradigm includes war, we are all a functional part of it. However, as a result of their training and work environment, there is a natural tendency for the military to look for military solutions to every problem. After all, that is their specialty, just as engineers tend to look for technological solutions to problems. It is the responsibility of each of us to recognize the limitations of the military as well as the limitations of technology (or any other specialized branch of knowledge) in the solution of a general problem. The well-educated person will learn that it is unreasonable to expect the government, the military, or any technological advancement to achieve peace. Every profession and individual citizen has a contribution to make. It does matter what kind of contribution, however. If we are thinking in terms of war, our contribution will tend to increase the likelihood of war.

Alfred Nobel (the inventor of dynamite), Hiram Maxim (the inventor of the machine gun), the Wright brothers, and the scientists who developed the atomic bomb all thought they were helping to end war. The process continues in the promises of the Strategic Defense Initiative (known as Star Wars) program. However, none of these people seriously considered rejecting the traditional way of thinking about the probability of war, and, hence, none seriously entertained the possibility of peace. In thinking about peace, we must look for opportunities to "give peace a chance." From my engineering background, I gained a philosophy that the state of society called "peace" is actually an unstable state that must be actively maintained as in balancing a broom. However, the cost of letting the broom fall is nothing less than catastrophic. In the past, humans have learned how to do this kind of balancing job on a smaller scale indefinitely (for example, standing on two legs). An essential ingredient for this balance is what I call the "theory of possibility."

PROBABILITY OF WAR; POSSIBILITY OF PEACE

Let me conclude with a brief commentary on the theory of probability, versus the theory of possibility. Warfare has always been based on an intuitive concept of probability. The theory of probability was formalized, several hundred years ago, as "the law of large numbers" when the subject of probability became a branch of mathematics. The idea is very easy to understand. If an experiment, such as the toss of a coin, is performed repeatedly, the number of "favorable" outcomes as a fraction of the number of trials approaches a fixed value as the number of trials becomes larger and larger. If the coin can be biased, or in the case of a gambling casino, if the house odds are biased, the long term outcome can be predicted accurately even though the outcome of a single trial may be unpredictable. Part of the science of war is to attempt to bias the outcome of each battle (for example, more men and/or better weapons) so that after many battles, the outcome of the war will be favorable to one's own side. Any military officer knows that the outcome of a single battle essentially is unpredictable, even if biased.

By comparison, there is the theory of possibility, known colloquially as "Murphy's Law" (if anything *can* happen, be prepared for it because it just *might* happen, even if it is not very probable). For example, contraceptives have a high probability of protection, but are not guaranteed. The possibility of nuclear war has changed the conditions of warfare permanently, but our thinking generally remains stuck in the concept of the probability of winning battles. We have failed to grasp the idea of a war with only one battle, and with no winner. Consequently, we continue to escalate the arms race without recognizing that the law of large numbers will insure the eventual occurrence of that last battle.

The only way out of the dilemma is to reject war as an option and get to work solving the problems of conflict without resort to war. This process of moving our thoughts beyond war is only the first step in thinking about peace. The converse argument begins with the conviction of the possibility of peace. If we are not convinced that peace is possible, we will not make serious plans to deal with that eventuality. We will be unprepared if "peace breaks out."

Many examples from other fields of study could be presented. Consider economic implications, for example. Probably, over half of our national economy is ultimately dependent on the preparation of war, and a large proportion of our national budget goes for interest on the debt of our unpaid bills for past wars. It is an enormous task to completely overhaul the economic base of a large proportion of the northern hemisphere. At the same time, the Third World must be treated with respect, as a partner in the process, otherwise the despair that accompanies poverty and injustice will lead to violent reactions that destroy any progress toward peace.

The point is that precious little thought has gone into the possibility of peace, because it is not generally accepted as "realistic"—it is not part of the paradigm. In fact, there are a multitude of opportunities for creative thinking and action in helping to bring about a conversion from a war paradigm to a peace paradigm. There is a great need for forethought in order to make the transition without causing unnecessary and widespread hardship. Not only is the need great, but also the time to begin is now. There is certainly no guarantee of success, but the possibility exists, and the alternative is extinction.

NOTES

1. Physicians for Social Responsibility, *The Last Epidemic: Medical Consequences of Nuclear Weapons and Nuclear War* (Cambridge, Mass.: Physicians for Social Responsibility, 1982), 16mm color film, 36 minutes.

2. Beyond War, *Beyond War: A New Way of Thinking* (Palo Alto, Calif., 1985).

3. Jonathan Schell, *The Fate of the Earth* (New York: Alfred A. Knopf, 1982).

4. Leon Festinger, *A Theory of Cognitive Dissonance* (Stanford: Stanford University Press, 1957).

7

Patriarchy, Peace, and Women Warriors

Christine Sylvester

It is common to think of women as being pro-peace. Women are highly
visible in such peace activist groups as the Greens, Women's Pentagon
Action, Greenham Common, The Women for Peace Movement and the
Peace People. Polls show that Western women oppose increases in
military expenditures and deployment of new weapons more frequently
than men.[1] Some feminist literature even suggests women may not be
prone to warlike abstractions, or soldierly expressions of power, as
dominance.[2] Yet, among the Women of the Year for 1986, designated
by *Ms.* magazine, are Sharon Gless and Tyne Daly, who play some-
times-armed cops on the television series "Cagney and Lacey". Lauded
for building characters who are good female buddies, these actresses
also have molded those characters either to like fighting in a man's
world (Gless), or, to have a closer relationship with a man than with
her children (Daly).[3] Winnie Mandela, another *Ms.* Woman of the Year,
says calmly: "...we are at war with white South Africa."[4] She speaks
as much for African women of that country as she does for her famous
husband and other male nationalists. She is unarmed in a region where
many of her sisters are, or were, combatants in national liberation
struggles. In addition to these "outstanding" women, there are other
"nonpeacefuls," like Margaret Thatcher, "the iron lady," who broke
the sex barrier of high public office and also directed the Falklands/
Malvinas war; and women who volunteer to train for war.

The purpose of this chapter is to consider some seemingly nonpeaceful women—women warriors. These women create and follow more antiestablishment, or establishment-skeptical, politics than woman serving in the police, armed forces, or high public offices of state. The latter are an integral part of dominant society and, through their careers, officially defend a public realm which "has always been defined in opposition to dangerous, disorderly, and irrational forces . . . consistently conceptualized as female."[5] Women who hold such positions may do so out of feminist convictions; that is, they may fight for power within an establishment that has heretofore excluded women and, in the process, actually strike a blow against that establishment. Women warriors are less well-adjusted to dominant society and, in fact, fight to make creative spaces for "irrational" and "disorderly" feminist projects which defy the rules and practices of social order. Their strategies are multiple, yet contain a common element of power through energy, capacity, competence, and effectiveness.[6]

This chapter will consider features of establishments which oppress women in war and in peace, and arguments that women would set societies on more peace-loving courses if they held power. In sympathy with the women-peace link, one wonders, nevertheless, if it is somewhat stereotypical and power-limiting in the sense of fitting too neatly into establishment-supporting gender expectations. To think/labor creatively about war and peace, women may have to labor as warriors (against male-dominated order, and for healthier pieces of disorder). Clues to women-warrior strategies emerge in branches of feminism, that reveal, delegitimate, and challenge, in unthinkable ways, the wars and peaces of patriarchal societies.

WOMEN: MORE PEACE-LOVING THAN MEN?

Birgit Brock-Utne thinks it noteworthy that "women have never institutionalized violence."[7] Would they do so if they held power? She thinks many might, unless they were to involve themselves in a different education to counter "the training in patriarchal thinking in formal school systems and political life [which] generally guarantees that women will think like men, will compete the way they do, and hold the same value systems."[8] Components of this education include "developing our 'women's logic,' continuing to care for others, feel compassion, share power, and become more assertive."[9] Brock-Utne is suggesting that women's experiences impart a privileged understanding of oppression, injustice, and that which passes for power in patriarchal society. If women could act on their special understandings in unity, and with an alternative power to that propagated by men's logic, they would not lead societies into war, tolerate rape and abuse, withhold resources, pollute, and injure through discrimination. But since women live in patriarchal societies, where all of the above practices dominate, it is difficult to find favor for peace-loving inclinations, let alone forge a social movement which advances "a morally and scientifically preferable grounding for our interpretations and explanations of nature and social life."[10]

Patriarchy is a system of power relations which creates and bolsters male supremacy, and "denotes the historical depth of women's exploitation and oppression."[11] Its emergence at different times in different societies may be linked to "man-the-hunter's" use of tools as weapons to assault and conquer others, acquire economic resources and control politics.[12] Understood this way, patriarchy is a form of colonialism that advances one group at the expense of others; in this case, at the expense of women who now systematically occupy less lucrative, less prestigious and influential statuses—the occasional woman politician or millionaire notwithstanding.

The power relations of male supremacy seem timeless and in the order of things when, in fact, they were socially created like other forms of colonialism. As with most accepted ideologies and practices, once in place, patriarchy is self-sustaining: If a majority of politicians, scientists, priests, ministers, popes, professors, chairs of corporate boards, physicians, job supervisors, judges, and peacemakers are always men, then challenges to that group's monopoly can actually seem unnatural, silly, or even harmful to social order. Those who push for changes in the structures and practices of power soon find that powerful men are the ones who decide how challenges to people like themselves will be handled. Such nonneutral decision makers have historically tried to ignore women's demands (women could not vote in this country until the 1920s, and just recently gained that right in Switzerland), or to accommodate them in incremental ways, so change will not seriously disrupt the existing hierarchy of power (American women got the vote, but it took decades for them to get equal access to credit).

Arguably, then, patriarchy is a system in which there is constant, covert, low-intensity, structural warfare against women—in "war" and in "peace." During shooting wars between states, the war-within-the-war often features male-dictated changes in the "normal" gender division of labor. Protecting national interests requires that male laborers leave for the battlefront and women "man" the factories at the homefront. Since women rarely hold positions in the public realms, where decisions of war and peace originate, those national interests, that shooting war to safeguard them, and the accompanying redivision of labor, are imposed. So, also, is the peace which comes when men who declare (or as often as not these days, nondeclare) the shooting war decide to stop fighting. With the cessation of "hostilities," women have been abruptly dismissed from the homefront jobs that pay, and sent back to their "natural" nonpaying jobs in the private household. Both the shooting wars and subsequent peaces contain hidden wars of dominance over women.

As a second example of patriarchal war-peace, consider the landmark U.S. Supreme Court decision in *Roe versus Wade*. The issue was abortion—whether women could decide to maintain or terminate their pregnancies. The Supreme Court handed down a decision lauded by pro-choice women around the country—their abortion rights had been "established." That some very powerful men had deigned to allow women to have some control over procreation was lost in the celebrations. Moreover, it can be argued that an exchange was implied in this decision: Women, with abortion rights, would put money in the pockets of mostly male physicians and halt self-gynecological practices that endangered, in the sense of undermining, accepted medical practices for example, giving each other pelvic exams and seeking mind-to-body abortions.[13] Under this interpretation, *Roe versus Wade* is not so much a victory for women as a war strategy designed to lull them into a false sense of power and security under conditions of patriarchal peace.

In each case, patriarchy wins because male "rights" to decide everything have become one of the mainstays of civilization. As well, there are rewards for women who accept patriarchy, play by its rules, and defend it from harm. These rewards include male protection from other marauding males, "freedom" to specialize in the labor of reproduction and caretaking or in public sector careers, approval for efforts to improve physical appearance (under patriarchy, "letting yourself go" has a negative connotation), and appreciation for handing over sons to the public realms which define war and peace. Under patriarchy, women may value something called "peace," and be peace-abiding. To paraphrase Brock-Utne, they need that different education to open their eyes to complicity in a violent, exploitative, and oppressive peace. The object-relations school of psychoanalytic theory suggests that even without a different education, women are more peaceable than men, more fundamentally disinclined to institutionalize violence. This difference has to do with preconscious responses boys and girls develop to the challenge of individuating from the women who mother them.[14]

For boys, there is an early and quite jarring realization that she who nurtures (with whom they feel symbiotic attachment), is a physical other, a not-I. This preconscious dawning sets up the structural personality conditions for male efforts to individuate from mothers in ways which repress and deny all associations with mother-world. To be male is to be not female. It is to be so defensive about the feminine sides of one's personality as to embrace opposing traits: "Real men," as the saying goes, are rugged individuals, competitive, independent, above cleaning dirty diapers, and, above all, rational. The appropriate model of masculine behavior is father, having himself been properly socialized to embody many of these "ideal" characteristics. This model, however, is often absent from the household, which means that boys learn to identify with an abstract figure who leaves home to work "out there."

Preconscious struggles and subsequent training to be properly masculine, prepare adult males to think in either/or terms and to feel most comfortable when distance is maintained from other people through mental comfort-zones of high abstraction. Customary social interactions reveal this: *Robert's Rules of Parliamentary Procedure* prevent meetings from becoming usefully disorderly by establishing intricate barriers to communication; men try not to cry or appear too emotional in public; they "hang tough" and never let another guy, or especially a woman, "get the better of them;" their friendships often center on "shop talk," competitive sports, and denigration of women and "wimps"—characteristics the 1987 hit movie, *Beverly Hills Cop II,* showcase.

In maintaining distance from anything "of women" and mother-world, men can unconsciously glorify war as the ultimate means of individuation. For the "good" battle (a just war against those who would take away what "we" have gained) men willingly undergo painful and humiliating training that, as shown in *Full Metal Jacket,* openly celebrates the fact that "here there are men and no women" (except for the few recruits who "don't make it").[15] The terror of battle temporarily breaks down rigid barriers to closeness and facilitates intense male bonding, about which men wax nostalgic once the war ends. Death in war is honorable and gains the soldier immortality as a "man"; he has faced the enemy. Yet, where intimacy and contempt are thesis and antithesis, and where fear of losing hard-fought identities as "not females" is omnipresent, those "just wars" continue into peacetime—consciously or unconsciously, patriarchal peace maintains the defenses against women.

For girls, the challenge of becoming individuals centers on resisting a mesmerizing and seductive sameness with "mother."[16] This individuating struggle, however, has fewer defensive components, because girls do not have to reject the first relation and adopt behaviors different from those of their mothers in order to be acceptably feminine. As well, their basic role model is concrete rather than abstract, self rather than other, and connected rather than distant. Accordingly, "girls emerge from this period with a basis for 'empathy' built into their primary definition of self in a way that boys do not."[17] Sara Ruddick maintains that daughters go on to learn special lessons in their mothers' houses, which norms of masculinity prevent sons from learning:

Women are daughters who learn from their mothers the activity of preservative love and the maternal thinking that arises from it. These 'lessons' from 'her mother's house' can shape a daughter's intellectual and emotional life even if she rejects the activity, its thinking, or, for that matter, the mother herself. Preservative love is opposed in its fundamental values to military strategy. Maternal theories of conflict are more pacifist than militaristic. A daughter, one might say, has been trained to be unsoldierly.[18]

As adults, women carry out their unsoldierly training by seeking more to preserve and enhance life than to jeopardize it. They look to the community as the realm of effective action, and learn from material experiences of childrearing that power is not a fixed, hierarchical, either/or thing; for example, they watch infallible parent power ebb as their children mature.[19] Of course, the world of "her" is not all laudatory. Although women might have less defensive and more connected postures toward the world, their gender lessons can freeze this potential around roles which sustain patriarchy. We can connect, for example, to the point of losing ourselves and our power in mesmerizing mergers with men or children. We can become a community of self-sacrificers that lacks the ability to challenge the "order" effectively.

The theories of men-women differences developed in object-relations scholarship and built upon by Brock-Utne, constitute a brilliant and useful case for linking women with peace and men with war. Yet, it seems that we might be digging our own graves within patriarchy when we think in the either/or terms of that dominant society. Is it not possible that war and peace are of a single piece, instead of being negations of each other, and that at this moment in time that piece is patriarchal? If so, one type of different education for women would consist of undertaking wars against the established patriarchal monopoly of war and peace, for the disorderly and irrational reorderings which feminize that piece, and change it fundamentally.

To state the problematique this way is not to say that women must become war- rather than peace-oriented in any patriarchal sense of those terms. It is not an argument that women secretly welcome rape or are impatient to institutionalize violence. Nor does it necessarily negate the idea that women may be more peace-loving than men. Rather, it recognizes that patriarchy may damage and distort women's perspectives as well as those of men: women may be embracing (and calling our own) peacemaker images that reflect and serve the prevailing gender order.[20] If so, this will limit the types of strategies women find acceptable for fighting patriarchal monopolies, and lead us to think, perhaps too righteously, that "real women" are totally opposed to destructive acts. In this respect, we often hear that women's liberation will liberate everyone, men and women, in nonviolent ways. Yet to say this is to deny that liberation brings pain, confusion, and loss—that it destroys as it generates new options. Also, an argument of this nature can deny the many women who take up arms in anti-colonial struggles.

The question we are led to is this: What constitutes patriarchy-alternative war-peace-lovingnesses, and what strategies will bring them into focus? The following section considers the different educations which feminist theories of social change represent, and highlights those which seem most conducive to educating women warriors.

FEMINIST STRATEGIES

Feminism is a diverse philosophical, political, and cultural movement to analyze women's oppression and to end it through the effective use of power. Some argue that feminism provides the framework for developing both the power of women and the power of peace, because feminists speak to issues of powersharing, egalitarian structures and freedom from direct as well as indirect or structural violence.[21] There is no such thing as *a* feminist perspective any more than there is consensus on what constitutes war and peace.[22] Lessons on war-peace-lovingness from feminism, therefore, vary widely within a set of parameters which focus attention on women's potential and the social changes needed to realize it.

Alison Jaggar enumerates four distinct types of feminist politics: Liberal, Marxist, radical, and socialist.[23] Of these, radical and socialist feminisms are women-warrior philosophies and politics. This does not mean there are no women warriors within the liberal or Marxist traditions, or that some feminists are misguided—all feminisms are so far from realizing their goals that should any come to prevail, the foundations of patriararchy would at least shake.[24] Women-warrior feminisms stand out for revealing the depths of the male-dominant order and for proposing strategies to combat it which differ from those used to sustain it. The warrior feminisms highlighted in this chapter simply suggest the possibilities.

Liberal feminism poses the challenge of women's power and goals as gaining equal rights with men within a marginally changed social system. To advance, women should have opportunities to participate fully in the heretofore male-dominated spheres of science, government, industry, commerce and education, without suffering pay and status discrimination, or sexual harassment on the job. As well, women who work within the household should be remunerated, or at least, their work should be highly respected. To accomplish what is essentially a goal of integrating women into mainstream society, liberal feminism uses two nonviolent strategies: Organizations such as NOW (National Organization for Women) and magazines such as *Ms.* work to raise women's consciousness by providing evidence both of women's accom-

plishments and of discriminations they suffer by virtue of being er-
roneously perceived as less rational and orderly than men. They also
lobby male powerholders to recognize and rectify inconsistencies and
injustices in the law and its implementation, proposing corrective
measures, like the Equal Rights Amendment, when appropriate. Both
efforts rely on reasoned argumentation and objective evidence of discrimination, as well as on shows of support through rallies and protests.

There are always disorderly or irrational elements in efforts to bring
women into the system. The goals and methods of liberal feminism,
however, are not especially disordering or irrationalizing—the aim,
women's "achievement in a competitive society,"[25] is based on a view
of the West as a "fair meritocracy;"[26] the methods, "demand articulation and aggregation," are accepted within liberal patriarchal societies.
Accordingly, liberal feminism can seem naive or bourgeois to Third
World women, who tend to think our system is always against "people
like them." As well, liberal feminists can work diligently for a demilitarized foreign policy and a nuclear freeze, but since their perspective
does not locate obstacles in deep structures of patriarchal power relations (among other sources), they may underestimate the challenge
and become bitter, frustrated, or politically ineffectual. Theirs is a
nonviolent, system-reforming peace-lovingness which can inadver-
tently work hand in glove with patriarchal peaces.

Classical Marxism is a warrior philosophy, but not especially a
woman-warrior philosophy. Its focus on the struggles of male and female workers for emancipation from exploitative structures, leads to
deeply antiestablishment proposals and practices, so long as the establishment is defined as capitalism. There is little or no recognition
within classical Marxism that capitalism may be the latest economic
arm of patriarchy. Hence, men-women relationships emerge as sec-
ondary contradictions within the large problematique of class exploitation. The women question has to do with women's usual job
assignment under capitalism—homemaking. Homemakers specialize
in reproducing new workers and reproducing existing workers' daily
needs. To many Marxists, these are nonproductive labors which put
women at the margins of history—reproducers do not sell their labor
power to the highest bidder and then experience their surplus value
drained in profits; nor is their labor subject to the types of technological
change which affect whole societies, as did for example, the invention
of steam engines. Isolated from economic activity in societies which
live by producing commodities for exchange in a market, homemakers
are thereby isolated as well from the lessons in exploitation which such
productive economic activity imparts, and from the revolutionary activities which propel societies towards increasingly progressive fu-

tures. The challenge for women is to join the lessons-imparting workforce as proletarians and fight alongside men for a new order.[27]

But what precisely will women thereby gain? Americans often think of Marxism as a monolithic, dangerous, disorderly and ever-so irrational "creed." Yet capitalists never caricature Marx as a woman, but as an anti-Christ—a turncoat male. This may be so because "Marxists have interpreted "labor" to mean primarily the production and exchange of objects—the kind of work that they associate with men."[28] Marxist feminism makes the important contribution of showing linkages between contemporary household structures that relegate women to subservient if not historically insignificant statuses, and the broader division of labor into haves and have-nots that fuels capitalist development. But, to the degree that classical Marxism does not usually acknowledge that one of its key concepts (production) is male-biased, Marxist women can naively believe that a socialist order will remedy women's exploitation by enlarging their opportunities beyond "backward" reproduction. In fact, socialism can be only a form of enlightened patriarchy in which women simply conform to economic activities which define socialist man, and men do not reciprocate by doing women's traditional work.[29] If so, the war-peace piece remains male-monopolized.

Radical and socialist feminisms are women-warrior philosophies and politics, although their proponents do not often label themselves as such. Each, in its own way and with permutations depending upon where one lives, fundamentally aims at disordering and irrationalizing the norms and practices which sustain patriarchal wars and peaces.

Radical feminists argue that women comprise an oppressed class in societies that they believe are characterized above all by patriarchy. Women's advancement in such systems is impossible, because the wars against them are omnipresent, multiple, and deep. Women must strive to emancipate from patriarchy by analyzing who they were before patriarchy descended on them, and how they should behave now to be true to themselves. The first step is to investigate and reclaim aspects of a buried, invalidated, and undervalued "her-story." Much, radical feminists argue, has been taken from women, and Mary Daly is brilliant in her search to "re-member" the lusty wanderers of the realms of pure lust and to separate them from the main demonic attackers of aggression and obsession.[30] Seeing no purpose in trying to persuade patriarchs to value the very qualities "the political community has been defined in opposition to ... forces which threaten its very existence and which require a masculine retreat to the well-defended barracks,"[31] and eschewing equality with men in a system of power through coercion, the second step for radical feminists is to separate or detach from dominant society and move wholeheartedly into woman-culture. This often entails creating women-centered communities where hierarchical power relations and the institutions they produce (war, rape, militarism and compulsive heterosexuality) intrude as little as possible. Basing the good life on women's revalorized experiences alone, makes radical feminism quintessentially disorderly, irrational and dangerous to legitimate patriarchal wars and peaces.

Socialist feminists infuse radical feminism with aspects of Marxist analysis. They claim that the problem facing women is not patriarchy or capitalism alone—although each system of unequal power relations is formidable enough. The problem is capitalist patriarchy, with its corollaries of racism and imperialism. Jaggar presents the issue in these terms:

Socialist feminists claim that a full understanding of the capitalist system requires a recognition of the way in which it is structured by male dominance and, conversely, that a full understanding of contemporary male dominance requires a recognition of the way it is organized by the capitalist division of labor.[32]

The two concerns come together in an analysis of interlocking components of a sexual division of labor which keeps women and other groups economically exploited, socially oppressed or both. These divisions are as follows: Between procreation and production of commodities for exchange in a market (the latter valued as men's "real" economic toil); within procreation, such that only women are childbearers while men control their sexual, procreative and emotional labor; and within commodity production, such that women's paid labor is often for different jobs than men perform, and compensated at a lower rate.[33]

The explicitly antiestablishment goal of socialist feminism is to eliminate those sexual divisions of labor in *every* realm of life, which means "women (and men) should disappear as socially constituted categories."[34] Moreover, these feminists argue that it is completely possible to accomplish this. For example, Western societies have the technology to enable men to carry and bear children, but lack the interest and will to make this a social option. Typically, the Strategic Defense Initiative (Star Wars) sounds more sane and desirable than men having babies.

To proceed to socialist feminist levels of disorder and irrationality, several strategies are useful. Organizations exclusively for women provide spaces for ideas, approaches to labor, and social agendas to percolate in semi-isolation from patriarchy. Becoming involved in complementary movements which chip away at the sexual division of labor (through fights for women's reproductive rights, childcare and comparable worth, and against rape, battering and abusive practices of animal vivisection which the strong impose on their subservients) also makes sense.[35] The key is self-education through struggles to "transform the social relations which define us."[36] This perspective inclines some socialist feminists to support women in armed combat against established states refusing to give up colonial conquests of a by-gone era, or those sponsoring particularly hideous policies like apartheid. In these cases, people's war is necessary labor, distinct from the unnecessary coercion imposed by colonialism. Moreover, it helps women build energy, competence, capability and effectiveness as shapers of new societies, and suggests that, against certain types of patriarchies, those which are fascist, genocidal, and racist, certain types of coercion become destructive-constructive.[37] Overall, socialist feminism draws attention to historical materialist structures of patriarchal culture, and the different and oppressive expectations which exist for males and females. It is a feminist politics of struggle on the terrain of patriarchal society, but against the very practices which make that society seem orderly and rational. It thus poses dangers to established roles, lifestyles and expectations.

Radical and socialist feminisms provide two different philosophies and politics to help women move beyond equality with men in societies created and led by men, and kept safe by patriarchal wars and peaces. We must realize that these are only rough guidelines for women-warrior thought, strategy, and labor, and may be inadequate to the challenges of diverse circumstances. In all forms, however, the woman warrior is actively skeptical of prospects for peace wherever and whenever order is a smokescreen for dominance.

WOMEN WARRIORS WHO ARE NOT FEMINISTS?

Do you have to be a radical or socialist feminist to be a woman warrior? Were there no women warriors in earlier times, that is, before the advent of contemporary feminist theories and politics? The evidence, limited as it is, suggests that women may need to develop and embrace some woman-warrior feminism to be effective in reshaping war and peace, and these are relatively new, as is some of the knowledge which underlies them.

There have always been women who actively or tacitly combatted aspects of patriarchal wars and peaces. Mies draws attention to slave women denying patriarchy its lifeblood by refusing to bear children.[38] Joan of Arc single-handedly threatened the established gender order by leading troops against the British in France. Pre-feminist "great women," however, became isolated within "his-stories." They acted irrationally by patriarchal standards, but lacked the "her-stories" and organized power bases necessary to formulate disorderly outcomes and fight patriarchal monopolies effectively. In the case of Joan of Arc, a man-god gave her the idea and a man-monarch accepted her help, and then allowed Joan to be sold to her enemies, tried instead of ransomed (the latter more the custom under such circumstances), and burned at the stake as a witch-heretic.[39] Similarly, for years preceding slave women's birth strikes, colonials discouraged slave childbearing, since this took time from productive labor in the fields. When antimotherhood became a form of resistance to slavery, one could argue that "the ideology of the ruling classes...became the accepted ideology of the oppressed."[40] These resistances, therefore, although momentous, contained double messages about who is rightfully in charge, and did not come out of powerful movements against patriarchy per se.

Even today there is evidence that women can enter into combat against some patriarchal pieces of war and peace, without challenging the entire monopoly. Such has been the experience of women in southern African people's wars.[41] There, women have power bases in the numerous women's organizations established to promote and support revolution, and often labor as combatants, which is irrational and role-altering. Yet, the press of events leads women to merge with "the" national liberation struggle without setting woman-centered conditions on their participation, such as equal numbers of command posts during the war and public authority after it. There is certainly strength in national unity. The problem, of course, is that the women sacrifice twice for the nation—they risk their lives, as do male combatants, and then refade into the background as the male warriors direct the newly liberated societies. Men like Robert Mugabe of Zimbabwe, or the late Samora Machel of Mozambique, are pro-women; indeed, they have ensured that the worst inequities in customary laws are rectified, such as the practice of treating adult women as minors. But it is clear that the education-labor involved in ousting foreign patriarchs provides only partial training for the task of dislodging accepted practices of local patriarchy, such as men running the public affairs of state.[42] Arguably, these pieces of patriarchal peace will ebb only when women with warrior inclinations become women warriors under terms of local warrior feminisms.

Along the way, women with warrior inclinations, who know nothing about or even reject warrior feminisms, can provide appropriate soldiering lessons for their daughters. Such was my upbringing. My mother had suffered war and peace at the hands of her alcoholic father who taunted her, killed her plans to attend college, and then forbade her to dissolve an unhappy marriage engagement with my father. In her mother's house, she was sheltered from all-out abuse by this patriarch, but was also taught to value, conform to, and defend male dominance. As an adult, mother was simultaneously warrior- and patriarchy-inclined—feisty in the company of patriarchs, she nonetheless worked to keep "fortress patriarchy" strong by training me, or trying to train me, to "act like a lady." Fighting patriarchal monopolies is not ladylike. I learned this through a war of survival brought on by the abrupt departure of father when I was twelve. Mother and I were reluctant draftees to this war because abandoned women often have few liquid assets, considerable guilty embarrassment, and a sense that "a woman who is not 'loved' by a man is a nobody."[43] Their households, however, often become the paragons of constructive irrationality and disorder, as mothers who may not have worked outside the household for more than ten years suddenly change their labor in order to hold off bill collectors, and daughters are stirred from innocence to clean houses, babysit, clerk, and sell magazines by phone as their war contribution.

My mother survived her war within patriarchal peace with considerable elan. She then, however, admonished the adolescent me to "let men do the driving." It did not work. Keeping the peace patriarchy-style was simply too dissonant with the other lessons I had learned about sacrificing oneself for a falsely secure order. Nonetheless, were it not for the new scholarship on women and my exposure to women warriors, I might not have nurtured the woman warrior part of me—to this day, mother sees herself as a warrior, not a feminist.[44]

CONCLUSIONS

It is inappropriate to draw sharp conclusions about interrelationships of women, peace-lovingness, women warriors, and strategies for tipping patriarchal war-peace pieces in more feminist directions. This thinking and action is very much in process and is also healthfully incoherent. Suffice it to say we should carefully examine claims that war and peace are negations of each other, and that women are unified in a natural or conditioned opposition to war and embrace of peace. Looking around the world, we see examples of mothers teaching their daughters to think in warlike abstractions, and of some women killing so as not to prolong community pain. We see others frankly appalled at the thought of violence, and still others who struggle first and foremost as workers or as citizens, entitled to equal rights with men under the law. We are all women; we are all learning about women, war, and peace; and all of our experiences have validity. Within this kaleidoscope of experience, women warriors are "nonpeacefuls" who expose patriarchal wars and peaces as bankrupt pieces of order. Count on them to stand in the way of any new, just, 'world order' that is not sufficiently disordering and irrational to challenge longstanding monopolies of power.

NOTES

Thanks to Morny Joy, Katherine Young and Nancy Hirschmann for helping me think about women warriors; to Warren Wagar, Linda Forcey, and the SUNY-Binghamton Peace Studies program for inviting me to present first thoughts; and to Louis Kriesberg and the Program on the Analysis and Resolution of Conflicts at Syracuse University for an opportunity to refine them. Bradley Klein, John Agnew, Joan Bokaer, and Mark Rupert had useful comments; and Gettysburg College supported this and all my work for the nearly seven years I taught there.

1. Birgit Brock-Utne, *Educating for Peace: A Feminist Perspective* (New York: Pergamon, 1985), 33.

2. Sara Ruddick, "Pacifying the Forces: Drafting Women in the Interests of Peace," *Signs,* v. 8, no. 3 (1983).

3. M. Gordon, "Sharon Gless and Tyne Daly, Stars of 'Cagney and Lacey,' " *Ms.* (January, 1987).

4. Winnie Mandela, "Interview," *Ms.* (January, 1987): 83.

5. Nancy Hartsock, "The Barracks Community in Western Political Thought: Prolegomena to a Feminist Critique of War and Politics," *Women's Studies International Forum,* v. 5, no. 3/4: 283.

6. The four aspects of feminist power are discussed in Nancy Hartsock, *Money, Sex, and Power: Toward a Feminist Historical Materialism* (Boston: Northeastern University Press, 1985).

7. Brock-Utne, *Educating for Peace,* 33.

8. Ibid.

9. Ibid., 148.

10. Sandra Harding, *The Science Question in Feminism* (Ithaca, N.Y.: Cornell University Press, 1986), 26.

11. Maria Mies, *Patriarchy and Accumulation on a World Scale: Women in the International Division of Labour* (London: Zed, 1986), 38.

12. Ibid., chapters 2 and 3, "Social Origins of the Sexual Division of Labour" and "Colonization and Housewifization."

13. This interpretation of *Roe versus Wade* extends a point Sonia Johnson made at Gettysburg College, November 2, 1987.

14. Nancy Chodorow, *The Reproduction of Mothering: Psychoanalysis and the Sociology of Gender* (Berkeley: University of California Press, 1978); and Dorothy Dinnerstein, *The Mermaid and the Minotaur: Sexual Arrangements and Human Malaise* (New York: Harper and Row, 1976).

15. For a discussion of masculine images in war discourse, see Bradley Klein, "The Textual Strategies of Military Strategy: or Have You Read Any Good Defense Manuals Lately?" paper for the International Studies Association, Washington, D.C. (April, 1987).

16. Nancy Hirschmann suggested this wording.

17. Chodorow, *The Reproduction of Mothering,* 167.

18. Ruddick, "Pacifying the Forces," 479.

19. See discussions in Marilyn French, *Beyond Power: On Women, Men, and Morals* (New York: Summit Books, 1985); and Hartsock, *Money, Sex, and Power*.

20. A similar point is made by Jane Flax, "Postmodernism and Gender Relations in Feminist Theory," *Signs*, 12, no. 4 (1987). Contrast this with the approach of Jean Bethke Elshtain, *Women and War* (New York: Basic Books, 1987).

21. Brock-Utne, *Educating For Peace*, chap. 1, "What is Peace"?; and Betty Reardon, *Sexism and the War System* (New York: Teachers College Press, 1985).

22. See discussion on defining peace in Christine Sylvester, "UN Elites: Perspectives on Peace," *Journal of Peace Research*, v. 17, no. 4 (1980).

23. Alison Jaggar, *Feminist Politics and Human Nature* (Totowa, N.J.: Roman & Allenheld, 1983), 5. Not all feminists think it is useful to categorize feminisms. See also Mies, *Patriarchy and Accumulation*, 12.

24. This argument runs throughout Harding, *The Science Question in Feminism*.

25. Jaggar, *Feminist Politics*, 194.

26. Ibid., 193.

27. See discussion in Selma James and Mariarosa Dalla Costa, *The Power of Women and the Subversion of Community* (Bristol: Falling Wall, 1973); and work by Clara Zetkin in *Socialist Register 1976*, Hal Draper and Anne Lipow, trans., Ralph Miliband and John Saville, eds. (London: Merlin, 1976).

28. Jaggar, *Feminist Politics*, 79.

29. For a discussion of why reproduction should be considered socially productive labor subject to technological change and consciousness-raising results, see Alison Jaggar and William McBride, "Reproduction as Male Ideology," *Women's International Forum*, v. 3, no. 8 (1985).

30. Mary Daly, *Pure Lust; Elemental Feminist Philosophy* (Boston: Beacon, 1984), ix.

31. Hartsock, "The Barracks Community," 283.

32. Jaggar, *Feminist Politics*, 124.

33. Ibid., 130–37.

34. Ibid., 132.

35. Mies, *Patriarchy and Accumulation*, chap. 7, "Towards a Feminist Perspective of a New Society."

36. Nancy Hartsock, "Feminist Theory and the Development of Revolutionary Strategy," in *Capitalist Patriarchy and the Case of Socialist Feminism*, Zillah Eisenstein, ed., (New York: Monthly Review, 1979), 62. In Mies, *Patriarchy and Accumulation*, chap. 7, "Towards a Feminist Perspective of a New Society," Mies argues it would be a sign of considerable self-education and power for men's groups to form around the issue of violence to women, and for women's groups to boycott industries which promote images of them needing constant beautification or romantic love to be happy and fulfilled.

37. See discussion in Mies, Ibid.; and in Christine Sylvester, "Some Dangers in Merging Feminist and Peace Projects," *Alternatives*, v. 4, no. 12 (October, 1987).

38. Ibid. chap. 3, "Colonization and Housewifization."

39. Marina Warner, *Joan of Arc: The Image of Female Heroism* (New York: Knopf, 1981).

40. Rhoda Reddock, *Women, Labour and Struggle in 20th Century Trinidad and Tobago 1898–1960* (The Hague: Institute of Social Studies, 1984), 17; cited in Mies, *Patriarchy and Accumulation,* 92.

41. See discussions in Stephanie Urdang, *Fighting Two Colonialisms: Women in Guinea Bissau* (New York: Monthly Review, 1979); and, "Women in Contemporary National Liberation Movements," in *African Women: South of the Sahara,* Jean Hay and Sharon Stichter, eds. (New York: Longman, 1984); Mies, Ibid.; and Sylvester, "Some Dangers in Merging Feminist and Peace Projects."

42. Olivia Muchena, "Are Women Integrated Into Development?" *African Report,* v. 12, no. 2 (1983); Stephanie Urdang, "The Last Transition? Women and Development" in *A Difficult Road: The Transition to Socialism in Mozambique,* John Saul, ed., (London: Monthly Review, 1985).

43. Mies, *Patriarchy and Accumulation,* 233.

44. For more discussion of this example, see Sylvester, "Some Dangers of Merging Feminist and Peace Projects."

8

Low-Intensity Conflict: A Growing Threat to Peace

Michael T. Klare

With the signing of the Treaty on Intermediate-Range Nuclear Forces (INF), we appear to be standing on the threshold of a pivotal moment in postwar history. The great engine of the cold war that has sustained the nuclear arms race for some forty years, finally appears to be running out of steam. Perhaps, it is a bit too early to call it dead in the water, but the INF agreement does represent a significant new stage in the U.S.-Soviet relationship—one in which the two superpowers are talking about *dismantling* nuclear weapons, not just controlling them. Moreover, the INF agreement (coupled to future Bush-Gorbachev summits) could lead to further arms reductions and increased superpower cooperation in other critical areas. We cannot be certain that events will follow this course—a new crisis can emerge in U.S.-Soviet relations to undermine this process. It does appear, however, that the populations of both the Soviet Union and the United States are eager to wind down the arms race, and that the leaderships of both countries perceive very significant incentives for doing this. Thus, I believe that we will see a lessening in superpower tensions and possibly some very real progress toward nuclear disarmament in the 1990s. It appears that the world has become a safer place than it was in 1981, when President

This chapter is based on a talk given by the author at Riverside Church in New York City on October 16, 1987. A modified version of the talk appeared in *Christianity and Crisis* (February 1, 1988).

Reagan launched a major buildup of U.S. nuclear forces, and the peace movement should take satisfaction from its critical role in changing public opinion on the nuclear issue.

While the risk of nuclear war seems to have declined, another peril has risen in its place—the threat of "low-intensity conflict," or LIC as it is known in military circles. Low-intensity conflict does not presently threaten our lives, or for the most part, those of our children. But it does threaten us in another, equally distressing way: It threatens the integrity of our values and the survival of our freedoms. Most people have heard the term "low-intensity conflict," and have some idea what it means, but for the record, let us review what it entails. From a military perspective, low-intensity conflict is warfare that falls below the threshold of full-scale combat between modern armies (the sort we saw in the Korean War, and at the onset of the Iran-Iraq War). Under U.S. doctrine, low-intensity conflict encompasses four particular types of operations: (1) *counterinsurgency,* or combat against revolutionary guerrillas, as is now being waged in El Salvador and the Philippines; (2) *pro-insurgency,* or U.S. support for anti-Communist insurgents, such as the anti-Sandinista contras in Nicaragua, and UNITA in Angola; (3) *peacetime contingency operations,* or police-type actions like the U.S. invasion of Grenada and the April 1986 bombing of Tripoli; and (4) *military show of force,* or conspicuous military maneuvers of the sort conducted by the Reagan administration in the Persian Gulf. These are not theoretical or anticipated forms of warfare; rather, they are military operations that the United States is conducting *now.* From a low-intensity conflict point of view, the United States is at war, extensively, aggressively, and with every evidence of continuing this activity.[1]

Before proceeding further, it is important to note that low-intensity conflict does not necessarily imply that the level of bloodshed and savagery in any given conflict is low (for instance, the low-intensity conflict in Guatemala has already claimed well over 100,000 lives, and similar numbers have perished in other low-intensity conflicts). What is crucial to recognize is that low-intensity conflict is a form of warfare in which *your side* suffers very little death or destruction, while the other side suffers as much damage as you can inflict on them without producing undue hardship for your own society. It is war with proxies, war with mercenaries, and war with modern military systems aimed at those with the most primitive of defenses.

In the United States today, low-intensity conflict has an even more specific meaning: Given the persistence of the "Vietnam syndrome," it means war in which U.S. involvement is kept sufficiently indistinct and inexpensive so as to not produce a hue and cry in Congress or the media. The U.S. military remembers the strident demonstrations and antimilitaristic attitudes of the Vietnam era, and is determined to avoid such responses for as long as it possibly can. Hence, by definition, low-intensity conflict is that amount of bloodshed, torture, rape, and savagery that can be sustained overseas without triggering widespread public disapproval at home. Or, to put it another way, low-intensity conflict is the ultimate in "yuppie" warfare—it allows privileged Americans to go on buying condominiums, wearing chic designer clothes, eating expensive meals at posh restaurants, and generally living in style without risking their own lives, without facing conscription, without paying higher taxes, and, most importantly, without being overly distracted by grisly scenes on television. *That*, essentially, is the determining characteristic of low-intensity conflict in the American context today. What, then, is the purpose of low-intensity conflict? Who are its victims, and what is the nature of low-intensity combat itself?

According to U.S. military leaders, low-intensity conflict is aimed at combatting terrorism, subversion, insurgency, and other forms of disruptive violence in the Third World. Such violence is generally portrayed in ideological terms, such as a Soviet- or Cuban-inspired assault on the pro-Western, democratic nations of the "free world." It is not just Marxist guerrillas whom low-intensity conflict is intended to defeat, but *anyone* in the Third World who calls for a radical restructuring of the global system, whether inspired by Marx, Mao, Christ, or Mohammed. Perhaps the clearest and most revealing formulation of low-intensity conflict was made by General Maxwell D. Taylor in 1974. Taylor is a significant figure in recent U.S. military history, and was one of the principal architects of U.S. intervention in Vietnam. Thus, at the end of the Vietnam war, when General Taylor wrote about U.S. military missions in the post-Vietnam era, his words carried great weight. He said, "As the leading affluent 'have' power, we may have to fight to protect our national valuables against envious 'have nots.' "[2]

This theme, the "haves" versus the "have-nots," is the underlying premise of low-intensity conflict doctrine. It states, in essence, that the privileged nations of the industrialized "North" are vitally threatened by the starving, non-white masses of the underdeveloped "South." Accordingly, we must be prepared to combat any forces in the Third World that seek to reconstruct the world system in such a way as to reverse the flow of wealth from "South" to "North." This theme was first articulated in a 1977 RAND Corporation study, *Military Implications of a Possible World Order Crisis in the 1980s*.[3] In this study, Guy Parker wrote: "There is a non-negligible chance that mankind is entering a period of increased social instability and faces the possibility of a breakdown of global order as a result of a sharpening confrontation between the Third World and the industrial democracies." Because of the growing gap between rich and poor, "The North-South conflict . . . could get out of hand in ways comparable to the peasant rebellions that in past centuries engulfed large parts of Europe or Asia, spreading like uncontrolled prairie fires."

In the 1980s, this sort of apocalyptic thinking became intertwined with the fervent anticommunism of President Reagan and his associates to produce the foundation for current low-intensity conflict doctrine. Perhaps the strongest exponent of this thinking is Neil C. Livingstone, a Pentagon consultant and counterinsurgency expert, who was a close advisor to Lieutenant Colonel Oliver North. In a 1983 speech at the National Defense University, Livingstone observed: "Unfulfilled expectations and economic mismanagement have turned much of the developing world into a 'hothouse of conflict,' capable of spilling over and engulfing the industrial West." The Soviet Union, according to Livingstone, sees in this discord "a means of undermining the West, wearing it down, nibbling away at its peripheries, denying it the strategic materials . . . critical to its commerce." Our response to this threat, he argued, "cannot be half-hearted or indecisive." Given the magnitude of the threat, "the security of the United States requires a restructuring of our warmaking capabilities, placing new emphasis on the ability to fight a succession of limited wars, and to project power into the Third World.[4]

In other words, the main thrust of U.S. power must be turned around: Instead of facing the putative threat from the East—from the Soviet Union and the Warsaw Pact—it must be rotated 90 degrees to face the *real* peril, the threat from the "South," from the envious "have-nots" who threaten to reverse the flow of global wealth. As expressed in the crisp language of Pentagon strategists, this means (quoting from Colonel James Motley in the Army's leading strategic journal): "The United States should reorient its forces and traditional policies from an almost exclusive concentration on NATO to better influence politico-military outcomes in the resource-rich and strategically located Third World areas." Moreover, given the West's growing dependence on these critical areas, "The United States will require forces with greater strategic and tactical utility to counter the more likely low-intensity contingencies that will confront the United States in ever-increasing numbers for the rest of this decade and beyond."[5]

While such views would have been considered heretical by most U.S. strategists in the early Reagan era, it has become prevailing doctrine in the late 1980s. Most revealing, in this regard, was the publication in 1988 of *Discriminate Deterrence*,[6] the report of the U.S. Commission on Integrated Long-Term Strategy (a panel organized by the Department of Defense and the National Security Council). Suggesting that "An emphasis on massive Soviet attacks leads to tunnel vision among defense planners," the report argues that U.S. strategists need to "deal with many important and far more plausible situations"—especially low-level conflicts in the Third World. Such conflicts may be "less threatening than any Soviet-American war would be," but they will have "an adverse cumulative effect on U.S. access to critical regions, on American credibility among allies and friends, and on American self-confidence." This being the case, "In the coming decades the United States will need to be better prepared to deal with conflicts in the Third World." Not only must we reorient our forces to face the growing threat from the "South," low-intensity conflict doctrine assumes, but we must be prepared to fight there again and again, for as long as we can see into the future. What will this mean in operational terms? How does a nation go about protecting itself from a world of envious "have-nots," assuming it is committed to a military solution? One could, of course, attempt to kill off a large part of the insurgent population, as European settlers did in the so-called "New World," or one could build walls, like the Great Wall of China, to try to keep the "barbarians" out. But killing three-quarters of the world's population doesn't seem very practical, or even profitable, since there would be no one left to buy our products; and building walls would disrupt the flow of strategic raw materials on which we depend so much. So what to do instead? Evidently, the cheapest solution is to hire or co-opt armies of thugs and mercenaries, and use them to starve and terrorize subject populations to the point that they are too dispirited, or too frightened, or too weak to resist.

Now, this may seem a rather extreme characterization of U.S. policy. But look at some of the so-called "success stories" of counterinsurgency: Guatemala under the generals, Nicaragua under Somoza, Chile under Pinochet, Iran under the Shah, and the Philippines under Marcos. In all of these cases, one finds that the essence of government strategy was precisely the eradication of protest through systematic murder, torture, and the "kidnapping" of disaffected individuals in social sectors such as labor, the peasantry, students, the clergy, Indians, and so on. It does not necessarily matter that the "right" people (the ones who are actually guilty of membership in an underground organization) are targeted. Rather, the idea is to so terrorize the population—by inculcating a constant fear of a knock on the door in the middle of the night, followed by blindfolding, torture, mutilation, and death—that it remains silent no matter what hideous crimes against humanity are being committed.

Frantz Fanon, the great black psychoanalyst, described this phenomenon in his classic book *The Wretched of the Earth*.[7] He describes those who give up the anticolonial struggle "because in the innermost recesses of their brains, the settlers' tanks and airplanes occupy a huge place." When they are told that resistance is necessary, "they see bombs raining down on them, armored cars coming at them on every path, machine-gunning and police action...and they sit quiet. They are beaten from the start."

This, more than anything, is the function of the kidnapping, the death squads, and the torture that occurs in so many Third World countries. It is not some irrational product of an underdeveloped mentality, but rather a pragmatic, cheap answer to the problem of three billion envious "have-nots," and it lies at the heart of the emerging low-intensity conflict doctrine. As suggested by Colonel North's mentor, Neil C. Livingstone, the United States failed at counterinsurgency in Vietnam because it was inhibited by excessive television coverage from using the most effective tactics. However, he noted, "They have learned this lesson in Guatemala, where the Guatemalan government has restricted the press to the urban centers and prosecuted the war against the guerrillas with efficiency, brutality, and dispatch."[8] Anyone who has examined Amnesty International reports on Guatemala knows what this means—the murder, starvation, or disappearance of an estimated 100,000 peasants, Indians, labor organizers, and church activists.

To engage in low-intensity warfare ultimately means to forge an alliance with the dictators, the death squads, and the psychopaths of the world—people who do not shrink from killing unarmed, unprotected women and children, who do not hesitate to apply electrodes to nipples and genitals, who are immune to the cries of the sick and starving. Such alliances, according to Livingstone, "would surely provoke an outcry from civil libertarians in the United States [but] the plain fact is that the United States is at war, and in wartime the only thing that counts is winning, because winning is surviving."[9]

Similar views were expressed by another low-intensity conflict expert, Professor Sam Sarkesian of Loyola University in Chicago: "The public must understand that low-intensity conflicts do not conform to democratic notions in strategy or tactics," he said in 1985. "Revolutionaries and counterrevolutionaries develop their own morality and ethics that justify any means to achieve success. Survival is the ultimate morality."[10] Those who can recall the Iran-contra hearings of 1987 will be reminded of the testimony of Lieutenant Colonel Oliver North, when he articulated a similar sort of "morality" to justify the subversion of U.S. laws and principles. It is this sort of behavior and thinking that leads me to assert that low-intensity conflict represents a vital threat to America's fundamental values.

What does it mean for a society to enjoy relative freedom and security at home, while aiding and abetting wholesale murder and mutilation abroad? Do we remain immune to the horror of it all? I think not. I do not believe that one can condone brutality somewhere else and not suffer some moral rot on one's own turf. We have ample evidence of this fact: Congress goes on voting "humanitarian" aid (food and fuel to sustain the killing of civilians in Nicaragua) for the contras, while denying food and shelter to the truly needy in our own country. The State Department offers a welcoming hand to death squad leaders from Central America, and the Justice Department prosecutes those who offer sanctuary to the victims of death squad violence. Former Secretary of State, George Schultz, spoke about our support for "freedom fighters" around the world, but persistently overlooked the terrorist crimes committed by the contras in Nicaragua and UNITA in Angola. When we turn away from these atrocities, when we avert our eyes from injustice, when we escape into indulgence and self-absorption, our values suffer a poisonous decay.

Is the United States succumbing to this poison? Not entirely, there are many people in America who believe in peace and justice, and thank goodness, they are not silent about their beliefs. Indeed, this is the greatest single obstacle to the triumph of the low-intensity conflict doctrine. So long as there are strong voices in America to protest the savage and immoral nature of U.S. military policy abroad, the White House and the Pentagon will be deterred from increasing the U.S. commitment to low-intensity conflict in the Third World. One final point about low-intensity warfare: It is a strategy aimed not only against the envious "have-nots" of the Third World, but also against those Americans who speak out against U.S. intervention in internal Third World conflicts. Make no mistake about it, Colonel North and the other exponents of low-intensity conflict doctrine are fully aware that domestic U.S. opposition is the greatest obstacle to the success of their policies, and they are fully determined to overcome such resistance.

Domestic public opinion is the *home front* in the global struggle against U.S. "enemies," and low-intensity conflict strategy is addressed as much to this front as to the overseas fronts in Central America, South Africa, and elsewhere. The weapons might be different—instead of rape, torture, and multilation, we are more likely to be threatened with lies, deceit and intimidation—but the will to combat is no less intense. This notion of a struggle for the homefront was clearly articulated by Neil Livingstone in his 1983 speech at the National Defense University: "It is vital that the American public and our policymakers be educted as to the realities of contemporary conflict, and the need to fight little wars successfully." In doing so, moreover, we must recognize that "The United States will never win a war fought daily in the U.S. media or on the floor of Congress, where members attempt to micromanage conflicts rather than making overall policy and leaving the implementation of that policy to others."[11]

The implications of this outlook are clear: To win a succession of "little wars" in the Third World, the U.S. government must muzzle the press, subvert Congress, and turn over management of its foreign wars to those like Colonel North who believe that any means are justified in the pursuit of victory. Low-intensity conflict and American democracy are incompatible. To preserve our democratic system and protect our basic values the low-intensity conflict doctrine must be repudiated. Our integrity, our humanity, and our morality are at risk in the Pentagon's campaign to carry out the strategy of low-intensity conflict. We can be intimidated by this, and become numbed to the violence we see in Central America (just as we can be numbed by the risk of nuclear war). But if we resist the numbing, and act to protect our rights and values, we can be liberated from despair and find a new sense of purpose in the common struggle we share with the many millions of advocates for peace and justice in the world today.

NOTES

1. For further discussions of low-intensity conflict doctrine and strategy, see Michael Klare and Peter Kornbluh, eds., *Low-Intensity Warfare* (New York: Pantheon, 1988), especially chapters 1 and 3.

2. Maxwell Taylor, "The Legitimate claims of National Security," *Foreign Affairs* (April 1974): 586.

3. Guy Pauker, *Military Implications of a Possible World Order Crisis in the 1980s*, report no. R–2003-AF (Santa Monica, Calif.: RAND Corp., 1977), 1–4.

4. Neil C. Livingstone, "Fighting Terrorism and Dirty Little Wars," in William A. Buckingham, Jr., ed., *Defense Planning for the 1980s* (Washington, D.C.: National Defense University Press, 1984), 166–67, 186.

5. James B. Motley, "A Perspective on Low-Intensity Conflict," *Military Review* (January 1985): 7, 9.

6. U.S. Commission on Integrated Long-Term Strategy, *Discriminate Deterrence* (Washington, D.C.: Government Printing Office, 1988), 13–14, 33–34.

7. Frantz Fanon, *The Wretched of the Earth* (New York: Grove Press, 1968), 63.

8. Livingstone, "Fighting Terrorism," 188.

9. Ibid.

10. Sam C. Sarkesian, "Low-Intensity Conflict: Concepts: Principles, and Policy Guidelines," *Air University Review* (January-February 1985): 11.

11. Livingstone, "Fighting Terrorism," 188, 195.

9

America's "New Thinking"

Daniel Yankelovich and Richard Smoke

I

The American public is willing to experiment with winding down the cold war. But this "new thinking" in the United States differs in at least one important respect from Mikhail Gorbachev's "new thinking" about Soviet-U.S. relations. Gorbachev seems to want to make changes swiftly. The United States insists upon proceeding cautiously, testing Soviet good faith at each step. The average American wants to explore new possibilities but cannot easily brush aside forty years of hostility and mistrust. The attitudes of the American public have been tempered by disappointment with the détente of the 1970s. The public feels that the Soviets took advantage of the United States, and does not want to be tricked again.

Without sensitive management of the superpower relationship from both sides, a disjunction could open between these differing tempos that could create difficulties for years to come. No new U.S. administration, Republican or Democratic, will want to, nor can afford to move more rapidly than the American public. But public attitudes are shifting. Despite ambivalences, a striking pattern of change in public attitudes is radically altering the boundaries within which U.S.-Soviet policies can be shaped in the next few years.

II

The current attitude of Americans toward the Soviet Union is different from anything we have seen in forty years. It is not the troubled mood of recent years, of worry about nuclear war. It is not the mood at the beginning of this decade, when Americans assertively endorsed a strong military buildup.[1] It is not the mood of the early 1970s, when Americans were overly optimistic about the possibilities of détente. Nor is it the cold war mood of the 1950s and early 1960s. The majority of Americans are now interested in neither a further military buildup nor instant friendship. The current mood can be characterized as a wary readiness. It is readiness of a special kind—distinctly hopeful yet cautious. The public is hopeful that far-reaching change, perhaps even an historic, fundamental change in relations with the Soviet Union is in the offing. As time passes, the nation is ready to embrace the prospect of fundamental change, if it meets America's needs. But the "if" is a big one, keenly felt. The country remains suspicious and mistrustful of the Soviets. If change proves to be a trap, Americans will be unsurprised; they are equally ready to embrace a new round of strenuous global competition.

This duality is easily misunderstood. However, on close inspection it proves to be a rational, hard-headed stance upon which a new national consensus can be firmly built. Because the change is so far-reaching, it is desirable to document it as carefully as possible. Fortunately, the evidence is exceptionally abundant. Not one, but two projects of unusual scope and depth, in addition to a variety of regular polls, have explored American attitudes on this subject in the past year.

One project is "Americans Talk Security" (ATS), an ongoing series of 12 bipartisan surveys of registered voters on national security issues, conducted on a rotating basis by three firms—a Republican polling firm, a Democratic firm and a politically neutral firm. This project has explored a rich menu of questions on the single topic of national security, and the ongoing nature of the project has also permitted ambiguous points to be probed by follow-up, elaborated questions.[2] The other project is "The Public, the Soviets, and Nuclear Arms," a joint effort by The Public Agenda Foundation (PAF), and the Center for Foreign Policy Development at Brown University.[3] The latter's research on policy options was interwoven with PAF's research on how the public uses information, to convey policy possibilities in a form accessible to the public.[4]

Both projects offer compelling evidence that Americans have changed their outlook on U.S.-Soviet relations. In the first two years of the Reagan administration, numerous polls showed that the public endorsed a strong "get-tough" posture. Fewer than one out of five voters supported a conciliatory "negotiating" approach. In the final year of the Reagan era, the public has completely reversed its emphasis. Now, only one in five support the "get-tough" posture, with large majorities endorsing the view that the United States should seek to reduce tensions through negotiations and agreements (see Tables 9.1 and 9.2).

Only two years ago, in October 1986, a Gallup poll revealed that only approximately one-third of the voters (37 percent) believed that relations between the United States and the Soviet Union were stable or getting better, and 60 percent thought they were getting worse. By July 1988, an astonishing 94 percent thought they were stable or getting better, with a strong majority (68 percent) convinced they are now getting better according to the seventh ATS survey.

In the summer of 1988, the seventh ATS survey, presented voters with a variety of options for U.S.-Soviet cooperation. Six were endorsed at a consensus level (more than seven out of ten voters): Working together to combat (1) environmental pollution (85 percent); (2) the illicit drug trade (85 percent); (3) terrorism (78 percent); (4) expanding cultural exchanges (84 percent); (5) working together to resolve conflicts in the Middle East and other regional trouble spots (72 percent); and (6) eliminating most nuclear weapons by the year 2000 (71 percent).[5]

Perhaps even more persuasive is evidence from the PAF/Brown study, which queried citizens about the long-term future (to the year 2010). In this study the public was asked not for predictions but for preferences. Before casting their ballots they discussed at length the arguments for and against each of four broad policy alternatives:

—The United States should seek to gain and maintain the upper hand over the U.S.S.R.

—The United States should cooperate with the Soviets in far-reaching steps to reduce the risk of nuclear war, but compete vigorously in all other ways.

—The United States and the Soviets should strive for as much "cooperative problem-solving" as possible, on a variety of problems facing them both.

—The United States should confine its defense commitments to the area around North America.

The participants were urged to consider not just their hopes but what would be feasible and realistic. Even after hearing a range of contrary arguments, people predominantly chose a future of cooperative problem-solving between the superpowers, giving it a decisive plurality of 46 percent. Fully three quarters named it their first or second choice (see Table 9.3).

Table 9.1
Public Attitudes in the Early Reagan Years

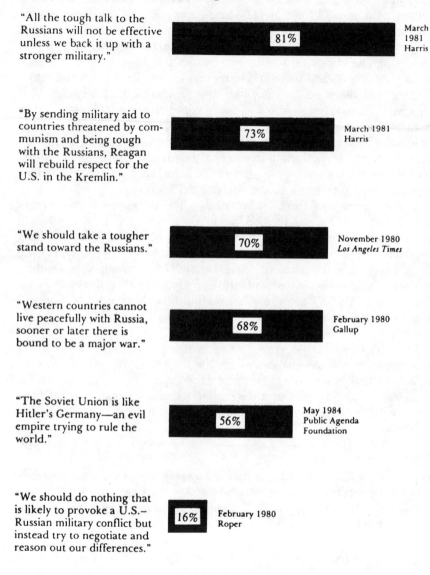

"All the tough talk to the Russians will not be effective unless we back it up with a stronger military."

81%

March 1981 Harris

"By sending military aid to countries threatened by communism and being tough with the Russians, Reagan will rebuild respect for the U.S. in the Kremlin."

73%

March 1981 Harris

"We should take a tougher stand toward the Russians."

70%

November 1980 *Los Angeles Times*

"Western countries cannot live peacefully with Russia, sooner or later there is bound to be a major war."

68%

February 1980 Gallup

"The Soviet Union is like Hitler's Germany—an evil empire trying to rule the world."

56%

May 1984 Public Agenda Foundation

"We should do nothing that is likely to provoke a U.S.– Russian military conflict but instead try to negotiate and reason out our differences."

16%

February 1980 Roper

Table 9.2
Changing Public Attitudes Toward a "Get-Tough" Posture

Agree that:
"The U.S. should try
harder to reduce tension
with the Russians
versus getting tougher
in its dealings with
them."

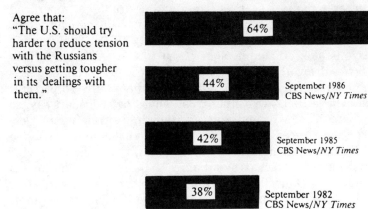

64% — October 1987 ATS #1

44% — September 1986 CBS News/*NY Times*

42% — September 1985 CBS News/*NY Times*

38% — September 1982 CBS News/*NY Times*

20% — January 1980 CBS News/*NY Times*

Table 9.3
Alternative Futures for the Next Century

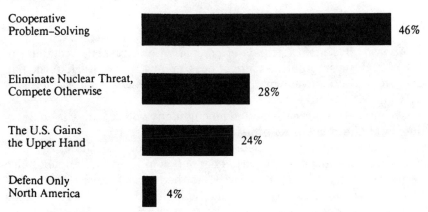

Cooperative
Problem–Solving — 46%

Eliminate Nuclear Threat,
Compete Otherwise — 28%

The U.S. Gains
the Upper Hand — 24%

Defend Only
North America — 4%

NOTE: Percentages add up to more than 100 due to rounding of figures. Figures here are for first choices only.
SOURCE: *U.S.-Soviet Relations in the Year 2010: Americans Look to the Future*, The Public Agenda Foundation and The Center for Foreign Policy Development.

These clearpowerful evidence that the American people recognize that important changes are now under way in U.S.-Soviet relations, with still greater changes seen as likely and desirable. A superficial reading of figures like these might suggest that the American public is as ready now as it was for détente in the early 1970s. That reading would be a mistake; other questions posed in the "Americans Talk Security" series draw a very different kind of response. The first ATS survey, for instance, shows that two-thirds of the public (68 percent) continue to believe that "we cannot trust what Soviet leaders say, so we should proceed slowly and with caution in responding to Gorbachev." The most recent ATS survey reveals that majorities agree with the following statements: "If we are weak, the Soviet Union at the right moment will attack us or our allies" (56 percent); "The Soviets lie, cheat and steal—they'll do anything to further the cause of communism" (64 percent). Just one month after the Washington summit of December 1987, at which the Intermediate-range Nuclear Forces (INF) Treaty was signed with much fanfare, 55 percent said that "the Soviets cannot be trusted to keep their part of the bargain on arms control issues, according to the second ATS survey.

The evidence is unmistakable that Americans continue to harbor deep-seated feelings of mistrust of the Soviet Union. Despite a strong favorable rating for General Secretary Gorbachev, the American people are definitely not prepared to drop their suspicions of Soviet leaders and their motives.

III

At least five major strands of perception and response combine to create today's singular mixture of hope and wariness. Each of the five is a response to developments over a span of years; none is merely a passing reaction to immediate events.

The first strand is satisfaction among many voters with the achievements of the Reagan administration. In the assertive mood of 1980, Americans believed the Soviets were gaining ground in the superpower competition. Majorities supported not only a military buildup, but also a demonstration of American will. At the start of the Reagan presidency, a substantial part of the public believed we had tried in good faith to make peace with the Soviets, yet the Soviets took advantage of this goodwill to make gains at our expense. The attitude was that the Soviet Union understands only strength and interprets goodwill as weakness. Therefore, the United States had to demonstrate strength. In the eight years since, these feelings have evidently been satisfied.

Significantly, the public today expresses aproval of the U.S. military buildup. Sixty-six percent consider that the buildup was necessary and only 31 percent call it unnecessary, according to the sixth ATS survey. Equally significant, however, the public (84 percent) now feels no need for any further buildup, according to the third ATS survey.

The backlash of the 1980–1982 period was in substantial measure a reaction to a specific situation (the invasion of Afghanistan), and not a long-term norm. But public attitudes have not returned to the norm of earlier years either, for two reasons. One is that, although the backlash is emotionally spent, "detente" has become a pejorative word in the American lexicon, one that all U.S. political leaders avoid no matter what their policy preferences. The public attitude is "once burnt, twice shy." Americans do not want to go through another cycle of superficial improvement in relations, excessive expectations, the exploitation and collapse of good relations, and yet another military buildup. They also are determined not to be seen as naive again. Despite their caution, Americans also anticipate real change. Not only does a strong majority think U.S.-Soviet relations are getting better, but 80 percent of that majority also expects improvement to be fundamental according to the sixth ATS survey.

The second strand is economic. In the 1988 presidential election year, voters were more worried about U.S. competitiveness in the world economy than about the Soviets. The third ATS survey showed that in choosing the next president, the public was more concerned, by a margin of nearly two to one (62 to 33 percent), that he be someone "who can strengthen our economy" over someone "who will protect our national security interests." Americans worry that excessive attention to national security may be sapping the economy. Asked in 1983, and again in 1988, whether the American military buildup of this decade has "been good for the overall economy," the proportions responding yes and no have almost exactly reversed: 53 percent to 41 percent said yes in 1983 while 53 percent to 39 percent said no in 1988. About three in five believe "the amount of money spent on defense is hurting our economic well-being," according to the third and fourth ATS surveys. Eighty-six percent of the third ATS survey respondents thought that we may "seriously damage our economy by spending too much to defend other countries."

The impact of Gorbachev and his reform comprise the third strand in the public's attitude today. Americans' regard for Gorbachev has been rising steadily. A June 1986 Harris poll showed that approximately half (51 percent) reported they had a favorable impression of him. By the first ATS survey in October 1987, the figure had risen to two-thirds, and by the seventh ATS survey in July 1988 it had reached 83 percent. A favorable impression does not mean that Americans are ready to trust Gorbachev. But the public now believes that he is trying to accomplish a change in the very character of the Soviet Union, not just in details of its policies. The fourth ATS survey found that 66 percent of the American public thinks that "new Soviet policies will eventually create a more free and open society, versus remaining the closed society it has been in the past."

The fourth strand is a change under way in Americans' perception of the nuclear danger. In the past, the Soviet threat and the risk of nuclear war were closely linked, but 67 percent of Americans now say that "nuclear weapons are more likely to be used by terrorists or countries other than the U.S. or Soviet Union," according to the fourth ATS survey. Seventy-five percent of the participants in the PAF/Brown study rejected the possibility of a direct nuclear attack by the Soviet Union; three out of five said that "a smaller country such as Pakistan, Israel or South Africa will eventually use nuclear weapons." Asked what they thought to be "the most likely scenario" in which a nuclear war in the Third World (for example, in the Middle East) will escalate and draw in the superpowers," only 15 percent thought a deliberate Soviet attack was the most likely possibility.

A mutual reduction in nuclear weapons by the superpowers enjoys strong public support. In spite of suspicion that the Soviets may cheat, the ATS surveys indicate that Americans consistently supported the INF treaty, month after month, at levels above 70 percent. And 70 percent also indicated in the fourth ATS survey, "any mutual reductions in nuclear forces makes the world a safer place and improves national security." However, Americans think that a basic change in the overall superpower relationship is more important than arms agreements, according to the fourth ATS survey. The PAF/Brown study reached the same conclusion. An argument participants raised repeatedly in the discussions was that, if the relationship were still competitive, the arms race might be relaunched; in the post-discussion questionnaire, 73 percent said this was "a convincing argument."

The fifth strand in the public's perception might be seen as an extension of the fourth. Though the evidence is less extensive, it appears that the public increasingly believes that important problems are no longer just East-West in nature, but global. New technologies and the spread of existing technologies are creating important new dangers. In the PAF/Brown study, one persuasive argument for the "cooperative problem-solving" option was that, in the future, a variety of global problems will confront the superpowers equally, including pollution, terrorism, overpopulation, medical crises like AIDS, the hazards of nuclear power plants, and nuclear weapons proliferation. This was the most popular argument for or against *any* of the alternative futures, and a remarkable 83 percent found it convincing.

In summary, there seems little doubt that in the late 1980s Americans are adopting a more global perspective on potential threats. U.S. economic strength is challenged not by the Soviets, but by new competitors from a different part of the world, who seem to be out-trading the United States on a global scale. To the American public, the fearsome possibility of nuclear war derives not primarily from the Soviets but from new nuclear powers (actual and potential) elsewhere around the globe. Finally, new dangers are appearing that are global in their impact.

IV

We can refine Americans' new thinking by clarifying what it does *not* mean. It certainly does not mean that the United States no longer needs to be concerned about military strength. Even though large majorities dismiss the possibility of direct Soviet attack, they clearly do so on the premise that the United States remains strong. In the latest ATS survey, a majority (56 percent) expressed their concern that the Soviets might attack us or our allies "if we are weak."

The public also questions whether Soviet foreign policy has changed in any material respect. A 1984 Public Agenda poll found that Americans agreed, by 56 to 38 percent, that "whenever there is trouble around the world—in the Middle East, Central America or anywhere else—chances are the Soviets are behind it." In 1987 the first ATS survey found that a majority of Americans still believed this, by the nearly identical margins of 58 percent to 37 percent. The Soviet Union is still seen as playing for gains in the Third World. In the PAF/Brown project about two-thirds of the participants considered it likely not only that the Soviets would "increase their support of countries like Libya and of terrorist groups," but even that they might "attack other nations in the way they invaded Afghanistan."

More broadly, the public doubts that the world powers will stop pursuing their interests, even though collisions could result. Because Americans do not think the Soviet Union has changed its basic foreign policy, only a third support any reduction in U.S. military spending, according to the third ATS survey. These views are usefully distinguished from those that are indeed new. One is a marked diminution in the fear of nuclear war. Between October 1987 and March 1988 the number of respondents who expect war within the next 25 years fell from 44 to 33 percent, according to the first and fourth ATS surveys. This is a large reduction in only five months.

The public believes that superpower nuclear arsenals are decreasing. This perception stands in notable contrast to actual fact, which is that the strategic arsenals are continuing to grow in number of delivery vehicles. The small reduction accomplished by the INF treaty will shortly be neutralized by normal growth in other forces. The public's view probably derives from policy declarations from both Washington and Moscow, that for several years have stressed reductions, not arms control or ceilings as the objective. The American public has accepted the view (somewhat controversial among specialists) that the Warsaw Pact enjoys a large advantage over NATO in the balance of conventional forces in Europe. For example, the PAF/Brown study found that by a margin of 53 to 33 percent, Americans think that eliminating nuclear weapons would leave the West exposed to the Soviets' "large advantage in non-nuclear forces, such as tanks and soldiers." And the public now believes that reductions in nuclear weapons must be linked to changes in conventional forces. The same study found that an impressive 70 percent said that either the Soviet Union must reduce, or NATO must increase, conventional forces "before another [nuclear] arms reduction." Only 22 percent favored going ahead with nuclear reductions without either option.

As marked as the contrast between a declining nuclear threat and a continuing global geopolitical threat, is the contrast between Soviet foreign and domestic policies. The American public now recognizes clearly not only that enormous changes are under way in the Soviet Union, but that the changes, if continued, could affect the Soviet system fundamentally. It has been a bedrock perception, endorsed for a long time by enormous majorities, that the Soviet system differs from the U.S. one in the most basic ways. If that perception starts changing in the years to come, the implications could be profound. If Americans come to the conclusion that the Soviet Union differs only relatively, not absolutely, from the United States, the ideological core of the conflict could start to melt away.

V

Because some of the hopeful thinking about the future of U.S.-Soviet relations is so new, it has not yet firmly jelled. It is useful, therefore, to assess where the public's views are stable and where they are in flux. While it is not true, as specialists have sometimes believed, that American opinion on foreign policy issues is always volatile and hence can be dismissed, it certainly is true that some opinions are volatile. From the policymaker's viewpoint, a quickly changing public opinion is more difficult to cope with than sustained oposition. Even stable and large opposition gives policymakers an unambiguous perception of where they stand. They can reach a rational decision about when to yield and when to cut losses. Stable majority opposition also has clear roots. Its sources and motives can be analyzed. Policymakers can better assess whether the opposition can be neutralized, or even converted to majority support, by acts of leadership.

Volatility does not offer these advantages, and it provides no firm basis for policy. Volatile opinion is often murky opinion. Uncertain itself, its sources and motives are even more uncertain. Volatility can sometimes mean that the public is in the process of making up its mind, and is thus especially receptive to strong leadership. But it can also mean that the public is only beginning to perceive or grapple with the question, or that important values are in serious conflict. Those are treacherous grounds on which to tread.

Opinion is volatile about the future of the Soviet reforms and their meaning for the United States. A majority of Americans has decided that Gorbachev himself is sincere in seeking reform. But, they ask, will he remain in power? Even if he does, can he succeed against great obstacles? And what will reform mean for future Soviet foreign policy— real and durable cooperation or, over the longer run, renewed political and military competition? The American people are divided and unsure about the relative importance of the Soviet threat, as compared with other threats to U.S. security. In March 1988, the fourth ATS survey found that 48 percent of the public thinks the United States should focus more on other threats such as terrorism and economic competition; yet 42 percent say that Soviet aggression is still the greatest threat, and should remain the top security priority. The complexity and ambiguity of the Soviet issue for the public was strikingly illustrated in the PAF/Brown study. Before the discussion, all four alternatives for future U.S.-Soviet relations received greater support than they did after the discussion. Thus the effect of hearing the arguments was to reduce people's initial enthusiasm for their preferences, whatever their preferences were at the time. Evidently, hearing the pros and cons lessened people's confidence in their off-the-top-of-the-head opinions. By the same token, a choice after the discussion represented a more considered judgment. (The figures shown on Table 9.3 are the after-discussion choices).

On certain matters, American views stand firm. One is the commanding importance of economic competitiveness. Worry about whether the United States can compete successfully in the world economy has reached the point where it is, perhaps for the first time, considered a vital issue of national security, according to the third and fourth ATS surveys. The fourth ATS survey found that a solid majority (59 percent) believes that "economic competitors pose a greater threat to national security than military adversaries do, because they threaten our jobs and economic security." The same survey offered options for what the United States should do. A decisive majority (61 percent) endorsed "improving the efficiency and productivity of U.S. industries" over "forcing other countries to adopt fairer trade practices" (24 percent). The third ATS survey asked people where they would cut spending if they were forced to cut it, and had to choose just one area. Many more chose "military spending" (55 percent) than "social and domestic programs such as health care and social security (18 percent), or "economic programs to create jobs and economic growth" (22 percent).

Equally commanding is the need to reduce the risk of nuclear war. A global nuclear holocaust remains so colossal a threat that even a small possibility of it, even in the distant future, creates continuing anxiety. Any measure that can credibly reduce the chances of nuclear war without raising other insecurities will receive overwhelming public support. The public appears firmly convinced that Gorbachev is sincere when he says he too wants to reduce the nuclear threat, according to the first and second ATS surveys. Americans believe that reducing the global nuclear threat is in the Soviet interest, and that the Soviets know it. They feel that the Soviets may also seek nuclear security from the additional, selfish motive that it could make their conventional superiority more important, according to the second ATS survey. But that does not deny Soviet pragmatism in wanting to avoid global destruction. Because of this perception and their own anxiety, Americans are firm that this is a time for negotiation, not confrontation. In three years, Gorbachev has done nothing especially threatening, and he wants to talk. So, says the public, let's talk.

Finally, Americans are firm that the United States bears global unrelinquishable responsibilities for peace and security. The PAF/Brown study offered an essentially isolationist posture as one alternative future. Both before and after hearing the arguments for (as well as against) this option, it was rejected almost unanimously.[6]

VI

Today's public attitudes and values permit some inferences to be drawn for policies that will win widespread public support. Four of them merit attention. The first, and most direct, is that the public wants to see U.S.-Soviet relations improve, but it wants U.S. policy to proceed with caution. Americans have little desire for any quick change in East-West relations. Policies that create a public impression of great changes to be achieved rapidly might well call up the memory of "detente" and evoke a negative reaction. The always useful distinction between short-term and long-term policy choices is unusually important at this juncture. The public itself is now making this distinction.

There is little doubt that over the next few years, Americans want the United States to proceed very carefully. The seventh ATS survey asked people specifically whether "we should act now to seek agreements on arms reduction, trade and other issues as rapidly as possible", or whether we would proceed "cautiously, step by step." A decisive margin of 76 percent endorsed proceeding cautiously, against 16 percent in favor of seeking agreements as rapidly as possible. Only four percent endorsed the third possibility offered, that "even under Gorbachev the Soviet Union remains an 'evil empire' and we should not have anything to do with them."

A second general inference is that Americans' strongest support will be reserved for strategies that do not depend on trust. A good example is the INF treaty. This treaty does not enjoy its great public support for traditional arms control reasons. Americans understand that the treaty means only a small percentage reduction in either side's nuclear forces. The first through third ATS surveys and the PAF/Brown study show that what the public finds interesting in the INF treaty is its novel provisions for on-site inspection in the Soviet Union. This is the secret of its appeal, winning public approval by margins greater than 70 percent at the very moment that a majority also thinks the Soviets are likely to cheat on arms control. The on-site inspection feature means, to the public, that Americans do not need to rely on trust in this agreement. Even if the Soviets do cheat, the small percentage of the total forces involved means the cheating will not make much military difference. A similar attitude would probably prevail regarding some kinds of limited agreements with the Soviets for mutual restraint in certain areas of the Third World. As long as the outcome meets the two conditions of being visible and low risk, such agreements would likely meet with public approval. Possible areas might include Cambodia and parts of Africa such as Ethiopia.

The principle of "verification," in fact, is moving to the center of the public's attitude toward U.S.-Soviet agreements. Only to a small degree does this mean "verification" in the technical sense employed by arms controllers. The PAF/Brown research indicates that the public knows little about, and does not entirely trust, unilateral and technical methods of verification such as satellites, over-the-horizon radars and electronic listening devices. What the public seeks is direct and unambiguous verification, such as U.S. inspectors on Soviet territory. The public wants the evidence to be so direct and clear, that if the Soviets do cheat, the whole world will know it and believe it. The public definitely does not want verification to degenerate into an arcane debate among technical wizards, with Washington and Moscow trading charges and counter-charges that few people can even understand, much less judge.

The desire of Americans not to rely on trust has sometimes been misunderstood. It is simply a common sense attitude, much resembling their attitudes in other spheres of life. For instance, many transactions in the world of commerce do not rely entirely on trust. Large corporations maintain internal auditors to follow the money trail, and also hire external auditors to check on them, then superimpose a third level of checks and balances, typically in the form of an audit committee of the board of directors. Businesses sign contracts that are legally enforceable, reducing reliance on trust. Businesses do not necessarily expect to develop blind trust over time, as some people apparently feel the United States and the Soviet Union should do. Americans would be relieved to find new mechanisms that permit agreements with minimal dependence on trust. There can be no enforceable legal contracts because there is no authority to enforce them. But independent verification by each side of the other's behavior can play an important role. If one side cheats, future "contracts" will not be signed, and other current ones may be jeopardized.

The word "verification" does not entirely capture what Americans are seeking, which is why they will sometimes express dissatisfaction with this term. What they want is a low-risk, working relationship that improves only if and when the good faith of the other side has been clearly demonstrated. The seventh ATS survey gives some indication of what Americans mean when they speak of trust and good faith. The elements of good faith that majorities feel are absolutely essential in the other party are that "they abide by treaty commitments" (68 percent), and "they tell the truth in dealing with us" (67 percent). Significantly, in judging good faith, the public draws a sharp distinction between a country whose "citizens enjoy basic human rights" (deemed absolutely essential by 53 percent), and a country that is "a democracy" (deemed absolutely essential by only 29 percent). Only 14 percent consider it absolutely essential to good faith that "their customs, culture and language are similar to ours."

The desire to verify is also part of our third general inference for U.S. policy: Americans will support strategies that test the Soviet Union's good faith while achieving something constructive. "Testing strategies" appeal to both the hopeful and wary halves of the two-sided readiness. The hope is that the tests may yield more weighty proofs that the Soviets are indeed finally changing. But convincing proofs are demanded—that is the wariness.

For many years Americans have heard numerous charges from their leaders in Washington that the Soviets have cheated on past agreements. An Associated Press/Media General poll shows that 61 percent believes that the Soviets do not keep their side of arms control agreements. Americans also see a new Soviet leader who is trying to change, at least in some ways, the very character of the Soviet state. Perhaps under Gorbachev the Soviet Union will continue to cheat, perhaps not. Again the public's attitude is pragmatic: Let's find out. This is another part of the INF treaty's appeal. The on-site inspection provision gives the United States an opportunity to probe whether or not Soviet behavior is truly changing. Will inspection provide adequate and reliable information in actual practice? Only experience will tell, but the possibility is worth exploring. Success could lead toward a "verification" type of relationship not requiring blind trust. Since the INF treaty involves such a small fraction of U.S. nuclear power, it also satisfies the desire to proceed cautiously. One of the creative challenges facing this administration will be to devise additional testing strategies that can speak simultaneously to both the hopeful and wary parts of the public's stance. Conventional reductions in Europe may be one area where the Soviets might be profitably tested at low risk.

Our last general inference is the simplest, and it applies to both superpowers: The temptation must be resisted to exploit short-term opportunities that could, in the public's mind, jeopardize the relationship. Today's constellation of American attitudes represents a balance that can be easily shaken and the implications could be tragic. There is a genuine readiness in the United States to evolve an altogether new relationship with the Soviet Union, if the Soviets will genuinely put their "new thinking" into practice. By almost four-to-one margins (59 percent to 16 percent) Americans would rather help than hurt the Soviet economy, in the interests of promoting greater freedom and democracy, according to the sixth ATS survey. The evolution will take time. Some major rupture in U.S.-Soviet relations could derail the evolution in ways that would make it very difficult to restore for a long time.

The on-again, off-again pattern (cold war-detente-cold war-detente) leaves a residue of skepticism in the public mind. At this point in the history of U.S.-Soviet relations, as the two superpowers are trying to build mutual confidence, it is essential that this confidence not be dashed. Were a "psychology of disappointment" to emerge, the result could actually be worse than what existed before. In our view, it would not just be equally difficult to rebuild confidence once again in the future—it might be impossible.

The American public is ready to accept that fundamental change in the Soviet Union can truly come to pass. It is also ready to accept that change may prove a chimera. Americans are feeling hope and wariness in equal measure. It is too soon—much too soon—to make decisions or start acting on the assumption that the Soviets mean what they now say. It is not too soon to begin some new thinking about the possibility.

NOTES

1. Daniel Yankelovich and Larry Kaagan, "Assertive America," *Foreign Affairs, America and the World* (New York: Pergamon, 1980).

2. The firm used by the Republicans is Market Opinion Research: by the Democrats, Marttila and Kiley, Inc.; the nonpartisan firm is The Daniel Yankelovich Group, Inc. Seven such surveys have been conducted to date. The first "Americans Talk Security" survey (ATS 1) was conducted by Marttila & Kiley, Inc., on October 15–18, 1987. ATS 2: Market Opinion Research, January 7– 14, 1988; ATS 3: The Daniel Yankelovich Group, Inc., February 17–24, 1988; ATS 4: Marttila & Kiley, Inc., March 22–27, 1988; ATS 5: Market Opinion Research, April 25-May 1, 1988; ATS 6: Marttila & Kiley, Inc., May 24–27, 1988; and ATS 7: The Daniel Yankelovich Group, Inc., June 25–30 and July 5–7, 1988. All of the surveys used a sample size of approximately one thousand. "Americans Talk Security" is sponsored as a public service by Mr. Alan Kay.

3. The Public Agenda Foundation and the Center for Foreign Policy Development, Brown University, *U.S.-Soviet Relations in the Year 2010: Americans Look to the Future* (1988).

4. The two projects include unique and innovative features. In the bipartisan ATS project, the three organizations checked each other's wordings of questions and interpretation of responses, thereby helping to ensure objectivity. In the PAF/Brown project, the challenge was to get beyond the public's superficial responses to well-considered judgments. This was accomplished by giving a cross-section of nearly one thousand eligible voters approximately three hours' exposure (including time for group discussion) to four broad directions for policy (to the year 2010), to the pros and cons of each, and to their short-term implications.

5. The following options received the least support: (1) sharing SDI with the Soviets as it is being developed (28 percent); (2) agreeing to stop work on SDI as part of a nuclear arms agreement (34 percent); (3) agreeing on a 50- percent reduction in long-range nuclear weapons without any reduction in Soviet conventional weapons in Europe (36 percent); or, (4) before seeing how the new INF treaty is working out (36 percent); and (5) selling "nonmilitary high technology, such as advanced computer equipment and software" (36 percent).

6. For more on elements of stability and potential consensus in public attitudes, see Daniel Yankelovich and Sidney Harman, *Starting with the People* (Boston: Houghton Mifflin, 1988).

10

Peace and War in the Modern World-System

Immanuel Wallerstein

Through the ages, people have developed many attitudes toward peace and war. There has been enthusiasm for war, and there has been enthusiasm for peace. There have been ambivalences and much indifference. Through history, these attitudes have led to many kinds of movements. There have been hawks and doves in almost every situation. There have always been people who have argued that war or violence is a constant of human behavior. I am very skeptical about any constants of human behavior. I am certainly skeptical about this one, but there is very little hard evidence in one direction or the other. What we are called upon to do is analyze how we can (given the real world that we live in) at least reduce war and perhaps eliminate it.

I do not like to discuss constants of human behavior. I do not believe they are very significant. I believe that social behavior is a function of historical systems. We live in a particular historical system I call the modern world-system. It is important to see the historical role of war within that system. For that purpose, I will distinguish three kinds of warlike behavior. It is not a sharp distinction; nonetheless, it is important for our analysis. One is social violence. A second is formal interstate war, which is what we usually mean by war (two states actually declaring war on each other). The third is world war. It is this form of war that preoccupies most people. However, it is very difficult to be preoccupied with world war without taking into account the other

two kinds of "collective violence." I will discuss each of them succes-
sively.

Let's start with social violence. In itself this is an enormous continuum of possible behavior. By social violence, we usually mean something which involves some relationship to the state-structure. If we
think of it in those terms, we have at least three kinds of social violence
related directly to the state-structure. The first, which has begun to
be discussed only in recent years, is state-violence—violence by the
state against some portion of its citizens. Violence by the state is in
some sense almost the raison d'être of the state. According to the classic
definition of Max Weber: A state is a structure which asserts the legal
monopoly of the use of violence. The state presumably engages in violence to *minimize* violence, but the question then arises whether the
state is not itself a promoter of another kind of violence (personal
violence). This discussion is very active today in the United States,
and in many other countries as well. The state, by not treating all
citizens equally, creates the situations which promote the likelihood
that some citizens will engage in violence toward other citizens. Then,
there is the relatively recent discussion of human rights as a protest
against the degree to which the state misuses its rights where violence
is concerned. Thus, we have state-violence that is very clear.

Antistate violence is a second form of social violence. There are
various kinds of protests. Those which ultimately can lead to civil war
are the most violent forms of protest. Such protests can be based on
class, ethnic, or racial considerations. The question then arises: To
what degree is personal violence a hidden mode of antistate violence?
The argument is often made that what the state may regard as a crime,
is in fact a form of social violence, which is more legitimate than if it
were merely personal violence.

The third form of social violence is intergroup violence. We have a
phenomenon everywhere called racism. One group, for whatever reason, disregards another group, looks down on it, and acts toward it in
some violent way to maintain it within its relative position in society.
The result is antiracist reaction.

Then there is interstate violence that we definitionally call war.
Some years ago, Quincy Wright calculated that in the last five hundred
years there were only two or three years in which there was not an
interstate war. That one state is at war with another state is a constantly repeated phenomenon within our modern world-system. At the
present time we tend to forget about the "formal" declaration of war.
Iran did not actually declare war on Iraq, or Iraq on Iran, but we all
know there was a war going on. One thing to note about interstate
wars is that they tend to be in the more outlying parts of the world-
system. But why does Iran fight with Iraq, why does Vietnam fight

with Cambodia, or China with Vietnam? Why is there this enormous frequency of interstate wars? Most of the explanations normally given make little sense, except if one sees it as groups of people maneuvering for some relative advantage in an interstate relationship, perhaps trying to maintain some internal cohesion of an existing regime. This is one standard explanation. Perhaps they are the unspoken agents of larger outside powers—another standard explanation. The constancy is worth noting, and the fact that if one of these small conflicts is resolved in one way or another (because of outside pressure, internal exhaustion, or conquest), it is more than likely that another will emerge somewhere else.

In addition to the interstate wars, there is another frequent phenomenon, almost an interstate war, that we now call anticolonial wars. An area which is jurisdictionally part of a state but asserts that it should not be, fights for its independence. If it is separated by sea, we usually call it an anticolonial war; and if it is separated only by land, we call it a secessionist war. Many of these wars occur, and, although we have had some concentrations of them, they are a constant phenomenon. They, of course, blend very easily into the intergroup violence we discussed as class-based or ethnic-based. It is almost a question of juridical definition when it ceases being an intrastate civil war and becomes a secessionist war.

What concerns most people is world war. The first point is, unlike social violence and unlike interstate wars, world wars have been rare. They are not a frequent phenomenon. World wars seem quite different from the run-of-the-mill interstate war and the run-of-the-mill social violence. Of course, it all depends on what is meant by world wars. A rather elementary definition may be that we call a war a world war because it includes many nations. A look at the history of world wars reveals that they never include literally everyone, but they do include most of the major military powers. Second, they are extremely destructive—destructive of land and destructive of lives. Third, they are quite long. World wars are generally a thirty-year phenomenon. They are long, but not necessarily continuous. They have enormous consequences—unlike inter-state wars, which are often only exercises in frustration. After Iran and Iraq had exhausted themselves over a period of seven to nine years, it may be that nothing significant changed. However, at the end of a world war, a considerable amount of change will have occurred in the world-system. World wars are clearly not about jousting for relatively small shifts in position. They are the culminating points of struggles for hegemony in the world-system.

The world-system we have been living in for several hundred years is a curious system in a number of ways. First of all, it *is* a system. It has rules, it has constraints, and it has processes which can be analyzed.

It is not, however, a single state in which there is a single overarching political process. It is an interstate system with a multiplicity of states, in which no single state is imperial (in the sense of having total power). We retain two images which are absolutely false. One image is that of total power over the system—which does not exist—and the other is total sovereignty (or equality of all states)—which does not exist either. These are myths. The founding myth of the interstate system is the sovereignty of all states. No state in our interstate system, from the most powerful to the least powerful, is sovereign—if by sovereign it is meant that it can decide fully what goes on within its boundaries.

Between these two myths of total power and total independence, there is a range of possibilities. At one end is the situation in which there is a hegemonic state—not a total power, but a very great power. At the other end is the more normal situation in which power is widely divided, leading to a reasonable number of strong powers. Hegemony is relatively rare and has to be measured in very clear ways. It is irrelevant how much power the United States has vis-à-vis Guatemala. The measurement that is significant is how much power the United States has vis-à-vis Japan, Germany, Great Britain, and France (substantial, significant powers). Hegemony is that relatively rare situation where one major power really can, to an extent, call the shots economically, politically and militarily vis-à-vis other major powers. Economically, it can outsell the others at home (although rarely) politically, it can effectively "twist their arms" on important issues (rarely, but it happens).

A real hegemonic power has emerged only three times. The first time was in the seventeenth century, when Holland, or rather, the United Provinces, emerged as the hegemonic power of the then world-system. From circa 1620 to 1672, the United Provinces was clearly economically able to outproduce and outsell all other significant powers. It had an extremely strong army, and was able to manipulate the world to its will. Britain played that role in the nineteenth century, roughly from 1815 to 1873, and the United States played that role from the end of World War II to approximately 1970. During all other periods of time, we have had what is classically called a balance of power—a system of multiple powers interacting with each other.

If one looks at the history of how countries became hegemonic and ceased to be hegemonic, a very interesting and clear pattern emerges. The hegemony generally lasts twenty-five to fifty years, and is brought to an end by a very normal economic process whereby other countries get stronger economically and undermine the basis of strength of the hegemonic power. The power of the hegemonic power declines relatively as new competitors emerge and attempt to seize the leadership-role. This goes on for a certain amount of time, followed by the beginning of a reorganization of the interstate alliance system. At the end of this process, the system arrives at an acute crisis.

Holland, Britain and the United States, in the period immediately preceding their roles as hegemonic powers, were countries that expended very little of their energy on the military. They had land armies of little significance. Insofar as they had a military force, it was a naval force (and recently a naval and air force), but relatively small. So, prior to hegemony those states spent very little of their energy on military expenditures. They concentrated their energy on increased internal productivity. They burst into hegemony as the result, finally, of a world war with their chief competitor, who in each case turned out to be the major land-oriented, military-oriented power of the time, and who seemed to be moving toward creation of a world-empire. The Dutch opposed a Spanish objective, the British opposed a French objective, and the United States opposed a German thrust.

There were three thirty-year wars. The Thirty Years' War of 1618–1648, had immense destructive consequences. It involved everybody of any significance militarily at the time, resulted in the definitive elimination of Spain as a power of any significance, and led to the hegemony of the Dutch. Immediately, the Dutch assumed certain responsibilities which were very heavy. As a state becomes hegemonic it has to expend heavily on the military during the world war and afterwards, which is also very expensive politically and economically, and becomes part of the process of undermining the hegemony.

During its long competition with the French, Britain was a sea power and never had a very large standing army. There were long discussions in Britain about that fact. In the 1802 to 1815 wars, Napoleon overran all of Europe and thereby exhausted himself. The British finally won and created the British era. At that point, they had to begin creating the military forces and political-economic structures which eventually undermined their hegemony. Similarly, the United States, up to 1940, spent very little on the military. In two successive wars (really constituting a single world war) Germany attempted to create a land-based empire. The United States came in finally, with a tremendous advantage, having escaped the earlier destruction. The United States won and was able to expand and expound its hegemony.

Notice a last common trait of these countries. As the Dutch hegemony began to decline, the French and the British began competing. What did the Dutch do? Over a fifty-year period, they became the junior partner of the other growing sea-power, the British. A similar thing happened after the British decline: The United States and Germany began competing, and Britain eventually became the junior partner of a rising United States, the other sea-power. We are beginning to see that pattern again with the relative decline of the United States, and the emergence of Japan as a new major competitor. Japan is also a sea-power, and there is the beginning of a United States-Japan linkage, that will strengthen over the next thirty years.

So much for the pattern of world wars. World wars are rare. They are the result of a long struggle for hegemony, they are destructive, and they do not occur again during the time that the new structures work. What that means right now is that world war is not an imminent phenomenon. However, in addition to this cyclical and repetitive process, there is another important element in the modern world-system. If one studies the last four to five-hundred year period, the trend in which the contradictions of the system work themselves out until the system begins to enter a crisis can be seen, but the cyclical patterns may not necessarily repeat themselves. Although there are these patterns in hegemony, they may not go on forever, because the capitalist world-economy will not go on forever as a system. We have been in the beginning of a long-term crisis of the system since 1914–1917, which has been accentuated since World War II.

The states and their relationships to world wars have been discussed. Now, the movements will be discussed. Movements are part of the trends of the capitalist world-economy. They have not been there forever. Movements are an invention of the nineteenth century, and they have been growing much stronger in the last fifty to seventy-five years. In the twentieth century, there have been three kinds of movements that have related to "peace" in various ways. We have had the world communist movement, which has had a very strong position on "peace." For many people, this has been a very suspect position. It was the position of groups who were siding with the Soviet Union in its "battle" with the United States.

One has to look at the post–1945 relationship of the United States and the Soviet Union as a very tense, extremely controlled game, in which the image of Yalta is the correct one. There was a "deal" made in 1945 between the United States and the Soviet Union. The Soviet Union would have a small corner of the world to "do its thing," and would stay out of the rest of the world. Then, each side would shout very loudly about a very serious ideological conflict, which would become its raison d'être. That game was played throughout the whole period of United States hegemony, and was part of the principle itself. It is only now beginning to break down. In fact, it has meant that all the talk of world war during that period was not real. That was not the game that either side was *really* playing.

There was, however, a real peace movement. It was made up of people who were very worried about the prospects of a world war. This movement had a certain strength, mostly within Western countries, but no strength at all in Third World countries. At no point was the peace movement other than a movement in Western countries.

The national liberation movements in the Third World constituted a third movement. They had a very curious position on peace. This is one of the reasons why the distinctions among social violence, interstate wars, and world wars were made. Had someone in the national liberation movement in the year 1950, or 1955, been asked if he or she were for peace, he or she would have said: Of course I am for peace— meaning I do not want the United States and the Soviet Union to go to war with each other. It would not have meant that he or she did not believe in interstate wars, particularly anticolonial wars. It also did not mean that he or she did not believe in social violence, because, of course, he or she did. The national liberation movements believed in antistate violence. So they were for peace. However, the minute detente was mentioned in the 1960s, Third World national liberation movements, after formal approval, became very uneasy about detente. They were afraid that a U.S.-Soviet détente, moving toward a U.S.-Soviet common position vis-à-vis them would be very negative.

Thus, there were three kinds of movements for peace. There was the communist-led peace movement, that was really not taken seriously. There was the more genuine peace movement, that although taken seriously, was always a minority movement and existed only in the Western world. Finally, the national liberation movements in the Third World did talk peace, but did not mean it at all in the sense that the other two did.

Now look at movements in power. This is a totally different story. The antisystemic movements emerged in the nineteenth century, and took the form of socialist and nationalist movements. Their analysis of the world was that it was a terrible place because there were great inequalities. A great debate about how this could be changed ran from approximately 1850 to 1890. Those people who said the way to change the world was to assume state power, thereby enabling change, won the debate within the movements. Within the world socialist movement, the Marxists triumphed over the so-called anarchists. Within nationalist movements, the political nationalists triumphed over the cultural nationalists. From approximately 1880 to about 1960, antisystemic movements throughout the world concentrated on achieving state power.

Between 1945 and 1975, these movements achieved state power virtually everywhere. All the social-democratic movements of the Western world, which are the heirs of the socialist movements of the nineteenth century, can be placed in this category. They achieved state power and put through their major programs. Then, there are the socialist countries, heirs of the Third International. A whole bloc of countries in Eastern Europe, the Soviet Union, China, Vietnam, and many others achieved state power. The national liberation movements have achieved state power in many Third World countries. There are some cases where the issue is not yet resolved, for instance, in South Africa. However, from India and Indonesia to Ghana and Algeria, state power has been achieved by popular movements able to lead a struggle of some kind and mobilize masses of people.

The events of 1968, occurring in the Western world, the socialist world, and in the Third World, have been going on ever since. The new movements in these three parts of the world are all criticisms of the old movements. The "New Left," or new social movements in the Western world are all basically criticisms of social democracy. These new social movements take many forms—ethnic movements, women's movements, ecology movements, greens movements, and peace movements. The many forms of new movements in the socialist countries, from the Cultural Revolution and the Prague spring to Solidarity and what is going on right now in the Soviet Union, are all basically criticisms of the Communist parties. The new movements in the Third World, many of them taking on religious forms, are all basically criticisms of the national liberation movements.

In each case, state power was achieved for the purposes of changing the world, but it did not change. It was still unequal, within countries and internationally. Therefore, the movements became skeptical about the "Western Enlightenment tradition." Not only the social democrats, but also the Soviet Communist, Nasserist and the Algerian national liberation movements are all based on the enlightenment ideas. They were skeptical of those ideas and of the achievement of state power, but they were not skeptical about the fact that something ought to be done. They are still very anxious to do something because they do not like the system and its inequalities. The post–1968 phenomenon produced a set of new movements challenging the old movements because, although successful, they failed to produce change.

Three pictures have been drawn. First, is the cyclical pattern of world war in the capitalist world economy, that has gone on for 500 years. By the logic of that system, this pattern ought to result in a world war a hundred years from now, with Japan and the United States fighting western Europe, perhaps aligned with the Soviet Union. In theory, this should happen, if that same pattern were to continue. The very early stages clearly can be seen. There are parallels today to what went on between 1873 and 1900, and in the late seventeenth to early eighteenth centuries. Second, the world-system, as a system, also has secular trends, and it is in a crisis. All these cycles cannot be constantly repeated. And third, one of the trends in the world-system has been the emergence in the mid-nineteenth century of the antisystemic movements, which, although actually succeeding in their middle-range objectives, turned out to be in one sense a big failure, breeding a whole range of new antimovements. Suddenly we have six varieties of movements exhibiting a great deal of uncertainty as to what strategies should be used. This uncertainty is shared by all; it is structural, and it is important. It is not a lack of clarity of mind. The world-system is in a crisis, and the movements that are supposed to transform it are wondering whether what they are doing is, in fact, going to transform it in the right direction.

Where does it leave us? On the one hand, world war is very unlikely in the immediate future. Of course, that may not be satisfying since one out of a hundred chances of a nuclear holocaust is still too much. Accidents could happen, and they could be catastrophic. Therefore, partial disarmaments are useful, and peace movements that keep the pressure on are socially very useful, but our primary problem is not to prevent a third world war. Our primary problem is certainly not to reduce the amount of social violence over the next fifty years, since nothing can reduce it, nor is it necessarily obvious that it is the most desirable thing to do.

Our primary problem is that we are living in a moment of historic social transformation—not a moment that is three years in length, but a moment that is fifty or a hundred years in length. The major agencies of this social transformation are in a dilemma as to what strategy would actually transform the world in the right direction. The world will transform itself. The question is, will it transform itself for better, worse, or the same? The transformation will occur, but this is a moment in which one can actually contribute to pushing it in the direction one wants it to go. There are more social possibilities in these moments of crisis than in normal times. The crisis of the movements is itself the critical ground in which the decisions will be made. The six varieties of movements are beginning to debate a new strategy for the next fifty to one hundred years. Perhaps a family of these movements will be created. Each of the six varieties of movements is very critical of the other, but they are beginning to talk to each other. There is no inevitability of progress, only a possibility of progress. One can attempt to change the world in ways that may make it better, but there is nothing in the historical process that makes this inevitable.

III

Strategies

11

Conflict Escalation and Problem Solving

Dean G. Pruitt and William Rick Fry

Conflict occurs across all levels of society, and ranges from disputes among playmates to war involving several nations. While it is recognized that the specific features of different conflicts will vary, it is believed that conflict is sufficiently similar from setting to setting, that meaningful general theory is possible. Therefore, the concepts and principles discussed in this chapter are assumed to apply across a wide range of conflicts. This chapter starts with the concept of escalation, using a hypothetical neighborhood dispute and the development of the cold war as examples. Then it discusses a number of conditions that affect the likelihood that conflict will escalate. Finally, it moves to ways in which conflict can be managed or controlled (de-escalated).

CRISIS ON ELM STREET

Conflicts between neighbors are a common occurrence, happening in small and large communities alike. Often they start over rather insignificant issues, but evolve into situations involving a great deal of animosity and even danger to the principals. Such was the case for the conflict between the Smith and Brown families, who lived next door to each other on Elm Street.

Preparation of this manuscript was supported by two grants from the National Science Foundation: BNS83–09167 and SES85–20084.

These families shared a common driveway. The Smith family had high school children, while the children in the Brown family were in grade school. The conflict started one afternoon when the husband in the Brown family pulled his car out of the garage to go to work and found another car blocking his driveway. Mr. Brown went over to the Smith's and complained rather vigorously. He was obviously upset, and by the time he left so were the Smiths. A few days later, the young Brown children wre playing near the Smith's open window which had a flower bed beneath. The noise irritated Mrs. Smith, who stuck her head out of the window and yelled "shut up." She then saw that some of her flowers had been trampled and broken, which led her to utter a curseword. Mrs. Brown, hearing this and clutching her surprised and fearful children, shouted some insults back at Mrs. Smith. After this exchange, things really began to heat up. The young Brown children would make faces and obscene gestures at Mrs. Smith when she was outside. The Smith family also received phone calls with no one responding on the other end, and the doorbell would sometimes ring and nobody would be there. The older Smith children began to scream insults in the direction of the Brown home as they rode past on their bicycles. The oldest Smith boy also began to make wide turns with his car as he drove into the common driveway in order to run across the Brown's lawn. This was particularly destructive to the lawn whenever the ground was wet. Mr. Brown went over and complained about this and other things that Mrs. Smith's teenagers were doing, and Mrs. Smith became extremely angry and told him never to come back. The Browns had been involved in a neighborhood block association for some years, and Mrs. Smith began to believe falsely that the Browns were now using the association to get them kicked out of the neighborhood. After a number of other incidents, the police were finally called when one of the Smith boys was accused of throwing firecrackers at the Brown children.

DEVELOPMENT OF THE COLD WAR

During World War II, the United States and the Soviet Union had been allies, but the Soviets emerged from the war with deep suspicions of the West. Concern for their territorial integrity led them to dominating the countries on their borders to develop a buffer between themselves and the West. They achieved control over many of the governments of Eastern Europe and put pressure on Greece and Turkey. The United States replied to the Soviets in three ways. It provided military aid to Greece and Turkey. It also began supplying vast amounts of economic aids to Western Europe to revitalize the economies of these countries in an attempt to weaken the Communist parties in them. And, working with its allies England and France, it began slowly to reunify West Germany. The latter move alarmed the Soviets, who feared Germany. Their initial response was one of protest. Then, as the Allies persisted in the unification of West Germany, the Soviets began sporadic interruptions of communication between West Berlin (an enclave surrounded by the Russian controlled portions of Germany) and West Germany. Finally, when the Allies introduced a currency reform in West Germany, the Soviets cut West Berlin off from West Germany and would not allow land travel into or out of the city. The allies responded by airlifting supplies and personnel into the city. They also began discussing formation of a military alliance, the North Atlantic Treaty Organization (NATO). This latter development led eventually to the rearmament of West Germany, which caused further alarm in the Soviet Union. The story of this conflict continues to the present day. It provides an example of a massive and extremely significant escalation.

TRANSFORMATIONS THAT OCCUR DURING ESCALATION

Escalation of conflict between two parties involves at least five transformations that take place as the parties' relations deteriorate (Pruitt & Rubin, 1986). These transformations occur separately in each party. But when they happen in one party, they tend to be reflected in the other, so we can speak of escalation in the conflict as a whole. All five transformations may not occur in every conflict that escalates. These transformations make the conflict more intense and harder to resolve. The five transactions are as follows:

1. Light to heavy. It is rare to see full blown hostility emerge spontaneously. There is almost always a prior build up. The process moves from light influence attempts (ingratiation, persuasive arguments) and escalates to threats, irrevocable commitments, and damaging statements about the other. In both of the examples given earlier, protests about the other party's actions were eventually supplanted by hostile actions that increased in intensity. The use of increasingly heavy influence attempts is the most common transformation in escalation.

2. Doing well–to winning–to hurting the other. Initially one's welfare is not linked to that of the other party. One's gains or losses are evaluated separately. Deutsch (1958) refers to this as an individualistic orientation in which one is concerned only about one's own welfare. As conflict escalates, however, the parties begin to evaluate their outcomes relative to the other, seeking to do better than the other does. And finally, as conflict escalates still further and both sides experience mounting losses, the goal becomes to hurt the other more than one is hurt by them.

3. Small to large. As conflict escalates, there is a tendency for issues to pro-
liferate. Commitments to the conflict becomes heavier as do the use of
resources, time, energy, and material in an effort to prevail.

4. Specific to general. As the conflict escalates, differencs over specified concrete issues tend to be replaced by more general, abstract differences, which
are usually more emotion laden. Parties become less tolerant of one another
and perceive the need for deep and fundamental changes by the other.

5. Few to many. Conflicts commonly move from involvement of just the principals to involvement of a progressively greater number of participants.
This is, in part, because close allies rush to the support of the participants,
and in part, because the participants solicit the help of less closely related
"others."

CONFLICT MODELS

Pruitt and Gahagan (1974) have identified three broad models of the
processes that produce escalation when it occurs: The aggressor-defender model, the conflict spiral model, and the structural change
model. These represent different schools of thought about how escalation develops. All three models are useful under some circumstances,
although none can be viewed as having a monopoly over the truth.

The Aggressor-Defender Model

The basic assumption of the aggressor-defender model is that the
aggressor is primarily responsible for the escalation of conflict. In an
effort to achieve its aims, the aggressor initiates influence attempts,
using progressively heavier tactics if the other resists. The defender
simply reacts to the aggressor's actions, escalating its response only
to match the aggressor's escalation. The terms "aggressor" and "defender" are not used in an evaluative sense in this model—they do not
convey information about who is right or wrong. They simply identify
the initiator and the reactor. The aggressor is a party who sees an
opportunity to achieve its ends by means of pressure tactics; the defender, a party who tries to resist the use of these tactics.

The aggressor-defender model helps to explain one of the stages in
the development of the cold war. This stage is the point at which the
Soviet Union adopted the goal of blocking the unification of West Germany. At first, the Soviets employed the mild tactic of protest. When
this did not work, they moved to a heavier tactic of sporadically in-
terrupting communication between Berlin and West Germany. When
this, too, was unsuccessful, and the West introduced a currency reform
that further contributed to German unification, they employed an extremely heavy tactic—a blockade of the city. While this explanation

is cogent, the aggressor-defender model is incapable of interpreting many other stages in the development of the cold war, and indeed, in most conflict escalation. Thus, this model provides a useful but incomplete account of the processes underlying most escalation.

The Conflict Spiral Model

The conflict spiral model of escalation is found in the writings of many theorists (North, Brody & Holsti, 1964; Osgood, 1962; and Richardson, 1967). The emphasis in this model is on the mutual and reciprocal nature of escalation. Neither side is the aggressor or the defender. Instead, each party's actions are both responsive and provocative at the same time, and conflict escalation involves a vicious circle of action and reaction. One party's hostile actions encourage a like response from the other, which contributes to more hostile actions from the first party, completing the circle and starting it on its next iteration.

A conflict spiral can take either one or both of two forms, a retaliatory or a defensive spiral. A retaliatory spiral involves a "hurt more" dynamic. After being hurt, a party feels the need to retaliate in order to hurt the other at least as much, and preferably more. An example would be the United States' bombing raid on Libya following the disco bombing in Germany in which U.S. servicemen were killed or wounded. A defensive spiral is one in which each side reacts to a perceived threat from the other by buiding up its defenses, which further increases the perceived threat and leads to an even greater defensive buildup. A good example is an arms race. In a defensive spiral, each party can be thought of alternately as the aggressor or the defender. Conflict spirals act as a ratchet for conflict intensity, each reaction tending to be more severe and intense than those preceding it, up to some asymptote. The conflict spiral model provides a good explanation of the escalation from light to heavy tactics. It also helps to understand the proliferation of issues and increased commitment to the conflict. Each retaliatory or defensive action in the spiral provides a new issue (a new grievance) for the targets of this action, producing a growing sense of crisis.

The conflict spiral model provides futher insight into the dynamics of the cold war escalation. In response to Soviet moves in Eastern Europe, Greece, and Turkey, the United States and its allies began to establish a West German state. In response to this action, the Soviet Union instituted a blockade of Berlin which, in turn, led to the development of NATO and so on. Although pure cases of the aggressor-defender model do exist, as in many of the battles that established the Roman and British empires, the conflict spiral model can help identify sources of such conflicts easily overlooked by the aggressor-defender model. Quite often the goal that impels the aggressor is, at least in part, a reaction to the defender's prior actions. This point tends to be missed by participants in conflicts, who usually attribute the cause of the conflict exclusively to their adversary's aggression.

The Structural Change Model

A third model of escalation is the structural change model that has been discussed in the writings of Burton (1962), Coleman (1957), and Schumpeter (1955, first published in 1919). The essential idea of this model is that the use of heavy tactics changes the parties in ways that encourage even heavier tactics, and detracts from conflict resolution efforts. For example: "Party's" yelling at "other" causes "other" to think of "party" as an unpleasant person (structural change), making it easier for the "other" to yell back, encouraging "party" to develop the goal of punishing "other" (another structural change), motivating "party" to take a further step such as making a harrassing phone call, and so on. Structural changes can take place in individuals, groups, or communities.

Changes in the individual are psychological in nature. The "other" triggers off emotional reactions of disgust, hostility, fear, or wounded pride. The "other" comes to be seen as less human, more selfish, or more to blame for the problem. The individual often becomes increasingly sensitive to status and position loss vis-à-vis the other. All of this causes the individual's goals to become increasingly more rigid, with less and less room for compromise, making it increasingly difficult to develop a creative solution to the problem.

When a group or organization is embroiled in a conflict, all the psychological changes just described occur in the individual members. In fact, they may even experience a deeper hostility or fear of the other group because these feelings become group norms. Additionally, structural changes may also occur at the group level. New, more militant leadership may emerge, further contributing to the collective orientation toward struggle. Subgroups that are "dedicated" to struggle with the other party may form or become strengthened. The group may also become increasingly cohesive, as a result of having an outside enemy, which tends to energize these changes and focus group member attention on defeating the enemy. Structural changes may also take the form of polarization in the broader community in which the antagonists belong. Third parties may join one or the other antagonist, forsaking the constructive neutral role they might otherwise play. All these changes whether occurring to the individual, group, or community, induce greater levels of hostility and tend to lock the parties into an escalated stance.

CONDITIONS ENCOURAGING AND DISCOURAGING ESCALATION

Some disagreements escalate. Other do not, and hence never develop into full-blown conflicts. How can these differences be explained? Once a disagreement has emerged, three conditions encourage it to escalate into a full-blown conflict:

1. High, inflexible aspirations on one or both sides. When aspirations are high, it is hard for both parties to get what they want. Thus, one or both of them are likely to seek a unilateral advantage by employing heavy pressure tactics against the other. This can start a conflict spiral.

2. Low-perceived integrative potential (a belief by one or both parties that problem solving is unlikely to be effective and, thus, a win-win solution is probably unattainable). Such a belief could be based on a perception that aspirations are too high, on personal experience with the other's intransigence, or on the other's reputation for being a difficult person. Such a belief implies that the only way to achieve one's goals is to defeat the other party, and thus engage in escalative behavior.

3. A belief on one or both sides that heavy influence tactics are an effective way of dealing with the other. Such a belief may result from a sense that one is more powerful than the other party in terms of money, the capacity to give love, arms, or any of a wide range of other dimensions of power. Escalation may result if only one party had this belief. It is especially likely if both do, which can happen, since there are so many dimensions of power.

There are also five conditions that inhibit escalation:

1. Bonds between the parties, for example, positive attitudes, respect, kinship, perceived similarity, common group membership, or future dependence. Ordinarily, the more bonds there are, the less likely the parties are to employ heavy influence tactics that run the risk of hurting the other party.

2. Social norms. Most cultures have devised rules of conduct that discourage the use of harsh tactics (It's not nice to fight.), and encourage the use of problem solving (You are old enough to figure out a way to play without fighting). These norms, taught when people are young and encouraged in adulthood, will be effective when differences are not too great and the parties involved are well socialized. Their effectiveness is valid to the extent that society has the capacity for enforcement—to the extent that third parties can learn about and punish norm violation.

3. Social institutions. Some conflicts stay within bounds because of the involvement of social institutions or forums that provide a peaceful means of resolving differences. Courts and legislatures are two examples, mediation services a third. An example of a formal mediation service is the Public Employee Relations Board in the state of New York, which has a series of steps for dealing with impasse in negotiations between public employee

unions and government agencies. Mediation is more commonly informal and relatively unstructured. A mother settles a dispute between her children, or a department chair steps in to resolve a disagreement between two faculty members.

4. Fear of escalation. One or both sides may avoid escalation out of fear of its consequencs. An example would be the case of two police officers who have to work together in a dangerous neighborhood. These officers will be reluctant to take escalative moves toward each other for fear of losing one another's support.

5. Fear of retaliation. Heavy or harmful tactics, of the kind found in escalation, tend to elicit retaliation from their target unless that target feels quite weak. Fear of retaliation often diminishes the likelihood that these tactics will be employed and, thus, the likelihood of escalation. Both parties may be deterred from escalation by the same fears. This is the logic of mutually assured destruction (MAD), a doctrine that argues nuclear weapons prevent military escalation because of the danger of their use. The same logic operates in less profound settings as well, for example, among children on the playground.

Fear of retaliation is a response to a threat, explicit or implicit. For this mechanism to be effective, it is necessary for the threat of retaliation to be credible, that is, for the threatener to seem both willing and able to retaliate. Less credibility is needed the greater the damage, if retaliation takes place (Pruitt & Snyder, 1969), but some credibility is always needed. The use of threats is a risky way to try to avoid escalation. In addition to requiring credibility, it requires that the recipient interpret the actions as a threat rather than actual hostility, because the latter interpretation can actually encourage escalation. Interpretation as hostility is less likely in situations where threats are appropriate or expected, as in the threat of jail for striking a police officer. History reveals many failures of the threat of retaliation in international affairs (Lebow, Jervis, & Stein, 1984). Threat-based deterrents are especially likely to fail, and escalation to materialize, when the responsible decision makers are mentally or emotionally incapacitated, making them unable to use the information available to them; regard the military future as so bleak, or the military balance as changing so fast against them, that they have little to lose by aggressing; or are impelled by foreign, or domestic political interests of such gravity, that they are willing to take large risks in a military adventure.

MOVING TOWARD DE-ESCALATION

In many conflicts where escalation has occurred, there is a point at which neither side is willing to escalate any further. The capacity to inflict greater pain and suffering may still exist, and accumulated levels of contentious behavior may persist, but conflict intensity increases no further. It is at this point that a stalemate emerges, a prelude many times to de-escalation. The shift from escalation to stalemate is due not so much to a change of heart toward the other, as a recognition that one is unable to achieve the earlier aim of defeating the other. Stalemates do not last forever. Conflicts are usually costly, and these costs tend to mount as neglected areas of business begin to demand attention. In the meantime, one is not getting anywhere in the conflict. These forces create pressure for settling the controversy. Three ways in which a party can respond to such pressures can be described.

The simplest, most direct way of ending a stalemate is for one side to yield. Alternatively, both sides may concede a little and agree on compromise. However, after a protracted struggle, it can be very difficult for either side to concede. The loss of face, that humiliation of forsaking one's cause after spending so much time, energy, and material on it, is often hard to swallow. Thus, while yielding can unlock the parties from a stalemate, it is unlikely to be a first choice.

Withdrawing

Leaving the house, neighborhood, state, or country are ways of moving away from the stalemate and reducing the potential for future conflict. After all, it takes "two to tangle" (Deutsch, 1973) and if either side is not present, conflict cannot occur. Withdrawal does not always have to be physical. It can be psychological as well, and this is often a less costly approach.

Problem Solving

Problem solving may be defined as any effort to find a mutually acceptable solution to a problem. No matter how much each may detest the other side, both parties may find they have to cooperate with the other to get out of the stalemate. In the process of doing so, they often soften their perceptions of the other, no longer viewing it as a hated enemy who must be destroyed. Problem solving is more likely to be pursued when aspirations are fairly rigid (yielding is not possible), and when dependence on the other party makes it difficult to withdraw from association with that party. Problem solving is also more likely when the sides are approximately equal in power, so that neither can push the other around. Further, the likelihood of problem solving increases to the extent that it seems possible to develop jointly acceptable alternatives. Parties who believe that it is nearly impossible to develop a deal are unlikely to put much effort into searching for one. Problem solving is often an excellent way out of a stalemate, because it frequently leads to the development of win-win solutions that tend to last.

The ideal form of problem solving involves a joint effort. Both sides share information about needs, priorities, interests, and values. They talk openly and frankly with each other in an effort to identify the issues dividing them. They offer a number of alternatives to bridge the gap between them and evaluate these collectively from the viewpoint of their mutual welfare. This ideal often fails to be fully realized, for a variety of reasons. One side may believe that, in making such an effort, they will miss an opportunity for competitive gains. Lack of trust can prevent the disclosure of critical information or the free discussion of options. It is still possible, in such circumstances, for one, and sometimes both parties to engage in unilateral problem solving in a private search for options that can subsequently be sold to the other. Indirect communication, through intermediaries or by means of signals, can also be employed in an effort to find a mutually acceptable solution (Pruitt, 1977). If all else fails, a mediator may be able to accomplish this goal.

OUTCOMES OF PROBLEM SOLVING

Three types of outcomes can emerge from successful problem solving: A compromise, an agreement on a procedure for deciding on a solution, and an integrative (win-win) agreement.

Compromise

A compromise is an agreement that splits the difference—both parties concede to some middle ground. Compromises are usually not as good for either party as integrative agreements. Yet, sometimes, a compromise is all that can be achieved, as for example, when there is only one dimension at issue, such as the price of a rug in an Eastern bazaar. More often, parties reach a compromise because of unfavorable circumstances. Time pressure may be great, or animosity so high, that the parties cannot engage in the creative thinking necessary to discover an integrative agreement.

Agreement on a Procedure

Another result of problem solving may be a procedure for settling the dispute. Examples of such procedures include tossing a coin, with victory for the winner, voting with victory for the party who can command a majority, and submitting the conflict to an arbitrator who will make the final decision.

Integrative Agreement

Follett (1940) has argued that most conflict situations have integrative potential—there are usually win-win solutions available if the parties will only employ the time and effort required to locate them. Such agreements are preferable to compromises because they tend to last longer, to reconcile the parties, and to benefit larger entities (a firm or community) of which the parties are members. Five types of integrative solutions can be identified (Pruitt, 1981; Pruitt and Rubin, 1986).

1. *Expanding the pie.* Conflict often derives from the existence of a limited resource such as time, land, or workers. The problem will be solved if a way can be found to expand that resource. For example, Follett mediated a dispute between two milk companies who were vying every morning to be first to unload their cans on a dock. The solution was to increase the size of the dock so that both companies could use it at the same time. This example illustrates the fact that resource shortages are not always apparent. Only the mediator was able to see that the problem resulted from the size of the dock.

2. *Compensation.* Another way to achieve an integrative solution is to compensate one party for agreeing to the other party's demands. For example, a husband might get extra love and attention for agreeing to a vacation at the wife's favorite spot.

3. *Logrolling.* When there are a number of issues and the parties differ with respect to their importance, it is possible for concessions to be exchanged so that each side gets what is more important to it, while giving up what is less important. For example, a husband and a wife who are buying a new car may differ with regard to the color and engine size. The wife may feel strongly about the color and be less concerned about the engine size; the husband may feel strongly about the engine size but care little about the color. A solution by logrolling is possible in such a case. The husband gets to pick the engine size and the wife to pick the color. Logrolling solutions are possible if one or both parties gains insight into the other's priorities. They can also be developed by trial and error.

4. *Cost-cutting.* In a solution by cost cutting, one party is granted its demands, and the other's objections to these demands are met. For example, suppose a husband and wife disagree about whether they should vacation in New York City. The husband wants to go, but the wife objects to the expensive lodging. If either party can find a way of reducing the lodging expense, such as staying with a friend, the problem can be solved in a mutually agreeable way.

5. *Bridging.* Bridging occurs when a new option is developed that satisfies both parties' most significant needs. Follett gives a homely example of two women reading in a library room. One wanted to open the window for ventilation and the other wanted to keep it closed to avoid a draft. An

integrative solution was found in which a window was opened in the next room, bringing in fresh air but avoiding a draft. Bridging resembles logrolling in that it is usually (though not always) necessary for both parties to make concessions on low-priority matters. But the two types of agreement differ in that logrolling involves a single additive combination of demands previously endorsed by each party, whereas bridging requires an understanding of the values underlying these demands and the discovery of a new way to achieve these values. This understanding can exist in one or both parties' minds, or that of a mediator who is trying to help resolve the controversy.

STEPS IN THE DEVELOPMENT OF INTEGRATIVE SOLUTIONS

The following steps are recommended for a disputant who is trying to develop an integrative solution to a controversy.

1. Determine whether there really is a conflict of interest. A first step in any conflict should be to ask whether differences truly exist between the parties. Sometimes conflict is more illusory than real. Misunderstandings about the other party's intentions can lead to a mistaken belief that the party endangers one's interests. Or the other's frustrating actions may seem arbitrary and illegitimate when really they are not. Thus, the first step is to ask whether the conflict is a real one.

2. Analyze one's own interests, set reasonably high aspirations, and be ready to stick to them. If a difference of interest is found to exist, the next step should be to determine what one wants and why. Basic needs and values should be clarified. Following this, it is recommended that one set high goals and remain firm about them while being flexible about how they are achieved. Such a firm but flexible stance enhances the likelihood that a solution will be found that is valuable to both parties (Pruitt & Rubin, 1986). Setting high goals enhances the likelihood of advancing one's own interests, and failing to do so may cause settlement for less than is available. Being flexible about the means to these goals makes it likely that a solution will be found that is also acceptable to the other party.

3. Seek a way to reconcile both parties' aspirations. Any or all of the approaches (expanding the pie, logrolling, and so on) described earlier can be useful for finding a way to reconcile the parties' aspirations. The nature of the problem, and the kind of information available, may make some of these approaches more useful than others. But one should try them all and not give up too soon on any of them. Every effort should be made to discover the other party's needs and values so as to combine them with one's own in an integrative solution. But sometimes such information is not available. For example, the other may reject one's proposals but refuse to give reasons or make a counterproposal. When this happens, a policy of trial and error must be adopted (Kelley & Schenitzki, 1972; Pruitt & Carnevale, 1982), in which one proposes a sequence of alternatives that satisfy one's own goals in the hope of finding an alternative that appeals to the other party as well.

4. Lower aspirations and search further. If, after a reasonable period of time, the previous steps have not led to agreement, it is necessary to lower one's aspirations and try again. One must re-examine one's needs and values, and develop priorities among them. Then one must concede on the less important issues and develop a new set of goals to be pursued as vigorously as before. Eventually, through this or a later recycle, it should be possible to find an agreement that will be reasonably acceptable to both parties.

CONCLUSIONS

Conflict escalation ordinarily follows a cyclical course, with each side reacting to the other side's reactions. Such a spiral is ordinarily accompanied by structural changes in the parties that produce increased hostility and lock the parties into an escalated stance. Many escalated conflicts eventually come to a point of stalemate when both sides recognize that they are not getting anywhere. If, as is usually the case, costs are also mounting, the parties will be motivated to try to escape the conflict. The best way to escape is through problem solving in pursuit of integrative (win-win) agreements. Sometimes the two parties are able to engage in joint problem solving, sharing information about values and priorities, and jointly developing new options. However, the prior escalation usually has produced too much distrust for this to happen. An alternative is for one or both parties to engage in individual problem solving, trying to develop new ideas on their own. Alternatively a mediator can take over the problem solving, working with the two parties, individually or together, to articulate the issues and develop a solution. Mediation, which is found at all levels of society, from the playground to the international arena, is often an excellent approach to escalated conflict. It is becoming an increasingly important part of our society, with the development of community, family, and divorce mediation services, and is generally quite successful. We have reviewed a variety of conditions under which escalation is more or less likely, and a variety of techniques for generating integrative solutions. Our approach is one of general theory, applying to conflict in all arenas, and such a theory should be achievable and potentially quite useful.

REFERENCES

Burton, John Wear. *Peace Theory* (New York: Knopf, 1962).

Coleman, James Samuel. *Community Conflict* (New York: Free Press, 1957).

Deutsch, Morton. "Trust and Suspicion," *Journal of Conflict Resolution*, v. 2 (1958): 265–279.

Follett, Mary Parker. "Constructive conflict," in H. L. Metcalf and L. Warwick, eds., *Dynamic Administration: The Collected Papers of Mary Parker Follett* (New York: Harper, 1940), 30–41.

Kelley, Harold H. and D. P. Schenitzki. "Bargaining," in C. G. McClintock, ed. *Experimental Social Psychology* (New York: Holt, 1972).

Lebow, Richard Ned. Robert Jervis and Janice Gross Stein. *Psychology and Deterrence* (Baltimore: Johns Hopkins University Press, 1984).

North, Robert Carver. Richard A. Brody and Ole R. Holsti. "Some empirical data on the conflict spiral," *Peace Research Society (International) Papers*, v. 1 (1964): 1–14.

Osgood, Charles Egerton. *An Alternative to War or Surrender* (Urbana: University of Illinois Press, 1962); and Osgood, Charles Egerton. *Perspective in Foreign Policy*, 2nd ed. (Palo Alto, Calif.: Pacific Books, 1966).

Pruitt, Dean G. and P.J.D. Carnevale. "The Development of Integrative Agreements in Social Conflict," in V. J. Derlega and J. Grzelak, eds., *Living With Other People* (New York: Academic Press, 1982).

Pruitt, Dean G. and J. P. Gahagan. "Campus Crisis: The Search for Power," in J. T. Tedeschi, ed., *Perspectives on Social Power* pp. 349–392. (Chicago: Aldine, 1974), 349–392.

Pruitt, Dean G. and J. Z. Rubin *Social Conflict: Escalation, Stalemate and Settlement* (New York: Random House, 1986).

Pruitt, Dean G. and R. C. Snyder, eds., *Theory and Research on the Causes of War* (Englewood Cliffs, N.J.: Prentice-Hall, 1969).

Richardson, Lewis Fry. *Arms and Insecurity* (Chicago: Quadrangle Books, 1967).

Schumpeter, Joseph A. *The Sociology of Imperialism* (New York: Meridian Books, 1955).

12

Interpersonal Factors, Structural Factors, and Conflict Resolution Strategies

Louis Kriesberg

It is obvious that peace must begin in each of us. Or is it? The relationships between interpersonal conduct and international conflict are not self-evident. Are nice persons necessarily nice in their international conduct? Undoubtedly, there were Nazis who loved their children and treated members of their family with sweetness and devotion. On the other hand, some valiant workers for peace have been interpersonally unpleasant and hurtful. There is an even more troubling question: Is being conciliatory toward others and renouncing violence an effective way of making peace with them? It can be and has been argued that acquiescence, or the refusal to use coercion and violence, simply invites an adversary to be more aggrandizing. It can also be argued that the alternatives are grossly oversimplified.

These are difficult issues, but they must be addressed. In this chapter, after examining how interpersonal factors can affect international peace, ways structural factors also affect international peace will be noted. Interpersonal and structural factors are then combined in an examination of the place conflict resolution has in peacemaking. Two phases of peacemaking are considered: First, preventing the emergence and escalation of international conflicts, and second, de-escalating an intense adversarial relationship. The first phase will be discussed in terms of the sources of international conflict, and the second in terms of the ways in which conflicts are waged (Macy, 1987).

RELATIONS BETWEEN INTERPERSONAL FACTORS AND PEACE

Three kinds of interpersonal factors can affect international peace: (1) personality factors and social psychological processes, (2) experiences in small groups and interpersonal interactions, and (3) shared subjective factors. As will be discussed later, interpersonal factors have effects on international peacemaking in conjunction with structural factors, varying in significance with different structures.

Personality factors include a wide variety of attributes relating to how individuals differently perceive and feel about the world in which they live. Additionally, there are widely shared social psychological processses affecting cognition and emotions. For example, among the general social psychological processes stressed in relationship to international affairs is the tendency to regard the same trait as favorable when it is ours and less favorable when it is exhibited by others (Jervis, 1976; White, 1981). This may be illustrated by the following changes in adjectives when the pronoun changes: I am firm, you are stubborn, and they are pig-headed.

Variations among individuals affect attitudes and opinions about foreign affairs. Some people tend to blame themselves when matters go poorly and some people are more likely to blame others. The former, those who are intrapunitive, are somewhat more likely to think the United States has been at fault in relations with the Soviets, while the latter, those who are extrapunitive, are somewhat more likely to think the Soviets have been at fault.

An emphasis on personality factors usually accords importance to nonrational considerations, affecting cognitions as well as emotions. Feelings of anger, distrust, love, and hate may be displaced or projected upon persons and objects unrelated to the original source of the feeling (Laswell, 1950). Thus, adversaries can be the targets of animosity arising from childhood distress. Beliefs, too, may be derived from experiences unrelated to the ostensible conflicting parties. Misperceiving the intentions of the adversary and attributing responsibility for a fight to the adversary, may derive largely from personality traits and only a little from the adversary's conduct.

The second set of factors encompasses attitudes about conflicts associated with small group and intergroup relations, which may be extrapolated to international conflicts. These attitudes include views about fights in the family and neighborhood, as well as intergroup conflicts based on ethnic and class differences. Thus, animosities generated by ethnic tensions may be generalized to international relations.

The third set of factors emphasizes widely shared cognitions and emotions. These subjective elements are basically acquired through socialization, particularly through major institutions such as schools and churches. They generate cultures, subcultures, identities, and ideologies. People sharing a culture within a society or civilization share views about the nature of conflict and conflict resolution. In addition, every culture has subcultures, variations of the major culture, that are also transmitted by socialization. Major subcultures are based on gender, class, and ethnic differences. Persons learn who they are through socialization. Learning to be part of a particular people is an important identification. Persons learn multiple identities, however, as members of an ethnic group, religious community, country, region, and so on. Such multiple identities have much relevance for international peace, being the bases for crosscutting and overlapping conflicts and affiliations.

Ideologies are also major subjective elements in conflicts. Specific political ideologies and general world views are sources for popular understanding of who the actors are in international conflicts, and how they conduct their struggles. To illustrate the possible relationships between interpersonal factors and international peace, a few research findings are cited. Additionally, some results from analyzing data from the General Social Survey, conducted by the National Opinion Research Center (NORC), are reported. These results are based on analyses made specifically for this chapter, and on analyses reported in more detail in other publications (Kriesberg and Klein, 1980; Kriesberg, Murray, and Klein, 1982; Kriesberg and Quader, 1982). These surveys were conducted annually or biannually, beginning in 1972.

Sources of International Conflicts

Interpersonal factors affect the emergence of major conflicts in the world in many ways. Individual and personality factors may contribute to antagonism toward available foreign targets. Similarly, intergroup tensions may be transferred to foreign adversaries. General subjective orientations may also help shape the views about foreign adversaries. To illustrate how individual personality characteristics or attitudes may affect feelings toward a possible adversary, consider the level of hostility among Americans toward the Soviet Union. Responses to two NORC questions help to assess such international animosities. One question asks respondents how much they like or dislike the Soviet Union, among many other countries, on a scale from plus five to minus five: the other question asks respondents how they feel about communism as a form of government.

One kind of personality factor which may affect animosity toward possible adversaries is the level of anomia—the degree of normlessness and estrangement a person feels. Statements that are regarded as indicators of anomia are often agree-disagree items such as: It's hardly fair to bring a child into the world with the way things look for the future. Generally, few statistically significant relationships appear between these anomia items and evaluations of communism. The relationships, when significant, are between agreement with the anomic statement and belief that communism is the worst form of government. For example, respondents who agree with the statement, "These days a person doesn't really know whom he can count on," are somewhat more likely to think that communism is the worst form of government, than respondents who disagree with the statement. The pattern is similar in regard to disliking the Soviet Union. There is a statistically significant relationship for some items in some years. The relationships are in the direction indicating the projection of personal feelings on international objects, but the relationships are weak. One kind of interpersonal and intergroup attitude is among whites about blacks. Respondents objecting to having children go to school with blacks are somewhat more likely than others to regard communism as the worst form of government. The relationship between race prejudice and antagonism to the Soviet Union, however, is not statistically significant during the years for which the NORC data are available.

Finally, I will consider possible effects of general subjective factors—the ways in which people in a society tend to view the world. Such world views are partly incorporated in political ideologies. In the United States, explicit and highly elaborated ideologies are not widely held, but people do differ in general ideological orientations. As an indicator of such orientations, ideological self identification can be used. Persons who identify themselves as liberal rather than conservative are much less likely to feel that communism is the worst form of government. Self-designated liberals are also less likely to rate the Soviet Union in the most negative categories.

On the whole, the findings indicate only weak relationships between personal factors and intergroup prejudice, and evaluations of the Soviet Union. The relationships are only a little stronger with attitudes toward communism. However, ideological identification is strongly related to evaluations of each.

Waging Conflict

Preferences regarding ways of handling international conflicts are illustrated by responses to a question asking whether the federal government is spending too little, too much, or about the right amount for the military, armaments, and defense; and responses to a question asking if it is a good idea for our government to remain in the United Nations (UN) or pull out of it now. The anomia items are usually statistically related to preferences about military expenditures and the UN. The relations are in the direction indicating the projection of personal feelings upon foreign symbols, but the degree of relationship is small. For example, respondents who agree that a person doesn't know whom he can count on, also tend to think the government is spending too little on arms. The results are similar in regard to pulling out of the UN.

As measures of preferences regarding the means to be used in interpersonal conflicts, answers to questions about favoring the death penalty, and approving hitting an adult stranger under various circumstances, are illustrative. Respondents who favor the death penalty for persons convicted of murder are somewhat more likely to favor withdrawing from the UN, and much more likely to think we are spending too little for the military. There seems to be a generalization of interpersonal rules of conduct to international ones. Respondents who could imagine situations in which they would approve a man hitting an adult male stranger, however, are usually not more likely to favor pulling out of the UN, or believe the United States is spending too little for the military. Rather than generalization, it is probably that views about the death penalty are elements of political ideologies, along with views about the UN and military spending. Whether or not it is right to punch someone under various circumstances is not incorporated within generally prevelant ideologies. Rather, attitudes about hitting someone may indicate the dimension of activism versus passiveness, or simply the situation-specific character of such attitudes.

Finally, there is the role of general political ideologies, such as liberalism and conservatism. Self-designated liberals are generally much more likely than conservatives to think our government should remain in the UN, and that we are spending too much or about the right amount for the military. The degree of correlation varies over the years, but it is nearly always statistically significant. In regard to views about military spending, the relationship is relatively strong.

Thus, several interpersonal variables are associated with preferences about foreign adversaries, and about ways of conducting international conflicts. The findings suggest some popular extension of interpersonal antagonism to international targets, and the generalization of rules for conducting interpersonal conflicts to procedures for international conflicts. General orientations or approaches, however, seem to play more important roles. For example, subjective factors about political orientations have significant effects. In themselves, these findings do not answer the questions posed at the outset. We need to consider how interpersonal factors operate within the context of social structures, and how they impact upon peacemaking.

STRUCTURAL FACTORS AND PEACEMAKING

The emergence, escalation, and resolution of international conflicts are shaped by three structural settings: domestic conditions, the interaction between the adversaries, and the international context. How interpersonal factors affect peacemaking will be discussed in each setting.

Domestic Setting

Official and nonofficial leaders are affected by their constituencies. Many analysts have argued that international conflict is a result of the actions, by leaders of one people or country, reflecting constituency or domestic considerations. Thus, Marxists may argue that wars result from the struggle by capitalists, controlling their respective governments, to expand their markets. Democrats may argue that nondemocratic societies are war prone because there are few checks on the aggrandizing leaders who identify themselves with the state.

Interpersonal factors function in many ways relevant for peacemaking, within the domestic context of international adversaries. The functions vary, depending in part on the social structure of the country; for example, its openness to influence by the public at large or by various elites. Personality factors are significant insofar as particular personal qualities are widely distributed within a society. For example, widespread and profound anomia would contribute to a constituency for antiforeign mobilization. This process has been pointed to as part of the explanation for the rise of fascism in Germany in the 1930s. Personal qualities are also important insofar as they are relevant in the selection of people for foreign policy decision making offices. Compare, for example, the analyses of John Foster Dulles and Henry Kissinger (Russett and Star, 1981:312–314). Do societies tend to select persons with qualities which foster the projection of animosity upon foreign targets? Election campaigns waged in terms of who is tougher than whom, obviously have implications for how such selections are made.

Interpersonal and group experiences have effects, depending on their distribution. Although not related to opinions of liking or disliking the Soviet Union, racial prejudice is positively related to anticommunism, but the relationships are very small. Other interpersonal and group experiences are more directly relevant to peacemaking. These involve the processes of decision making and crisis management. For example, some writers have warned against groupthink—a process in which members of a decision making group try to move quickly to a policy and discourage disagreement (Janis, 1972).

Subjective factors such as ideology have an impact insofar as they are widely shared and are authoritatively interpreted. For some political, language, religious, and ethnic communities, certain office holders are given the authority to make definitive interpretations of ideologies. That often exacerbates conflicts, but it also allows for sudden reconciliations, as was the case with the 1939 Nazi-Soviet nonaggression pact.

Adversarial Interactions

Many structural features of the interactions and relations between adversaries are relevant to peacemaking. Some analysts stress the relative power of the adversaries, arguing that conflict is inhibited when the adversaries are about equal in strength, while others argue that de-escalation occurs when there is a hurting stalemate that is costly to all the adversaries (Touval and Zartman, 1985).

Interpersonal factors affect interactions among major adversaries in many different ways. First, personal qualities of adversary representatives may match each other well, or poorly, for mutual understanding and liking. For example, in the Egyptian-Israeli peacemaking efforts in late 1977 and 1978, the personal bonds established between Anwar Sadat and Ezer Weizman were useful, and helped overcome some of the interpersonal difficulties between President Sadat and Prime Minister Begin (Quandt, 1986; Carter, 1982; and Weizman, 1981). Second, small group and interpersonal interactions can be structured to facilitate communication. This has been done through small workshops at which adversaries meet with each other (Kelman, 1972; Burton, 1969; and Mitchell, 1973). Additionally, a variety of informal and nonofficial intermediary action can provide channels of communication otherwise unavailable to adversaries. Third, subjective factors such as world views, linguistic formulas, and specific ideologies affect adversary interactions. The adversaries may share such world views, styles of discourse, and ideologies, based upon their shared religion, ethnicity, language, civilization, or political theory. Such commonalities facilitate accurate communication and reduce misunderstanding.

International Context

Some analysts argue that the international context, consisting of sovereign states, is necessarily war-prone. It is an anarchic system lacking institutionalized rules for managing major disputes. Personal qualities probably are not very important at that level, except through the workings of the dominant institutions, including the mass media. But networks of international interactions are varyingly available for communication and influence. This can and does occur informally as well as formally within international governmental organizations. It also occurs through the expanding network of international nongovernmental organizations.

World views and ideologies in the world system are usually seen, for good reason, as grounds for division and animosity. Their multiplicity, however, could also provide the basis for crosscutting ties and identities. Theoretically, at least, such crosscutting ties mitigate hostility across any one division (Kriesberg, 1982). This theoretical possibility becomes a reality when many other conditions are conducive. For example, the shared European identity and culture helped alleviate the enmity between France and Germany only after three even more devastating wars, the division of Germany, and the development of the U.S.-Soviet cold war.

Having noted some ways interpersonal factors work through social structures domestically, in adversarial interaction, and in the international system, we must also recognize that interpersonal factors are shaped by structural ones. For example, certain kinds of people tend to be selected as leaders, and elite groups are able to greatly influence, if not control, the media and institutions which contribute to the formation of people's conceptions.

Other aspects of the international system also play a role in conflict emergence and de-escalation. Thus, every dispute is interlocked with many others. As the salience of one conflict increases, the de-escalation of others is often facilitated. For example, when the conflict between the People's Republic of China and the Soviet Union escalated in 1969, and the U.S. engagement in the war in Vietnam became increasingly burdensome, the prospect of détente between the United States and the Soviet Union became increasingly attractive. Another important aspect of the international system is the availability of institutions and persons who can play mediating roles in international conflicts. The United Nations is one such institution, and particular governments and nongovernmental organizations can, and often do, play mediating roles in specific conflicts.

CONFLICT RESOLUTION AND PEACEMAKING

Conflict resolution is an approach to reducing the too often disastrous consequences of conflicts. It has been rapidly developing in theory and practice in many social spheres, including the international. Some of its major features can be best understood in the context of combining insights from approaches emphasizing interpersonal as well as structural factors.

Peace is not a static condition, and a stable world of harmony and justice will never be attained. Peace may be regarded as a process in which conflicts are managed, or resolved, in ways that prevent them from escalating into large-scale violence. It is true that within the world there are pairs or sets of countries which are so integrated that the threat of a conflict escalating into armed struggle is barely conceivable. These are called security communities (Wright, et al., 1957). They have highly effective institutionalized ways to manage conflicts. Many persons working in the field of conflict resolution examine how sets of international actors, who are not in such circumstances, can be moved toward it. That involves altering the bases of conflicts and the way the conflicts are waged. Such alterations have both structural and interpersonal components.

Consider the bases of conflicts. In this chapter, some interpersonal approaches which help explain variations in animosities and other sources of conflicts have been discussed. For example, animosity between international entities is affected by the extent to which adversaries share ideas and feelings. Thus, consensus among adversaries should facilitate accurate communication, make appropriate responsiveness more likely, and provide a basis for shared identities. There is some evidence supporting this. Societies which share language and religion are less likely to have been at war with each other than societies which are dissimilar in these respects (Rummel, 1979:279).

In an ideological age, wars are likely to be fought over differences in religion and political thought. Theoretically, however, differences in ways of thinking could be the basis of harmony, since the differences could underlie complementary relations. On the other hand, with consensus, adversaries have the same values and preferences, and therefore, they would be in conflict if what they both want is limited, and each believes what it gets is at the expense of the other. In reality, consensus and dissensus enter into every fight. Thus, even if power or other resources are differently valued, they are valuable instruments to achieve whatever goals are felt to be important.

Aside from the degree to which values, beliefs, and feelings are shared, their content is important. What seems particularly important for peacemaking is the relative significance of ways of thinking that are tolerant of other ways of thinking. Being convinced of the superiority and even holiness of one's own belief system, combined with great power, is a formula for trying to impose those beliefs upon others, and thus, for intense mutual hostility. For example, consider the sources of the decline in tension in U.S.-Soviet relations in the early 1970s. It was facilitated by the gradual shift in U.S. public opinion in the 1960s toward increased tolerance for the views of others, including domestic communists (Kriesberg and Quadar, 1984). Such subjective orientations, it should not be forgotten, are in part, shaped by structural conditions. For example, tolerance and mutual respect are more likely to emerge between parties who are relatively equal in power and have common interests.

Much conflict resolution work is focussed on how a conflict is conducted. In this chapter, it has been emphasized that rigidity in approaches, and especially great reliance upon coercion and the threat of violence, often fosters conflict escalation. The usefulness of expanding the repertoire of ways to wage a conflict has also been suggested. This includes the utilization of noncoercive inducements in combination with coercion. It also includes using persuasion to reframe a conflict so that it is regarded as a shared problem, at least in some measure. Additionally, the repertoire may be expanded to include new ways to conduct negotiations that facilitate the search for fresh options regarding the parties involved and issues selected, as well as regarding possible outcomes. Conflict resolution techniques may be used to increase the likelihood that negotiations will result in agreements. Furthermore, some methods have been developed that can help maximize the mutual benefits the parties to the agreement gain (Fisher and Ury, 1981; Raiffa, 1982).

As discussed, subjective factors affect the way conflicts are conducted and thus the likelihood of war or peace. One major aspect of the way conflicts are conducted is the reliance on actual or threatened coercion, especially violence. We have seen that there are ideological, and to some extent personal qualities, that affect the tendency to rely upon the threat of violence in international conduct. That evidence does not tell us whether or not such reliance is conducive to war, or to peace. Insofar as reliance or coercion is derived from interpersonal and intergroup experience, however, it is likely to be used rigidly and inappropriately in international conflicts. Using threat as a means of defense is likely to be perceived by an enemy as an offensive threat, and not as a defensive response to its own appearance of threat (White, 1984).

One set of relevant studies pertains to the effects of arms races. The studies generally support the view that arms races tend to end in wars rather than in extending peace (Naroll, Bullough and Naroll, 1974; Wallace, 1972; Smoker, 1964; and Beer, 1981:270). Research on U.S.-Soviet relations also indicates that coercion has not been an effective instrument of U.S. policy (Leng, 26). There is even some evidence that noncoercive inducements can be useful in gaining de-escalating objectives in international conflicts (Kriesberg, 1987). This has been noted in studies related to Osgood's ideas of Graduated Reciprocal Initiatives in Tension-Reduction (GRIT) (Mitchell, 1986; Etzioni, 1967; and Kriesberg, 1981).

Conducting international conflicts in ways that minimize the probability of war is more likely if the parties are flexible about the means they use. Therefore, the availability of alternative ways of conducting international relations is conducive to peacemaking. This means that constituencies, as well as leaders, should have a large repertoire of alternative ways to pursue their goals. The repertoire will include the use of positive sanctions, and official and nonofficial intermediaries.

The conflict resolution approach also stresses the many kinds of activities that intermediaries can perform to initiate de-escalating negotiations and to reach stable, mutually beneficial agreements. Many such activities are performed by nongovernmental persons and organizations, as well as governmental ones. The activities include helping to exchange information, suggesting new options, and facilitating the conversion of the conflict into a problem to be solved (Bendahmane, 1987; Bercovitch, 1984).

Finally, adherence to rules of conflict management that have been developed over time can limit the escalation of international conflict. Such adherence to international law, or to United Nations decisions, depends on normative constraints and feelings of propriety, as well as calculations of short-term self interest in extrinsic terms.

In closing, what should be stressed is the importance of specificity in applying approaches to peacemaking. It is necessary to analyse the concrete and unique case for which peacemaking policies are being proposed. This includes taking into account the nature and stage of the conflict. It also includes being clear about the time frame in which policies are being proposed.

REFERENCES

Beer, Francis A. *Peace Against War* (San Francisco: W. H. Freeman & Co., 1981).

U.S. Department of State. Foreign Service Institute, *Conflict Resolution: Track Two Diplomacy*, ed. by Diane. B. Bendahmane (Washington, D.C.: U.S. Government Printing Office, 1987).

Bercovitch, Jacob. *Social Conflicts and Third Parties: Strategies for Conflict Resolution* (Boulder, Colo.: Westview Press, 1984).

Burton, John W. *Resolving Deep-Rooted Conflict: A Handbook* (Lanham, Md.: University Press of America, 1987).

Carter, Jimmy. *Keeping Faith* (New York: Bantam Books, 1982).

Etzioni, Amitai, "The Kennedy Experiment," *Western Political Quarterly*, v. 20 (June 1967): 361–380.

Fisher, Roger and William Ury, *Getting to YES: Negotiating Agreement Without Giving In.* (Boston: Houghton Mifflin, 1981).

Janis, Irving L. *Victims of Groupthink* (Boston: Houghton Mifflin, 1972).

Jervis, Robert. *Perception and Misperception in International Relations* (Princeton: Princeton University Press, 1976).

Kelman, Herbert C. "The Problem-Solving Workshop in Conflict Resolution," in A. L. Merritt, ed. *Communication in International Politics* (Hobson: University of Illinois Press, 1972), 168–204.

Kriesberg, Louis. "Noncoercive Inducements in U.S.-Soviet Conflicts: Ending the Occupation of Austria and Nuclear Weapons Tests," *Journal of Political and Military Sociology*, v. 9 (Spring 1981):1–16.

Kriesberg, Louis. *Social Conflicts*, 2d ed. (Englewood Cliffs, N.J.: Prentice Hall, 1982).

Kreisberg, Louis. "Carrots, Sticks, De-escalation: U.S.-Soviet and Arab-Israeli Relations," *Armed Forces and Society*, v. 13 (Spring 1987):403–423.

Kriesberg, Louis, and Ross A. Klein, "Changes in Public Suport for U.S. Military Spending," *Journal of Conflict Resolution*, v. 24 (March 1980):79–111.

Kriesberg, Louis, Harry Murray, and Ross A. Klein, "Elites and Increased Support for U.S. Military Spending," *Journal of Political and Military Sociology* v. 10 (Fall 1982):275–297.

Kriesberg, Louis and Abdul Quader, *"L'opinion publique americaine et l'U.R.S.S.*: les annees 70," *Etudes Polemologigues* v. 29, no. 1 (1984):5–36.

Laswell, Harold D. *World Politics and Personal Insecurity* (Glencoe, Il.: The Free Press, 1950 orig. pub. in 1934).

Leng, Russell J. "Reagan and the Russians: Crisis Bargaining Beliefs and the Historical Record," *The American Political Science Review*, v. 78 (1984): 338–355.

Macy, Mark, ed. *Solutions for a Troubled World* (Boulder, Colo.: Earthview Press, 1987).

Mitchell, C. R. "Conflict Resolution and Controlled Communication: Some Further Comments," *Journal of Peace Research*, v. 10, (1973):123–132.

Mitchell, C. R. "'GRIT and Gradualism—25 Years On," *International Interactions*, v. 13, no. 1 (1986):51–90.

Naroll, Raoul, Vern L. Bullough, and Frada Naroll, *Military Deterrence in History: A Pilot Cross-Historical Survey* (Albany: State University of New York Press, 1974).

Quandt, William B. *Camp David* (Washington, D.C.: The Brookings Institution, 1986).

Raiffa, Howard. *The Art and Science of Negotiation* (Cambridge: Harvard University Press 1982).

Rummel, Rudolph. *Understanding Conflict and War*, vol. 4 (Beverly Hills, Calif.: Sage Publications 1979).

Russett, Bruce and Harvey Starr, *World Politics: The Menu for Choice* (San Francisco: W. H. Freeman and Company, 1981).

Smoker, Paul. "Sino-Indian Relations: A Study of Trade, Communication and Defense," *Journal of Peace Research*, no. 2 (1964):65–76.

Touval, Saadia and I. William Zartman, "Introduction: Mediation in Theory" in Saadia Touval and I. William Zartman, eds. *International Mediation in Theory and Practice* (Boulder, Colo.: Westview Press, 1985).

Wallace, Michael. "Status, Formal Organization, and Arms Levels as Factors

Leading to the Onset of War," in Bruce Russett, ed., *Peace, War and Numbers* (Beverly Hills, Calif.: Sage Publications, 1972).

Weizman, Ezer. *The Battle for Peace* (New York: Bantam Books, 1981).

White, Ralph K. *Fearful Warriors: A Psychological Profile of U.S.-Soviet Relations* (New York: Free Press, 1984).

13

Game Theory, Cooperation, and Conflict

Glenn Palmer

In this chapter, a framework for analyzing some causes of conflict and peace in international relations is examined. The aim is to outline a method of analyzing social phenomena (game theory) to be used to understand the sources of peaceful interaction, or conflict. We will look at specific examples of conflict in international relations to illustrate the type of analysis one might do with game theory. The emphasis, however, of this chapter is on the *method* of analysis, rather than the particular conclusions to be drawn from the specific examples. At the conclusion of this chapter, the reader will be able to look at international situations other than those discussed through the use of game theory, and derive both predictions regarding the outcomes of specific situations and some solutions to conflictual international circumstances. We begin by exploring the theoretical background of the use of game theory in international relations. Game theory assumes that nation-states are the most important actors in international relations. Game theory further assumes that nation-states are capable of recognizing their interests, and of acting in the pursuit of those interests. It finally assumes that the interactions of those nation-states take a certain form. These assumptions are shared with the approach to the study of peace, based on the nature of the international system. First we will look at the perspective from which game theory operates at the international level.

GAME THEORY AND THE INTERNATIONAL SYSTEM

The study of international relations and the prospects for peace has several starting points—or assumptions. Different schools of thought emphasize different aspects of the political world, and base their discussions, questions, and conclusions on those aspects. Some scholars emphasize the relationship between a country's domestic political structures and its war- or peace-proneness. For instance, one often hears that democratic countries are less violent in their international behavior than totalitarian countries. Others may study the effects of individual leaders, and discuss how, for instance, Hitler was responsible for the outbreak of World War II.

One of the more prominent ways of studying international relations is based on the nature of the international system. The type of political analysis that is called "power politics" starts with the belief that all states in the world want similar things. They all desire to increase, or at least maintain the level of their own security, and perhaps increase their power, or ability to persuade other states to behave in certain ways. Because all states share these common goals, it is not necessary (according to this perspective) to analyze the internal political make-up of countries or study the character of individual leaders. The nation-state is "black-boxed" (all nation-states are basically the same, and vary only in the amount of power they have). Thus, this form of analysis concentrates, instead, on how the structure of the international system and interaction of the goals of the countries affects the possibilities for the attainment of peace.

The analysis of the ways the international system affects the prospects for peace enjoys a long history. One of the first writers to concentrate on this type of analysis in understanding causes of war and the prospects for peace is Jean-Jacques Rousseau, who in *The Social Contract* presents the illuminating tale of the "stag and the hare." This tale is one of the earliest uses of what we now call "game theory," and it highlights Rousseau's beliefs about how peace can be achieved.

Imagine that in the formative stages of society a group of hunters band together to try to capture a stag, which will give them each sufficient nourishment for some time. To capture the stag, they agree to encircle an area where they suspect the stag to be, to close in on that area, and eventually capture the animal. Each hunter is assigned a part of this circle, and no hunter can see any of the other hunters. Now suppose a small hare runs by one of the hunters. That hunter is faced with the choice of abandoning his or her area (through which the stag may then escape) to pursue the hare, or continuing to maintain his or her place, foregoing the opportunity to get the hare. What would the hunter do? The hunter may believe that the group's interest is paramount, and that the proper course would be to ignore the hare and continue to move in on the stag. But, the hunter may think, suppose the other hunters have also seen a hare run by. How do I know that the others have not abandoned their responsibilities to our group to pursue their hares, and I am the only one left? In fact, if only one of my fellow hunters has pursued a hare, the stag will probably escape and I will go hungry, unless of course, I go after my hare. And away goes the hunter in pusuit of the hare. There are many lessons to this story, and scholars are still arguing the merits of the example. But the lesson to be highlighted is this: The hunter is placed in a situation of trying to predict the acts of the other hunters. Our hunter makes that prediction based on the recognition of common interests. That is, the very thing that brought the hunters together (the common need for food) leads our hunter to expect that the other hunters have already pursued their interests individually.

What has this story to do with international relations and the search for peace? States today enjoy sovereignty. That is, they have the legal right to make and enforce laws within their boundaries. As is the case with the hunters, there is no greater entity or authority telling them what to do. They live in a system of *anarchy*. International law has no enforcement mechanism. Neither the United Nations nor the World Court can force countries to act in accordance with international law if they do not wish to do so.[1] Nation-states, like the hunters, have common interests such as access to resources, economic prosperity, and national security, to name but three. Consider national security for a moment. If two countries want to provide more security for their citizens, each may build arms. An arms build-up by one country may be seen to diminish the security of a second country, forcing that country to build arms as well. The first country is now less secure and may build even more weapons than before, necessitating a response by the second country, and so on. Why don't both countries simply stop building arms, and by doing so become more secure? We will look at this question later.

The international systems perspective that is captured in Rousseau's story is the dominant one for scholars interested in the causes of conflict in international relations (at least in political science). There is voluminous research on such questions as how the "balance of power" may lead to war; how relative growth rates in military and/or economic power may lead to war. All these questions share the belief that the structure of international relations is at least conducive to conflict, if not its fundamental cause.[2]

We will now explore a particular form of analysis that follows from this perspective. If we assume that states have goals, are capable of making decisions on their own (which is what sovereignty means), and are dependent on the actions of other states for the realization of their goals, we can apply a method of analysis called "game theory" to determine how the interactions of states can lead to peace. Game theory is simple and, if done well, can be fun.

GAME THEORY AND THE ANALYSIS OF CONFLICT

Game theory is a way to analyze social phenomena. It views actors as "players", connected in a situation by rules, and interacting in an interdependent fashion to determine the outcome, or result of their game. For example, let us look at what is probably the most fruitful game (*Prisoner's Dilemma*) and discover its relevance to understanding the prospects for peace.

The story that establishes the prisoner's dilemma is simple. Two people suspected of committing a major crime, for example, a robbery, are captured by the police. The police can prove a lesser crime against these people, such as possession of stolen property, but they lack sufficient evidence to obtain a conviction for bank robbery. The prisoners are separated, and not allowed to communicate with each other. The police present each prisoner with a choice: They can keep quiet, or confess to the bank robbery. If each prisoner keeps quiet, each will be convicted of the lesser crime and go to jail for one year. If each confesses to the bank robbery, each will be convicted of that charge and go to jail for five years. However, if one prisoner confesses and the other remains quiet, the prisoner confessing will go free, while the one keeping quiet will be convicted of bank robbery and receive ten years in jail.

Let us call the prisoners A and B. They each have a choice of keeping quiet (Q) or confessing (C). The results of this game depend on what each prisoner does. The game is presented in the matrix below. It can be seen that if each prisoner remains quiet, each receives one year in jail (−1); if both confess, each receives five years in jail (−5); if A keeps quiet while B confesses, A receives ten years in jail (−10), while B goes free (0); and if B keeps quiet while A confesses, A goes free (0), while B gets ten years in jail (−10).

What will the prisoners do? Recall that they cannot communicate with each other, but each is aware that the other is facing the same choice as he or she. Consider A's situation. This prisoner may think, If B keeps quiet, I can keep quiet and go to jail for one year, or confess and go free. Obviously, I would prefer to go free, and thus confess. What if B confesses? In that case, I can keep quiet and go to jail for ten years, or confess and spend only five years in jail. Again, I would prefer to confess. So A would prefer to confess *no matter what B does.*

Figure 13.1
The Prisoner's Dilemma

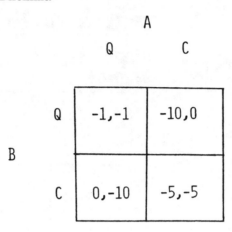

B's thinking would be the same, and under the circumstances specified by the game, each would confess and each would go to jail for five years. But of course, each is worse off than if they both kept quiet and received only one year in jail. We call the situation where both prisoner's confess a "dominant strategy." This is when one player is better off (or at least not worse off) making a particular choice, regardless of what the other player does. The concluding point of the game is that if both actors pursue their individual interests, they will achieve an outcome that is worse for each of them than if they had not. We refer to this as a "socially deficient outcome", since everybody is worse off than they could have been by doing something else.

   Before continuing, it is useful to discuss some of the objections that are raised to this story. First, one might argue that the prisoners will not confess because they feel sympathy for their partner. Perhaps, but the story does not allow for sympathy. We could make it more complicated (and we will below) by asking what would happen if each actor cares about the welfare of the other. But the story establishes that each prisoner is interested in his or her own well-being, surely an accurate depiction of most aspects of international relations. Second, it may be believed that a confessing prisoner might face retribution from some outside authority like organized crime, and would therefore prefer to keep quiet. It is worth pointing out that the inherent threats to the confessing prisoners, presented by the existence of organized crime, are something the prisoners want. If each prisoner knows that anyone confessing will be killed, each, then, prefers to keep quiet and go to jail for only one year. This is better for the prisoners than what happens without these threats. However, this belief introduces the

Figure 13.2
Arms Buildup Game

U.S.

		N	B
USSR	N	3,3	1,4
	B	4,1	2,2

equivalent of an international government, and the anarchic international system does not have such a thing. Finally, one might wonder what the future relationship of the prisoners will be if each knows the other cannot be trusted. That is, suppose the prisoners can anticipate dealing with each other (or some other prisoner) again. Does this change the prisoners considerations? Yes it does, and we will examine this below.

Let us use an example of the Prisoner's Dilemma applied to another situation to see what we can learn. Two countries, the United States and the Soviet Union, have the following choices. Each can build more arms (B), or not build arms (N). There are four possible outcomes in this simple game. Let us assume that the worst outcome for the United States is not to build arms, while the Soviet Union does and that this is the best outcome for the Soviet Union. We will give this worst outcome for the United States a value of "1"; and since this is the best of the four outcomes for the Soviet Union, we will give it a value of "4". Similarly, the best outcome for the United States is to build arms while the Soviet Union does not; and this is the worst outcome for the Soviet Union. Thus, in this case the United States gets "4" while the Soviet Union gets "1". The two remaining possible outcomes are that both countries build arms, or both do not. We will assume that because arms are expensive, each country would prefer the situation where neither builds arms to the situation where both build. The game is presented below.

This game is identical to the Prisoner's Dilemma in its logic and, in fact, this is the more generalized form of the game. Each country prefers to build its arms no matter what the other country does—each has a

Figure 13.3
Game of Chicken

A

	V	S
V	3,3	2,4
S	4,2	1,1

B

dominant strategy. And, if each country follows the "best" course of action, each will build arms and will be worse off than if neither built arms. Again, see the "socially deficient outcome."

Not all games take the form of the Prisoner's Dilemma. Some games are zero-sum. In this type of game, whatever one actor gets, the other actor loses. Sport events are zero-sum—one team wins, the other team must lose. Elections are also zero-sum—if one candidate wins, the other(s) must necessarily lose. It is sometimes asserted that much of international relations is zero-sum. One hears on occasion, for instance, that if the Soviet Union "gets" Iran, the United States must lose it. But this is an overly simplistic view, and one can explain "socially deficient outcomes" without believing that the world is the purely conflictual place that zero-sum games assume it to be. The Prisoner's Dilemma, for instance, has a mixture of conflict and cooperation in it.

Chicken is another game that has a mixture of conflict and cooperation, and is often used to analyze international relations, which is derived from the "James Dean" school of international relations. The story is straightforward. Two people (A and B) in cars face each other on a long, straight road. They drive toward each other at great speed. Each has an option of veering off (V) or of going straight (S). If both go straight, a horrible accident will follow, and, if one veers while the other goes straight, the former is a "chicken" (better than being involved in an accident) and the latter is seen as brave. The game is presented below. Recall that "4" means "that outcome" is the best for a given player, "3" is the second best, and "1" is the worst.

This game is different from Prisoner's Dilemma because neither player has a dominant strategy; each wants to avoid the worst out-

Figure 13.4
The Persian Gulf

IRAN

		A	I
U.S.	M	3,1	2,A
	W	4,B	1,4

come—each goes straight. What motivations do the players have in this game First, each player has an incentive to prove to the other that she/he is commited to going straight, and that the other has what is called "the last clear chance" to avoid a collision. For instance, if B throws the steering wheel out of the car so that A sees B do this, A now knows that she/he has the choice of going straight and causing the collision (which is the worst outcome), or veering to stay alive. Second, each player has a very strong incentive to avoid the outcome that both players go straight. These two incentives conflict with each other, and make Chicken a very dangerous game.

It is sometimes asserted that the deterrent relationship between the United States and the Soviet Union takes the form of Chicken. For instance, some argue that if the Soviet Union could attack Western Europe (the equivalent of going straight) and know that the United States would not respond to the attack, the Soviet Union would begin war immediately. However, it is the fear of a U.S. retaliation to that attack (both countries going "straight") that dissuades, or deters the Soviet Union from starting a war. And thus, the logic continues, to deter them, the United States must make clear to the Soviet Union that a U.S. response will automatically follow any Soviet attack on Western Europe. This response, if the war were to start, *is something the United States would prefer not to do*. To put the matter differently, the United States must convince the Soviet Union that it will respond in an "irrational" manner to Soviet military actions. This perverse logic is sometimes referred to as the "rationality of irrationality". It is this logic which underlies some aspects of current U.S. strategic doctrine.

Game theory, as mentioned, is a method of analysis. The task of a user of game theory is to determine the preferences of the actors in a game. Is some outcome (a) better for an actor than another outcome (b)? Is it better than (c)? Is (b) better than (c)? As an example of applied game theory, let us examine a situation in international relations.

In 1988, the United States had a large naval presence in the Persian Gulf, whose task was to protect shipping as it passed through the Gulf. The United States had a choice between maintaining that presence (M) and withdrawing its naval forces (W). Iran and Iraq periodically attempted to interdict that shipping. For purposes of illustration, we will concentrate on Iran. Iran had a choice between continuing to interdict that shipping (I), or allowing general free passage (A). From my reading of U.S., including Pentagon, statements, it appeared that the most preferred outcome for the United States would have been to withdraw its forces if Iran had allowed free passage of shipping. To withdraw while Iran continued interdiction efforts was the least preferred outcome for the United States. And, given that the United States maintained its naval presence, it would have preferred Iran to allow shipping rather than attempt interdiction. For Iran, the best outcome would have been to continue interdiction while the United States withdrew its forces. The worst outcome for Iran was to allow free passage while the U.S. naval forces stayed in the Gulf. But what about the other two outcomes? Which was better for Iran: To continue interdiction while the United States maintained its forces in the Gulf (outcome a), or to allow shipping to pass while the United States withdrew its forces (outcome b)?

If we, as analysts, believe that Iran prefered (a) to (b), then Iran had a dominant strategy—to continue interdiction. Given that, the United States would have preferred to maintain its forces in the Gulf. If, however, we believe Iran preferred (b) to (a), the game becomes a little more complicated. Then, both Iran and the United States would have rather seen a cessation of interdiction and a withdrawal of American forces, than a continuation of the situation. If this were the case, diplomatic efforts toward a resolution of the problems in the Persian Gulf could have been expected to succeed. The point is that if we can identify the preferences of a country (in the example, Iran), we can make some predictions about what will happen.

Space considerations prohibit a detailed examination of the uses of game theory to analyze conflictual situations in international relations. Hopefully, the reader has been presented with sufficient information regarding the nature of the analysis to apply game theory to other situations in the contemporary world. Now, let us consider some more general lessons of game theory applied to the prospects for peace.

LESSONS FROM GAME THEORY

The Prisoner's Dilemma is an extremely useful game in two regards. First, many situations in international relations, and in domestic politics, can be captured accurately by the game. In international relations, such decisions and actions as whether to build more arms or not, or whether to impose trade barriers or not, can be captured by the Prisoner's Dilemma. The characteristics of Prisoner's Dilemma are present in the following situations: Whether an individual should join a labor union; whether one should work to support the Equal Rights Amendment; and whether a company or municipality should dump waste material in a river. Second, and what will be concentrated on here, are the reasons one might be hopeful that nations can peacefully resolve areas of conflict, and develop cooperation with other nations, using a Prisoner's Dilemma game. Those reasons fall into two general categories: Repeated play of the game itself; and the strength of the assumptions underlying the game.

Repeated Play of the Prisoner's Dilemma

Return for a moment to the U.S.-Soviet arms build-up game. At first glance, the implication of this game (if it is correct) are grim. But of course, the two countries do not decide to always build arms or not build arms. Each year the United States and the Soviet Union decide on their respective defense budgets, in which there are provisions to build (and sometimes not to build) specific weapons systems. Thus, the arms build-up game is played repeatedly, virtually every year. If we view the Prisoner's Dilemma as an iterated game, do the predictions of what the countries will do change? The following discussion is based on Robert Axelrod's *The Evolution of Cooperation.*[3]

Research that has been done on whether to play the *iterated* Prisoner's Dilemma, or *how people actually play it*, suggests that the one-shot dominant strategy (for instance building arms in the U.S.-Soviet game) is not the best thing to do, because people often do not behave according to their short-term interests. The reason is that the players tend to view the moves in each round of play as signalling their probable future actions. If the United States, for example, were to signal the Soviet Union that it is willing to stop building particular weapons (at least temporarily), the Soviet Union may see that signal and stop building these weapons themselves. The Soviet Union must know that the United States is capable of responding in the future to its own weapons increases, and also know that if they continue to build arms, the United States will respond. Thus, each year's defense budget decisions may consider the reactions of the other player. In this way, an iterated Prisoner's Dilemma may lead to more cooperative, or more conciliatory moves, than one might expect from the one-shot game. And, as for the question of international cooperation, if the countries can expect their interaction to last a fairly long time, correctly perceive their adversaries' actions, and, understand that their actions may provoke undesirable reactions by their adversary, an arms build-up is not an inevitable outcome.

The Assumption of Egoism

An assumption in game theory that needs to be made explicit is that of egoism. Violation of this assumption may allow one to be more optimistic about the prospects for international cooperation. Game theory assumes that the actors care only about getting the best outcome possible for themselves. The players hold no direct animosity toward each other, but neither are they sympathetic. They are egoistic. This is not always true in the real world.[4] For example, the United States shares many interests with its allies, and generally believes that what is good for them is also good for the United States. But the United States also values the well-being of its allies for their own interests. Just as a married couple cares about each other, so, too, may some countries genuinely value another country's welfare. This is most obviously true among military allies and trading partners. But it can also be true of states we normally think of as adversaries. The American government's support for the Soviet Union's restructuring of its political and economic system is based primarily on the U.S. belief that if successful, that restructuring may lead to a modification of Soviet foreign policy behavior. But it also, in part, rests on an altruistic desire to see the lives of Soviet citizens bettered. In this way, an increased emphasis in world politics on society-to-society relations, as opposed to the more traditional state-to-state relations, may erode the egoism assumed under game theory. And if this were true, and applied to the Prisoner's Dilemma, states would have less incentive to pursue their own interests unilaterally.

CONCLUSION

In this chapter, it has been shown that an approach to the causes of peace and conflict based on the nature of the international system is a fruitful one, and one that enjoys a long history. This approach starts with the assumption that states in the international arena share basic goals, but the realization of those goals may be impeded and not helped by shared interests. This is also the starting point of game theory. Game theory is a method of analyzing social interactions. Game theory helps us understand peace and conflict in two ways. First, by applying the appropriate game to specific situations, we may better understand the possibilities (and unfortunately at times the impossibilities) for cooperative behavior. Second, by a careful consideration of the assumptions we make when we apply game theory to the world, we can discover how to control or eliminate the egoism that game theory assumes. It is hoped that by undertaking these two tasks, we can better understand the ways in which peaceful cooperation can be developed in international relations.

NOTES

1. It should come as no surprise that Rousseau's solution to the problem of war is to develop a powerful, federated world government, capable of enforcing peaceful international behavior, an idea which has enjoyed a very long, if somewhat fruitless, life.

2. The readers interested in finding out more about the international systems approach to peace are urged to read Kenneth Waltz, *Man, the State and War* (New York: Columbia University Press, 1954), and *Theory of International Politics* (Readings: Addison-Wesley, 1979); Morton Kaplan, *System and Process in International Politics* (New York: John Wiley & Sons, 1957); and Robert Gilpin, *War and Change in International Politics* (New York: Cambridge University Press, 1981).

3. Robert Axelrod, *The Evolution of Cooperation* (New York: Basic Books, 1984).

4. Rousseau, for example, argued that his hunters will not go after the hare if they develop sympathy for one another.

14

What of Peace History?
Lessons from World War I

Donald S. Birn

It used to be said of military history that its readers were those who studied past wars in order to make better ones in the future. This field has changed markedly in recent years, some of its readers less so. As one of its distinguished practitioners, Michael Howard, reminds us, "so long as the organized use, or threatened use, of force still remains an instrument in the conduct of international relations," there will be a place for analytic studies on the art of war.[1] What of "peace history"? Can we isolate techniques or institutions that helped keep the peace in the past, in the hope of building an appropriate model for the future? Most historians are wary of didactic exercises of that kind. However, we can enlarge our understanding of the past by studying the institutions, which fostered or undermined peace, in their proper context.

The period between the two world wars is the obvious place to begin, but also the most treacherous. For, just as the books which our parents read are the easiest to criticize, the political shortcomings of the preceding generation seem the most glaring. The "Munich syndrome", the well-worn tales of guilty men cringing before dictators, formed a kind of modern morality play against which Western leaders since 1945 have set off their own policies. We were determined not to disarm, not to appease, and we set our course accordingly. That the analogy did not quite fit—that the world was a very different place after the war soon became apparent. Yet, the challenge which the Western alliance has equipped itself to face, is still the old challenge updated, with the swastika replaced by the hammer and sickle. The weapons with which we have equipped ourselves are too dangerous to use and, sensing that we have lost our way, we search for other approaches to peace and security. The search could begin with those lessons learned before the last war, the lessons that we overlearned or misapplied. Did we miss anything the first time around because we were asking the wrong questions? A better understanding of the structures governing war and peace at that time would serve us well today.

World War I was so destructive that those who survived it felt they had the right to a better world. It had been a war of massed armies, the last of its kind between major powers. Many of its casualties were civilians, and even those civilians who had not come under fire became part of the war effort in ways they could not have imagined before 1914. The war had destroyed the European state system, and ushered in a revolution which threatened the social order as well. Despite all this, people still hoped for a just and lasting peace. Yet, those very hopes, nurtured through years of sacrifice, were so far-reaching and contradictory that they could never be satisfied.

One lesson military leaders learned during the war was that their training had failed them; trench warfare had been an unhappy experience that they hoped to avoid in the future. Some of them, remembering the awful price their troops had to pay when launched against the combination of barbed wire and machine guns, began to plan less costly defensive strategies. The Maginot Line, the ultimate trench, was the embodiment of this line of thinking. Others were more impressed with the way new technologies had been able to affect the course of the war. Tanks, submarines, and aircraft were not only weapons of immense potential in themselves, their use also underscored the changing nature of warfare and its increasing domination by weapons technology.

That industrial societies could harness their vast resources to produce elaborate weapons systems was nothing new. Before the war, Britain and Germany had engaged in a naval-building race that introduced most of the elements of a modern arms race. Battleships were the ICBMs of their day, costly offensive weapons that enabled their possessors to play the great power role in global politics. In 1905, the British, fearful that the Germans might be trying to get the jump on them with some new battleship design, introduced the *Dreadnought*, a ship so revolutionary in design that it outdated all earlier battleships. Moreover, it introduced this new weapons system under a cloak of secrecy, an innovation which so intrigued journalists that their curiosity was peaked, and they began to speculate about Admiral Fisher's "hush-hush policy." John Fisher, the first "sea lord," was able to play on this public fascination with his bold and wonderful projects, just as Tirpitz, his opposite number in Germany did.

Secrecy, reliance on espionage and worst-case capability analysis of the adversary, blatant efforts to drum up press and public support with inspired stories, lobbying by armaments manufacturers, and, above all, the driving force of a kind of technological imperative, were all present before 1914. Only after the war did other features characteristic of contemporary arms races appear. One of these features was introduced as part of an effort to curb the competition in armaments, which the public saw (not without reason) as a cause of war. It was arms control, which was first introduced at the Washington Naval Conference in 1922.

After the war, disarmament was often preached from pulpits and political platforms. A measure of disarmament had been imposed on defeated Germany, supposedly as a first step towards a wider disarmament program under the aegis of the League of Nations. But the League had been unable to make headway on the issue—military men asked to advise the world body seemed ready enough to label the weapons others had acquired as dangerous, but could not understand how anyone would want to get rid of essential, defensive armory. Moreover, France was reluctant to reduce her forces, the most powerful in Europe, until her concerns about security were addressed. The League was stymied, unable to achieve disarmament without security, and unable to see how security was possible without disarmament.

The Washington Naval Conference appeared to be a breakthrough. The five leading naval powers agreed to a ten-year naval-building "holiday" for battleships, and established a ratio among their fleets. Together with the pacts regulating affairs in the Pacific, which the conference also enacted, the naval arms agreement was heralded as a useful step that succeeding conferences could build. Washington's "ratio approach" could not be extended to land armaments, however. When the League of Nations tried such an extension, it discovered that it could not duplicate Washington's direct approach to disarmament. For one thing, Washington's approach was not direct. Only a security agreement assuring Japan of her sphere of influence in the Pacific made disarmament possible. Even more to the point, Washington had not really sought disarmament. Some ships were actually scrapped, of course, and the conference won great praise from peace movement activists. Exaggerated appraisals of the work of the conference came from everywhere. H. G. Wells, who attended the meeting, wrote that it "may prove to be the nearest approach the human will and intelligence has yet made to a resolute grapple against fate upon this planet."[2] Behind the fog of rhetoric, it was clear that this conference on the limitation of armament was motivated by concerns of economy and strategy. Disarmament, that longtime pacifist goal, had little in common with arms control, which assumes that armaments competition will continue, but can be regulated in the interest of efficiency and economy. Governments might appeal to public opinion and morality, as Britain did at Washington, when it tried to get submarines banned, but this was only opportunism, not a sign that the lion had turned into a lamb.

Arms control ratios only served to transfer the competition from what was regulated to what was not. Since capital ships over 10,000 tons displacement were banned, navies began a fierce competition to build the best ships they could, just under that limit—so-called "treaty cruisers." That the really promising new technologies of underseas and air warfare were left unregulated was no accident. Arms control, in fact, freed up resources for work in these areas; that was part of its appeal to military leaders.

Airpower was central to the new doctrine of strategic warfare that emerged in several countries after World War I. In their efforts to find an alternative to the demoralizing warfare of attrition from which they had just emerged, military strategists thought airpower provided a way out. If air forces were used, not as adjuncts to armies and navies, but as separate strike forces capable of attacking the enemies' homeland, wiping out their productive capacity, then, wars might be won at an acceptable price. It meant holding civilian populations hostage, of course, but in this age of total war, the line between combatants and noncombatants had become too faint to discern.

The doctrine of strategic warfare emerged a few years before the weapons—the heavy, four-engine bombers and the atomic bombs that would make it workable. Its acceptance in the 1920s and 1930s is still noteworthy. Governments that only a few years before had been railing about the atrocities committed against innocent civilians by their enemies, now, in essence, adopted the mass destruction of civilians as official policy. There were debates on whether the doctrine would really prove to be an effective deterrent to war, whether it was technically feasible, and whether it was prudent to drain off resources from infantries to bombers, and, of course, it was not adopted universally. But scarcely a voice was raised questioning its moral implications.

Thus, in the aftermath of "the war to end all wars," the modern war system was established, the horrors of future conflict were being planned, and the whole process was rationalized and controlled by international agreements. These agreements, popularly thought of as "disarmament," were not necessarily bad ideas. They did save money and resources, and, in some cases, fostered international trust. However, the uncritical public acceptance of arms control and limitation made the work of establishing the system too easy. Statesmen could point to the very modest limits that had been achieved in a few categories of weapons and win widespread adulation. The peace movement in the 1920s, so outspoken about the need for disarmament, did not perform what should have been its most important function—educating the public. To some extent, this failure can be ascribed to the tendency of peace activists to shirk the unpleasant duty of informing themselves properly about military matters. Weapons and strategies were for war and their concern was for peace. Yet, if this inclination was natural, it was damaging. It lessened their credibility in preaching to the unconverted, and did not allow them to understand what was happening. However, this inclination to shy away from the technical aspects of the arms race was certainly less pronounced in the 1920s than it was to become in the nuclear age.

The failure of peace movements can be explained in other ways. In the Western democracies, where they were strongest, they tried to play the role of pressure groups that could appeal to members of all political parties. They welcomed the support of established political leaders, even when the price for that support was too high. Politicians found it easy to neutralize peace opinion, because issues like armaments policy were not considered important enough to override party loyalties or force significant shifts in political alignments. No one generalization fits all groups in all countries, but the largest and best publicized peace groups, such as the League of Nations societies that flourished in Western Europe and the United States, displayed the greatest timidity. They had the "support", after a fashion, of so many influential national leaders, that they dared not jeopardize it.

More than political tactics kept the leaders of major peace groups polite and conciliatory; they had their own status and respectability to protect. Peace work had a middle class flavor to it, and it would not do to allow it to be contaminated by concern with side issues—"distractions" such as social and economic equality, imperialism, or women's rights. A wider audience might have been drawn to the peace cause if these issues had been addressed.

Internationalist and peace groups were able to break out of their narrow middle class ambit a few times in the interwar era. Their most notable effort came with the International Peace Campaign which developed in 1935. It sought a wider basis of support for collective security against the mounting forces of fascism by enlisting the help of existing organizations—trade unions, educational, youth and religious groups, primarily. The campaign spread to forty-three countries, and at its peak in 1937, could claim to speak for organizations representing four hundred million members.³ These were impressive numbers, but the effort came too late to have much impact. The fact that communists were active in it led to considerable infighting. Moreover, the peace movement as a whole had, by this time, become hopelessly divided between internationalists, who wanted rearmament against Hitler, and pacifists who did not.

Even when peace groups were able to expand their audience or modify their tactics, they still failed to change their conception of their role. In a world divided along lines of national sovereignty and imperial conquest, and where gross economic equality and exploitation remained the rule, they focussed on armaments and alliances. There was some work done in the health and social fields by the League of Nations, but it was a purely political organization, compared to the United Nations.

Peace activists in Britain and a few other countries did begin to address concerns about economic injustice in the late 1930s, but with a doubtful motive. In response to Mussolini's and Hitler's complaints about the peace treaties that had ended World War I, and their ravings about "have" and "have-not" nations, a number of peace leaders urged accommodation. Many peace groups proposed dealing with economic grievances, revising the Covenant of the League, and settling the colonial problem. However, they appreared to be, and often were, simply proposing appeasement. Their solution to the colonial problem was to give Hitler a bigger slice of the pie. The idea of championing the liberation of oppressed people was not proposed.

During World War II, in the shattered remains of the peace movement, a broader conception of what peace work might entail emerged. Even with the British League of Nations Union, the largest and most conservative of all peace societies, espoused a commitment to far-reaching economic and social change, to the rights of minorities, and to an end to colonialism. Some of these hopes were realized after 1945—within Britain once the Labour Party had come to power, and in a United Nations that had a much broader conception of its role than the League had had.

The interwar period yields more than one lesson. It has often been read as a case study in the need for military preparedness. In this reading of history, the experiments in disarmament launched in the period were ineffective, because they weakened the will of the Western powers to resist the dictators. However, it would be more accurate to say that the real trouble with the approaches of that era toward disarmament and conciliation is that if those approaches went far enough to satisfy public demands for progress, they did not go far enough to matter. The system remained, indeed it was able to coopt the disarmament process, and put it to its own uses.

NOTES

1. Michael Howard, *War in European History* (New York: Oxford University Press, 1976), ix.

2. H. G. Wells, *Washington and the Riddle of Peace* (New York, 1922), 18–19.

3. Donald S. Birn, *The League of Nations Union 1918–1945* (New York: Oxford University Press, 1981), 173.

15

Structuralism and World Peace

W. Warren Wagar

Peace scholars sometimes draw a distinction between "structural" and "interpersonal" approaches to the analysis and resolution of armed conflict. The dichotomy may be false, but like so many others, it has merit because it exposes perceptions. It puts on the table, for all to see, the growing rift between scholars who view the peace process macroscopically and those with microscopic vision. The two groups explore the same realities, but through different lenses. The dichotomy also draws, or at least implies, moral distinctions. In this case the villains are the hard, unemotional, tough-minded social scientists who argue that wars result from the mechanical operation of certain social structures, fundamentally economic and political, and that peace will break out only when profound changes occur in these structures. By contrast, the heroes (or heroines, since the macroscopists are mostly men, and the microscopists include a large proportion of women) contend that society—and peaceful or warlike behavior—originates in the psyche, the self, the family, and the clan. What happens there gives shape and impetus to our behavior in nations, economies, and the world community. For the heroines (the majority of microscopists are), peace will break out only when profound changes occur at the level of personality and interpersonal relations.

The structuralists, so far, have done most of the talking and publishing; and, lest we take the macroscopic/microscopic dichotomy too literally, it should be added that structuralism also flourishes in studies

of the human microcosm, as illustrated by the many schools of behav-
iorist psychology, sociobiology, and structuralist anthropology, that
share the hard, unemotional, tough-minded posture of all the "villains"
in political science, economics, and sociology. By reducing human behavior to the mechanical operation of what might be called microstruc-
tures, these schools can be accused of committing the same atrocities
as their counterparts in the other social sciences—in effect they banish
consciousness from the peace process. It can even be argued that the
structuralist approach is part of the problem, not part of the solution,
because it reduces human beings to objects, to automata behaving like
ants or bees, and this is precisely what ails warlike societies. In short,
they transform men and women into faceless instruments of state policy, into *means* rather than *ends*. Anyone who viewed a fellow man or
woman as a unique, ultimately spiritual entity possessed of will, consciousness, and choice (so the argument runs), would find it difficult,
and perhaps impossible to clothe that person in a uniform and march
him or her into battle with a million others, to assert the eternal
grandeur of Graustark, or the master race, or the working class.

Dyed-in-the-wool structuralists, of course, have a response to such
charges. As a historian, who deals professionally with the gray area
between free will and necessity, with the mysterious interplay of
unique self and systemic forces, the author of this chapter is anything
but an ideal representative of the structuralist school, but he will do
what he can to rescue it from the calumnies heaped upon it by ardent
interpersonalists. Surely the structuralists are correct in the assertion
that social structures exist, have a life and dynamic all their own, and
determine a great part of our behavior as historical beings living in
this or that unique point in time, in this or that corner of the world,
and in this or that class and cultural configuration. No one should be
happy to make such an observation. The final goal of human endeavor
is an order of society in which the power of structures to condition
behavior is reduced to the barest minimum, and necessity has been
replaced by freedom. But meanwhile, our humanity is hugely compro-
mised by our animality. With every word we speak, every gesture we
make, every value we cherish, and every ritual we re-enact, we betray
our place in social time and circumstance.

In brief, the best defense that structuralists can offer for their views
is candor. It would be more pleasant, and indeed the world might seem
like a better place, if we could shake off the conviction that human
behavior is so massively determined by structures, but, in fact, it is.
To be sure, structures are never static. They move in three ways,
according to their own internal logic. That is, they move mechanically,
repeating themselves over and over again; they move cyclically, which
is just a more elaborate sort of repetition; and they move along an

evolutionary path, in never repeated stages of world-historical development. In this third kind of movement, structures also undergo changes, and become other structures.

Drawing on the ideas of structuralists as different from one another as Karl Marx, H. G. Wells, Arnold J. Toynbee, Theodore Von Laue, and Immanuel Wallerstein, let us take as our guiding assumption that in modern times humankind has advanced from a congeries of relatively separate civilizations to a world order. This world order is a single organism in an economic sense, but divided into rival polities and a variety of traditional cultures in varying stages of internal decay as they struggle to withstand, unsuccessfully in the long run, the manifold pressures of modernization. Some polities thrive in an economic context that is nominally capitalist, others in a nominally socialist context. But the differences between them are more ideological than real. In fact, all belong to the capitalist global economy, whether the capital is owned by states, corporations, or a mix of the two.

In the modern world system, it becomes imperative to speak of world wars and world peace. Wars can still be, and usually are, localized geographically, but because of the profound interconnectedness of the global economy, and the many other unifying forces at work in the system, they inevitably involve all of us. Thus, even the current civil wars in Central America, just like the late wars in the Falklands or in Vietnam, are in a quite tangible sense world wars. The difficulty with moving from world war to world peace in the version of the structuralist perspective argued here is that warfare is not incidental or extrinsic to the modern world system, but part and parcel of it. The various peace movements that have flourished in this century are programmed for futility because they oppose only fragments of the system: Weapons, or certain weapons; military contractors, or certain military contractors; war ministries, or certain war ministries; and capitalism or nationalism or fascism, or certain kinds or aspects of each; the list is endless. Remedies proposed almost invariably stress how little of the world will be changed if this or that remedy is adopted; how the remedy will make the world safe for everything else we already do and have, including such things as the "American way of life" or the "one true church" or "our country right or wrong."

But if warfare is intrinsic to the modern world system, as it was also intrinsic to most earlier civilizations, then no amount of pruning or grafting, even if achieved, will make any difference at all in the long run. Likewise, attempts to create a new kind of self or family or community more pacific, less exploitative, and more androgynous, will also fail, or be unavailing, because they will leave the system intact, just as the supposed conversion of Russia or China or Cambodia to socialism did not and could not remove Russia or China or Cambodia from the capitalist world market, with all of its pressures and irresistible temptations. This is not to say that conventional peace movements can do nothing. They may help prevent or delay or terminate specific wars, when circumstances are otherwise favorable. They may help to make wars less destructive or brutal, when circumstances are otherwise favorable. They may help keep the conscience of humankind alive in days of wrath.

But if warfare is intrinsic to the modern world system, it follows that only when the modern world system itself passes away, through world-historical processes that we as individuals and as peace-lovers can perhaps accelerate at least a little (provided we understand them), will there be any hope at all of a lasting world peace. The essential precondition of peace is the replacement of the modern economic and political system, which is a warfare system, with something fundamentally and profoundly different. Indeed, this is the deeper meaning of the all too familiar phrase, "working for peace." It may even be necessary to find a new word or phrase for "peace" itself. In our dictionaries, "peace" is simply the absence of war, the absence of armed conflict between and within states, which so far has meant the dialectical moment that lies between wars, the interwar phase of the war process.

What we really seek when we use this inadequate word is a higher species of world order in which the structures that breed and require war no longer exist, in which it is no longer possible for sovereign states to advance their interests by the resort to armed force, because they will no longer be sovereign. In short, what we really mean by "peace" is *life*, the life that can be lived only when the war option has been withdrawn, the life not between wars but *after* war. Such a view is in some ways discouraging. It tells us that willing and wishing are not enough—the existing world system, with its capitalism, nationalism, militarism, and all the rest, has to shake itself apart, has to decay and disintegrate from within, before we can bid it farewell, although we may be able to aid this process and, in effect, speed it along. Also, because any realistic analysis of the prevailing system discloses that the system is still in most respects quite robust, it follows that we have a long and dangerous wait on our hands, even if we are able by our own efforts to hasten its demise. The system is probably strong enough to last at least another century, and longer than that if not effectually opposed.

Redefining peace as the life possible in an integrated postnational world order is discouraging, finally, because if we want to advance from here to there safely and expeditiously, we must double and redouble our efforts to understand the dynamics of the prevailing system. This means herculean feats of learning and research, directed not just at global capitalism or any other single component of the system, but at the system as a whole—economic, political, and cultural. We need to know how the system works so that we can do whatever is feasible to prevent a terminal nuclear war, and accelerate the collapse of the system. And we all know how much easier it is to carry a placard, or hold a conference, than to sit down and engage in protracted study!

But in time, in the fullness of time, in what the early Christians liked to call the *kairos* (meaning, the *right* time), when the modern capitalist-nationalist system has exhausted its possibilities and lost its paralyzing grip on the loyalties of the mass of the world's people, the peace movement of the future may well adopt a tactic for which the appropriate term is "civilian-based *offense*." Peace scholars are already familiar with civilian-based *defense*, the idea promoted in the United States by Gene Sharp and others, which asserts that if the civilians of a nation are trained, equipped, and prepared to carry on a relentless campaign of non-violent obstructive resistance to any would-be invader, the need for professional armies largely disappears, and countries organized to mount such a defense can do without them altogether. This strategy might actually work in the case of selected small neutral countries, faced with invasion by neighbors trying to stage attacks on other countries from their territory. If adopted, which seems highly improbable, it might even constitute a better defense against Soviet aggression than the NATO "shield" for the countries of Western Europe now allied with the United States, although how it can succeed in repelling an attack by ballistic missiles in the event of a major world war remains unclear. But civilian-based *offense* speaks of something quite different: Concerted militant action by citizens, preferably organized as a worldwide political party with aboveground or underground formations or both, as local conditions dictate, to replace existing governments and corporate usurpers of public wealth with a revolutionary world republic of workingpeople.

Needless to say, under the social conditions of late capitalism, the term "workingpeople" (as Rudolf Bahro and others have contended) must be stretched to include anyone who works for a living. Most so-called middle-class people, from managers, technicians, and salespersons to doctors and lawyers, belong to the contemporary working class if their principal source of income is payment for labor. In the advanced capitalist societies, proletarians in the nineteenth-century sense are clearly a vanishing breed, and may some day vanish altogether.

Yet there is no need to shy away from the nineteenth-century sense of the word "revolution." Of all the dreams and false hopes that dog peace movements, the saddest, in some ways, is the fantasy that the prevailing world system and its various national state components are likely to dismantle themselves, or at least surrender their monopoly of armed forces, if citizens just implore them often enough to do so. What we oppose is not a collection of fools and drones (although certain recent denizens of the White House may appear to have fit that description), but rather a fairly well-organized worldwide network of politicians, bureaucrats, generals, and corporate moguls who know exactly what they are doing, and who have the muscle and money to do it and keep on doing it for generations to come. If these potentates are to be replaced with an authentic worldwide democracy, working-people must be prepared to form an oppositional system no less well organized or powerful, and no less resolved to use whatever means are required to build a new world order without exploitation, and without war. This will be an immense revolutionary task. It will involve electoral politics wherever such things are tolerated, but also active and passive civil disobedience, including general strikes and selective use (if absolutely necessary) of armed force. It will require vigorous cooperation across national and ethnic frontiers. A movement to transform the world is destined to fail if it does not swiftly become worldwide.

The revolution will also demand the wisdom and patience to know when to act, and to act when the time is right and not before. It must carry on its work in the full realization that a century or more of struggle may be needed to achieve its goals. We are speaking of a race that can be won only by long-distance runners, not by sprinters bent on finishing in a blaze of sudden glory. Continued and intensified peace activism of a more conventional sort is essential in the interim, to try to avert a terminal third world war, which may break out at any moment, before we can hope to forestall it by long-run strategies. It may even be desirable to draw up contingency plans for action in a postapocalyptic world, should our efforts to prevent such a holocaust fail. If there are survivors, at least in the Southern Hemisphere, the opportunity to unify them and save what is left of civilization should not be missed.

But conventional peace activism cannot give us enduring world peace. At most it can buy us time. Nor can crusades to change interpersonal behavior by instilling peacelike habits of mind and heart succeed in a world system predicated on exploitation and the warfare state. Even structuralist remedies for war will prove equally futile, unless they take into account the holistic nature of the modern world system. The system is all of a piece. Its propensity for warmaking cannot be extracted, as one would extract a diseased tooth. If we want a warless world, we must be prepared, when the opportunity arises, to raze the modern world system all the way down to its foundations, and build anew.

16

A Rational Basis for Hope

Charles Hauss

When I teach about France or the Soviet Union, my students are happy if I explain what is happening, and reach conclusions they find intellectually satisfying. Not peace studies. Students flock to courses on questions of war and peace, because, like so many adults, they are frightened and are searching for some reason to believe that there will be a future. They want a rational basis for hope. Providing that hope will require a fundamental shift in what the peace movement and peace educators do. We have succeeded in reaching a first goal by convincing the vast majority of people and political leaders around the world that we cannot fight and survive a nuclear war. Now we face a new challenge. The time has come to talk and teach and write less about the problems we face, and focus instead on how we can solve them.

As Peter Sandman and JoAnn Valenti put it:

> People require short term achievable goals as benchmarks along the way to build confidence that progress is being made. But progress toward what? While the movement has done an excellent job of articulating visions of nuclear apocalypse, it has only just begun the much harder job of envisioning a plausible world that has renounced nuclear weapons. It is in that new vision that new activists will find their hope and against that vision that they will measure their efficacy.[1]

If my experience is representative, convincing people (students and adults alike) that there is reason for hope, and that they can contribute to the creation of a more peaceful and just world, then it has to start with Sandman and Valenti's notion of "envisioning a plausible world that has renounced nuclear weapons," but go even farther. When I began teaching about the threat of nuclear war, I found myself unable to give my students any good reason to be optimistic. I helped them analyze the best ideas of the arms control experts,[2] but those discussions invariably led to the conclusion that the experts did not have the answer. Their suggestion of negotiating more treaties, improving communications with the Soviet Union, or taking advantage of some technological breakthroughs, might well reduce the risks of war. But, my students and I demanded more, because we felt that reducing the risks just would not be enough, given the fact that the very existence of humanity is at stake.

Frustrated, I cast my intellectual net wider, and began seeing that the danger lies not just in nuclear weapons, but also in a broader global crisis that cannot be solved by our leaders in Washington, Moscow, or Geneva alone. What they do, of course, is critical, but the underlying cause of the crisis, and the way out of it, lie far deeper in basic perceptions and assumptions we all share, and which governs how we deal with conflict at the interpersonal and international levels, and all other levels. It is that paradigm or basic way of thinking about the world that has us in trouble, and only by shifting to another one that enables us to end war, and overcome the global crisis, will we be able to survive and solve the seemingly unsolvable problems that plague our lives as we near the end of the twentieth century. What that new paradigm might be, and how we can turn the dream of a world beyond war into reality is the subject of this chapter.

THE GLOBAL CRISIS

We find ourselves at an unprecedented moment in history. For the first time, a species is capable of rendering *itself* extinct. Never before have we been able to use the weapons of war to threaten the end of civilization. Never before have we altered the climate in ways that will harm all life for centuries, if not forever. Never before have we thinned the layer of ozone that protects us from lethal solar radiation. Never before has acid rain killed so many lakes and forests. Never before have there been so many people on the earth, and never before have so many yearned for food, shelter, dignified work, and simple human respect. We are unraveling the delicate social, political, and ecological threads that hold civilization together.[3] The prospect of our extinction is frightening. Psychologists say that it deadens many of us, leaving us fearful of the future, unable to see a way of overcoming the threats to our planet or the stresses of our daily lives—psychic numbing, future shock, alienation, the turned-off or me generation. All of these, and more, are terms used to describe a growing fraction of the world's population that seems to have lost hope not only in the future, but also asks will there be a future at all?[4]

There is a way out that begins with the first of two common denominators underlying life in what we call the nuclear age—the changed role of war. For the last two hundred years, war has been thought of, in the terms coined by the great German military theorist, von Clausewitz, as an extension of normal politics through other means. It was a way, we thought, of getting our way if nicer methods failed to work. That is no longer the case. We can no longer use war to settle our differences. Most of us know that a nuclear war would end life as we know it on this planet. More and more of us realize, too, that the conventional wars being fought around the globe have turned into bloody and costly stalemates that never put to rest the issues that sparked them in the first place.

But in the nuclear age, the problem of war runs deeper yet. Even without a shot being fired, war takes an unacceptable toll. There is, most obviously, that fear we all live with, that some day all the safeguards will collapse, and the nuclear holocaust will begin. There are also the massive and increasingly unbearable social and economic costs to the preparation for war, that we see in everything from the unfilled potholes in our streets, to the unfilled stomachs of millions of children in the Third World. The governments of the world spend approximately a trillion dollars a year on the military, costs that are graphically demonstrated by Harry G. Shaffer:

With that amount of money . . . we could build a $75,000 house, place it on $5,000 worth of land, furnish it with $10,000 worth of furniture, put a $10,000 car in the garage—and give this to each and every family . . . in Kansas, Missouri, Iowa, Nebraska, Oklahoma and Arkansas. . . . After having done this, we would still have enough out of our trillion dollars to build a $10 million library for each of 250 cities and towns throughout the six-state region. After having done all that, we would still have enough money left out of our trillion to put aside, at ten per cent annual interest, a sum of money that would pay a salary of $25,000 per year for an army of 10,000 nurses, the same for an army of 10,000 teachers, and an annual cash allowance of $5,000 for each and every family throughout that six-state region—not just for one year but forever.[5]

The effect of war on the minds and bodies of people, who may be thousands of miles from the fighting, has reached a level that we just cannot accept, and, in fact, is breeding the anger and frustration that will be the seeds of more wars in the future.

The problem of war does not stop with conflict between nations. It includes all conflict in which violence—psychological or economic, as well as physical—is used by people to impose their will on others. Viewed in this way, war becomes not just a problem "out there" caused by "them," or even something only perpetrated by men who beat their wives, or adults who molest their children, but something we all share in our daily lives—in the way we deal with our families, friends, and fellow workers. Our very language is filled with examples. "Wars" between the sexes, races, or classes, the warlike imagery of our sporting events and even "battles" of rock and roll bands. We also need to think of our continued destruction of the environment as a form of war. It is war because it is so destructive. It is also war because it reflects the assumption that we can do what we want to someone or something else, without thinking about the consequences of our actions. In short, any attempt at exploitation of country over country, group over group, individual over individual, or humans over the rest of nature is a kind of war. We are at war against each other, against ourselves, and against our environment. At first glance, seeing our difficulties in this light might make things seem even more depressing. After all, we have had little success in tackling any one of these problems.

However, if we take one more step in examining war, and ask what leads us to act this way, we can find the second common denominator, and with it, a ray of hope. Each of these kinds of wars has the same underlying cause, a set of values and assumptions about how we "have to" deal with conflict. The problem lies not in conflict itself, which is an inevitable outgrowth of human interaction, but in the way we deal with it. It begins with two assumptions from which everything else flows: that in most areas of life there are not enough resources to go around; and that individuals, the groups and nations they form, pursue their self-interests. The two together amount to a "tinderbox." If you and I are both out to get as much money, power, or prestige as we can, and there is not enough for both of us, we are bound to compete—to enter into conflict. That makes conflict something neither of us look forward to. Since I *know* you want what I want, I have to be wary of your actions and intentions. It is all but impossible to avoid thinking of conflict in adversarial, or "we" versus "they" terms. Since we both want the same thing that is in short supply, we assume that only one of us can win, and I am going to do everything possible to see that it is not you. Since neither of us looks forward to losing, the conflict will end only when one of us imposes our will on the other, and that means employing force of one kind or another. In fact, political scientists define power as getting someone to do *something they otherwise wouldn't do*. Assuming someone has to lose, I will strain every nerve and muscle to make sure it is not me. When those with whom we disagree seem to do something that could benefit us, we dare not trust them. We fear that friendly gestures are probably just tricks designed to lull us into letting our guard down. We feel the need to be eternally vigilant and suspicious.

At the heart of such a view of the world is what psychologists call the "image of the enemy."[6] At least, when conflict becomes intense, we see a world divided between "us" and "them." "We" are good; "they" are dangerous. Whatever the real conflicts between individuals, groups, or nations, dividing the world into "we" and "they" turns all parties into caricatures, and rules out the possibility of genuine resolution of the issues that spawned a conflict in the first place. Once this dehumanizing process is allowed to take hold, people extend their differences far out of proportion. Constructive response becomes more and more difficult as both sides blame and then depersonalize the other. Each becomes convinced that the other is out to do it in, and cannot be expected to behave in a civilized fashion.

Our identities are bound up in what defines "us" *as opposed to* "them." If I define myself as white, orientals or blacks must be something less than other human beings who are my equals. If I define myself as management, labor becomes the opposition, rather than the people with whom I work. If I define myself as Iraqi, the Iranians can seem different and dangerous enough, that I can justify not only killing them, but do so with chemical weapons. It is not the way we think all the time, or even the way we would like to think. But it is how must of us tend to act when the "going gets tough."[7] We react to "them" as something to be feared, something that is likely to harm us only if we are not as vigilant as we can be. Why else would we turn our fellow people into something less than human, into stereotypes that look like cardboard figurines?

This way of thinking opens the door to violence, despite our best intentions to avoid it. Under the circumstances, it is not surprising that we think of conflict as destructive, to be avoided whenever possible. We are not evil or uncaring people, and it seems natural that we would try to stay away from situations that we assume will only make a bad situation worse. But by putting conflict on the back burner rather than facing it, we actually are making matters worse. The anger, the fears, the antagonisms do not disappear, instead, they intensify, the chasms widen, and the costs we think we will incur by losing grow. So, when we finally do have to confront the conflict, the stakes are higher and then we are farther apart. All that increases the likelihood that we will panic, or misunderstand the actions of the other side, or, overreact to what it is doing.

Violence remains the ultimate recourse we know we can, and may have to, turn to. If intense forms of conflict can have only one winner and one loser, and if we know that this will happen only if one side can force the other to go along, we *know* that violence is something we will have to employ from time to time. It is because we *know* that only one of us can win a struggle that we each consider to be of a life and death nature, that we read the worst into each other's intentions. It is because we *know* we are competing for the same scarce resources that we assume peace comes only through strength, that we must match an eye for an eye and a tooth for a tooth. Again, violence is not the only outcome. But as the oh-so-apt cliche puts it: When push comes to shove, is it surprising that we so frequently respond with violence? Fear of attack, of outsiders, of differences, and of the unknown, lead to the assumption that when someone we think of as fundamentally different threatens us, we have no choice but to respond with a violent attitude or act. It is difficult for people to grasp the idea that there is this single set of values and assumptions that leads to war and violence in all its forms. Many find the whole idea of a "mode of thinking" difficult to grasp. Some have trouble seeing evidence that it exists, still others cannot easily see how the way we think shapes the way we act.

To help people get a first glimpse of the importance of the way we think, I often ask a class or community group to do the following exercise. I start by asking them to discuss why the United States and Soviet Union have had so much trouble working out their differences. Invariably, they come up with two sets of reasons. First, there are the objective differences between the two: Culture, history, language, political, social, and economic structures, and ideologies. Second, there are the forces that keep us from being able to handle those differences effectively: Fear, hostility, miscommunication, lack of trust, and suspicion about each other's intentions. Then I ask them to discuss a divorce situation. The same two lists emerge. There are always real differences in interests, personalities, or tastes between two spouses. However, as with the United States and Soviet Union, what keeps a marriage from working are those same attitudes of fear, hostility, and suspicion. Those attitudes are the root cause of our problems, and therefore, what we have to change.

NEW THINKING

How are we going to change the way we think? The so-called "realists" are convinced that our present way of thinking and acting is inescapable. It is how things are and how they have to be. Pleas for a new, different, and better way of handling conflict are dismissed as dreams or fantasies. But things do not have to be that way. Paradigms can be changed, and indeed, must be changed when they have outlived their utility, as is so obviously the case today. Throughout history, when a crisis became so overwhelming that it threatened what people held dear, they developed a response to get them beyond it. That response took the form of change, and never came easily. It always involved shedding ways of thinking and acting that were so deeply ingrained, that many people were not even aware of them. And there have always been doubters, who denied people could change. But the fact of the matter is, people have always been able to do it.

That is the situation we find ourselves in today. The paradigm we use today is deeply embedded, but not etched in stone. I see that each time I lead one of those discussions about U.S.-Soviet relations and divorce. As people begin to see the root cause of our problems more clearly, they also begin to talk about examples of international and interpersonal conflict, in which participants have been able to overcome those subjective differences, and truly settle their differences in ways that satisfy everyone involved. Those discussions mirror what researchers are increasingly finding: That our violence and aggression are learned behavior and we have grown more cooperative, not more competitive, over the centuries.[8] It is in those research findings, and in those everyday experiences, that we can begin to see the basis for hope in the future.

At the heart of this new way of thinking is the second common denominator of the nuclear age, our growing understanding that we are a single, totally interdependent people, sharing a single, totally interdependent planet. Transportation by jet and communication by satellite, for instance, have made the world seem smaller than ever before. The London stock exchange is open twenty-four hours a day to service the global financial markets. The planet we call home is a single environment, a single life support system for every creature who lives here. Our problems transcend national boundaries and cannot be overcome by any individual nation acting on its own. No one nation, alone, can maintain an environment that is hospitable to life. No one nation, alone, can lift all the suffering and indignity experienced by billions of human beings. No one nation, alone, can dismantle the system of independent and fearful countries, which have embraced nuclear weapons and the preparation for war, hoping to find security. Together, we created these problems, and we will have to solve them together. Today's problems require cooperation across national boundaries and other lines of division, yet, that is not how we have dealt with them. Our refusal to think about our actions in terms of global repercussions is at the root of all our problems. Our continued reliance on pre-nuclear age thinking is making things worse, not better. We release huge quantities of carbon dioxide and chlorofluorocarbons into the air, without thinking about the greenhouse effect or the ozone layer. We, in the developed world, consume a tremendous proportion of the earth's wealth and resources, without thinking about how little we are leaving to be spread among so many others. We continue supporting wars around the planet without really thinking about how much destruction they cause and how little they really accomplish. We maintain an arsenal of nuclear weapons without thinking how vulnerable it has made everything that humans have worked for over the centuries.

What is needed is a shift to a paradigm that puts the planet and our interdependence first. If the thoughtlessness of our narrow, selfish views of the world lies at the heart of our deepest troubles, then learning to think from broader, global perspectives can become the key to their solutions. Doing so will bring our thoughts and actions into line with what we now know the world to be like, and seeing that we are one, that we are all in this together, will lead us to act in ways that will take us away from war and toward something far better. The planet has proved to be an emotionally powerful symbol of our age. Astronauts who have had the privilege of seeing the earth from space talk about experiencing it as a whole without frames or boundaries. The pictures they have sent back have become an inspiration for us all, helping us to see both the beauty and fragility of life. As Joseph Campbell put it in a remarkable series of interviews with Bill Moyers, "new myths"— and with them new paradigms and operating principles—emerge out of new dreams and new realities. In the nuclear age, the new myth and the new inspiration will be the planet itself. As Campbell also said, "The only myth that's going to be worth thinking about in the immediate future is one that's talking about the planet, not this city, not these people, but the planet and everybody on it."[9]

Basing our lives on the reality of our interdependence will require us to rethink everything, including what success, prosperity, and security mean. As Anatoly Gromyko said regarding national security:

In a world of nuclear overkill and growing interdependence, it is impossible to secure a unilateral advantage for oneself to the detriment of the other side without ultimately impairing one's own interests. Recognition of this basic fact provides the basis for establishing one of the main principles of the new way of thinking. The stark realities of the nuclear age demand a revision of such basic notions as strength, superiority, victory, and security.... Genuine security in the present nuclear age must always mean universal international security.[10]

Putting the planet first rules out violence, in all its forms, as a way of settling disputes. In an interdependent world, everything we do affects everyone else, while their actions affect us in return.[11] In short, violence today lays the seeds for more, and often, worse violence in the medium or long term. There's nothing new to this idea. Each major religious tradition has its own version of the golden rule. But until we began to think in terms of whole, interdependent systems, these rules remained ethical principles which "realistic" observers thought could not be implemented in daily life. Now, however, we see that those principles are not just ethically but empirically correct as well.

Unless we find "win-win" solutions that benefit all parties in a conflict, it will not be resolved, and the potential for violence will still exist. Recently, researchers have discovered that almost any conflict is subject to a "win-win" solution, and dozens of techniques have been developed to help people get there.[12] But even more important than the techniques are the principles that grow out of our interdependence, four of which seem to be at the heart of all successful conflict resolution.

First, we have to take the initiative to address conflict. Too often, we ignore it, hoping somehow it will disappear, or be taken care of by someone else. We have all read about people who sit back and do nothing as a crime is being committed or an argument turns violent. We have all been in situations where we could have done something, but did not, assuming that someone else would. Because we now know that everything we do, and do not do, matters, we really have no choice but to act, to be the ones who begin the process of finding the options that will satisfy all of us. This will mean actively confronting all the problems responsible for the global crisis. If we are to have peace, we will have to deal with injustice, unmet human needs, the decay of the environment, and all the other unresolved issues that are the breeding grounds for violence today. We will have to become initiators of change, calling into question the practices that lead to global crisis and posing alternatives that could lead to something better.[13]

Second, we have to commit ourselves to an attitude of good will. As we have seen, our current way of thinking leads us to blame others for conflict and turn those with whom we disagree into dehumanized enemies. To think this way all but closes the door on successful conflict resolution, because it absolves us of any responsibility and deepens the divisions between us even more. Maintaining good will toward someone does not solve a problem, but it makes a solution possible. Maintaining good will during conflict entails a realistic acknowledgement that we may disagree, but we are both responsible for the conflict, and it can be resolved only if we work together. Good will is not some "sappy sweet" denial of our differences, but an understanding that no matter how deep our disagreements, we are part of the same human family that has created, and now must resolve its conflicts.

Third, thinking globally means taking responsibility for creating a world that works for everyone. A world beyond war will have to be one in which the basic needs of all people, and the life support system on which we all depend, are concerns for all of us. If not, we will continue breeding the resentment and ill will that has us on the brink of extinction today. Not only will we have to become more involved in dealing with the problems of the planet, we also will have to look at them in a new light. Instead of asking what is best for "me" and "mine," we will need to develop policies that are best for all. Instead of looking for quick fixes and simple solutions, we will have to commit ourselves to the long haul.

Fourth, the aphorism, "think globally, act locally" has to be extended to include the conflict in our daily lives. Changing only our political thoughts and actions will not be enough. If we continue relying on blame, coercion, and violence in our daily lives, we will be helping sustain the crisis. Applying these principles in the microcosm of our personal lives can become an important testing ground for developing approaches to conflict we can adapt for use at the international level.

Thus, this new thinking will lead us in a dramatically new direction. It is, first of all, a "no" to war, and to the thinking that has brought us face-to-face with our own extinction. Even more importantly, it is a "yes" to a better future—the next step in human evolution.

NEW ACTION

While there is no simple blueprint or road map for us to follow, there are historical precedents and current events that suggest it is possible to build a world that has renounced war and settles its differences in a constructive way. If we look back at history over the last century or so, we see that lasting positive change occurs when a population reaches agreement about a new principle. When it does, two things happen. First, dramatic political changes follow in the form of new legislation, court decisions, regulations, and so on. Second, the change lasts because people have dug deeply, questioned their fundamental and basic beliefs, and discovered the need and oportunity to change.

That happened in this country as recently as the 1950s and 1960s, with our acceptance of the principle that all people are equal, regardless of race. We have, by no means, achieved anything resembling equality between the races or the sexes. Nonetheless, we have made significant progress in the last forty years, and, in how that progress was made, can be seen some signposts for paths we can take in dealing with the global crisis. Think about race relations in this country in the early 1950s. Nearly a century had passed since the end of the Civil War. Despite the efforts of thousands of men and women, there were still plenty of staunch segregationists, and most Americans, among them even those who opposed segregation, were willing to accept a value system that made blacks second-class citizens. Quickly, however, things began to change. Sparked by court decisions such as *Brown v. Topeka*, that outlawed segregated schools, and demonstrations throughout the south, millions of Americans started thinking about racism and equality. The demonstrations and the violent reaction of segregationists made the headlines, but change occurred, because millions of Americans started talking about segregation and injustice around the dinner table, at work, and wherever else they gathered. It was through those discussions, and the thinking and questioning that went into them, that people began to change their basic principles. As the pollster Daniel Yankelovich put it: "The process... proceed[s] by way of a dialogue that is so active and effective and highly charged that it leaves none of the participants untouched and unchanged. At the conclusion of such a dialogue, no person is quite the same person he or she was before the dialogue began."[14]

Once large numbers of people begin changing as a result of their participation in that kind of dialogue, the possibility of real change begins.

It was at that point that a constituency began to be built. At first, progress was slow. For most of this century, the principle that blacks and whites are equal was accepted by a small fraction of Americans, who were not especially effective at communicating their ideas to other citizens. However, they persevered, and by the late 1940s, they were beginning to attract more people. By the mid–1950s, established community leaders such as the young Dr. Martin Luther King had begun support and actively work for integration. Sociologist Everett Rogers has estimated that once a new idea has the support of approximately five percent of the population (as was probably the case with civil rights by the late 1950s) it begins to take off.[15] When important opinion leaders have taken it on, supporting a new idea becomes less risky. If Rogers is right, once it has the support of one in five of us, the idea is unstoppable. At this point, two things have happened. First, key local leaders, who shape the way the rest of us think, have come on board. Second, political leaders (even if they still have doubts) have no choice but to change. Thus, once that threshold is reached, an agreement on new principle has been reached. In the case of civil rights, both Senate Majority Leader Lyndon Johnson and Minority Leader Everett Dirksen held up civil rights legislation during the late 1950s. But by 1964, public opinion had changed enough that the two reversed their decisions and played a major role in passing the Civil Rights Act of 1964, and other key pieces of legislation.

Thus, by following this process, the impossible can be made possible, and it can be made to happen quickly. It happens whenever people engage in the dual process seen in the example of the civil rights movement. First, they begin educating each other. Second, they focus the efforts of those who have changed to create what Norman Cousins has called a "wall of insistence"—a statement that is so loud and powerful that our leaders have no choice but to respond. This is not just an historical phenomenon. All we have to do is look around us to see dozens of examples of individuals and organizations who have already begun the process of building agreements using principles developed above. One does not want to go too far in assessing the positive steps that have already been taken—this chapter, for example, was written during the most depressing weeks of the 1988 presidential campaign—but it is important to note what has happened.

To begin with, we, the people have changed. During the 1980s, almost all Americans, Soviets, and others about whom we have data, have come to the conclusion that we cannot fight and survive a nuclear war. American attitudes toward the Soviets have also shifted substantially away from the "evil empire" image that dominated the renewed cold war rhetoric of the late Carter and early Reagan years.[16] And there is little doubt that the pressure of public opinion in the United States, in Europe, and in the Soviet Union played a major role in getting the two superpowers back to the bargaining table, leading to the INF treaty. More and more of us are aware of the costs of conventional war, the military budget, and our assault against the environment.

Furthermore, the sale of millions of copies of books, such as Roger Fisher and William Ury's *Getting to Yes*,[17] M. Scott Peck's *The Road Less Traveled*,[18] and Tom Peters' *Thriving on Chaos*[19] suggest that many of us have been exposed to alternative forms of constructive conflict resolution. Admittedly, little of this has reached the political arena, but in American corporations and non-profit organizations, these ideas have at least gained a toehold.

Finally, we can even see some encouraging political changes. Most obvious is the INF treaty, which, for the first time in the nuclear age, eliminated an entire weapons system. At the Moscow summit, both President Reagan and General Secretary Gorbachev made it clear that they understood that there must not be a nuclear war, and that the two superpowers have to learn to work out their differences peacefully. It was equally clear that one of the main reasons the two superpowers were able to work out the agreement was the popular demand to reverse the arms race. During the past year, a number of wars have ended or, at least, been scaled back: Iran and Iraq, Central America, Angola, Namibia, Afghanistan. Similarly, for the first time, there is a substantial movement among Jews both in the United States and Israel, calling for non-violent resolution of the escalating conflict in the occupied territories, while the PLO has taken a major first step toward recognizing Israel's right to exist by endorsing UN General Assembly Resolution 242. There seems little doubt that we can learn to cooperate in confronting the global crisis. The first theories about nuclear winter led Soviet and American scientists to explore the frightening possibility together, and showed leaders of the poorest nations in the Third World that they, too, had to participate in the struggle to rid the world of nuclear weapons. Events such as Chernobyl show us not only that we must but that we can change. In that moment of crisis, people from around the world put aside their political differences and came to the aid of the poor men and women who were exposed to dangerous levels of radiation. And while it is but a small and insufficient first step, most of the major industrialized nations have agreed to cut their production of chlorofluorocarbons.

NEW HOPE/NEW RESPONSIBILITY

Intellectual arguments, historical analogies, and even the importance of new thinking in our personal as well as our political lives, will not be enough. That "wall of insistence" can be built only if we are able to overcome the cynicism and pessimism so many people feel today. How often do we hear, "I just don't make a difference?" Or, "What can I do, I'm no expert?" Or "Nobody has any good ideas these days?" There is no shortage of reasonable proposals for slowing down and then ending the arms race, or cleaning up the environment, or meeting the developmental needs of the southern hemisphere. There is no shortage of grass roots organizations working on these issues and/ or developing support for new thinking. Even more importantly, we all come into contact with friends, family members, and fellow workers, most of whom share the same concerns we do, and most of whom are looking for some reason to believe that there can be a better future. The fact of the matter is, the hopelessness that underlies the above questions has no basis in reality. In an interdependent world, we each make a difference, whether we want to or not. If we do not act, our inaction helps sustain the *status quo*. One's action alone, will not change the way the world works, but one can be part of a larger movement of people demanding change. And, as with the civil rights movement, progress can come quickly. If in the course of a year, each of us could convince four other people to become involved in changing the way people think, and if each of those people in turn involved four others, we could involve many people in a relatively short time.

The students in our classrooms and the adults with whom we work in our communities do come to us looking for hope. The hope lies not just in Sandman and Valenti's vision of a world that has renounced nuclear weapons, but in adopting the new paradigm, living it every minute of every day, helping others see the need for change, and building that "wall of insistence" that will forge global agreement on these new principles, obliging our leaders to join in with us. Because we have the capacity for vision, because we can foresee alternate versions of the future, we can be masters of our own destinies. Time and again in the past, human beings have succeeded in meeting a seemingly impossible challenge because they believed that something could happen and, living as if it were possible, worked to make it real. Today, the burden is with each of us. We cannot depend on politicians. They can do very little without the strong political will of the people behind them. *We* set the direction and issue the mandate for change. Until new political candidates come along who will willingly lead us in a new direction, we each need to exercise our own individual responsibility. Whatever our talents are, there is an urgent need for them. We do not all have to do the same thing, but we must all do something, because ours is the generation that will determine whether humanity survives or not. In fact, we are limited in making a difference only by our imagination and creativity. It is our move.

NOTES

I would like to thank Arthur Ledoux and Winslow Myers, who are writing *The Challenge to Change: Building a World Beyond War* with me. All the ideas and many of the words in this chapter are theirs as much as mine.

1. Peter Sandman and JoAnn Valenti, "Scared Stiff—Or Scared Into Action," *Bulletin of the Atomic Scientists* (January 1986):15.

2. For the most compelling works along these lines, see the following two books: Joseph Nye, Graham Allison, and Albert Carnesale, eds, *Hawks, Doves, and Owls* (New York: W. W. Norton, 1985); and Nye, Allison, and Carnesale, eds., *Fateful Visions*, (Cambridge, Mass.: Ballinger, 1988).

3. See, for example, Rushworth Kidder, *An Agenda for the Twenty First Century*. (Cambridge: MIT Press, 1987); and "Agenda 2000," *Christian Science Monitor* (July 25, 1988): special report.

4. The literature on these themes is immense. Two especially useful recent works are: *Psychology Today* (June, 1988) special issue; and, David S. Greenwald and Steven J. Zeitlin, *No Reason to Talk about It: Families Confront the Nuclear Taboo*. (New York: W. W. Norton, 1987).

5. Harry G. Shaffer, "A Trillion Dollars," *Republic Airlines Magazine* (May 1986):24.

6. Sam Keen, *Faces of the Enemy: Reflections of the Hostile Imagination*, (San Francisco: Harper and Row, 1986); and, Jerome D. Frank and Andrei Melville, "The Image of the Enemy and the Process of Change," in Anatoly Gromyko and Martin Hellman, *Breakthrough: Emerging New Thinking: Soviet and Western Scholars Issue a Challenge to Build a World Beyond War* (New York: Walker; Moscow: Novosti, 1987), 199–208.

7. For an intriguing discussion about the use of this paradigm in economics, biology, and psychology, see Barry Schwartz, *The Battle for Human Nature* (New York: W. W. Norton, 1986).

8. In particular, the "Seville Statement," issued by a panel of leading psychologists and other scientists sum up much of that research.

9. Joseph Campbell with Bill Moyers, *The Power of Myth* (New York: Doubleday, 1988), 32.

10. Anatoly Gromyko, "Security for All in the Nuclear Age," in Gromyko and Hellman, eds., *Breakthrough*, 113.

11. The most accessible presentation of our interdependence and its broader implications remains Fritjof Capra, *The Turning Point* (New York: Bantam, New Age, 1983). This whole line of reasoning is an extension of systems theory, which is often criticized by the left and the peace studies community for being inherently conservative. That is the case in large part because the social scientists who imported systems theory from the "hard" sciences rarely, if ever, discussed "eufuncutional" systems that can grow and become literally greater than the sum of their parts.

12. Most influential is the work of Roger Fisher. See Roger Fisher and William Ury, *Getting to Yes: Negotiating Agreement without Giving In* (New York: Penguin, 1981); and, Roger Fisher and Scott Brown, *Getting Together: Building a Relationship that Gets to Yes* (New York: Houghton Mifflin, 1988). Also see Robert Axelrod, *The Evolution of Cooperation.* (New York: Basic Books, 1984).

13. See George Lakey, *Positive Peace-Making* (Philadelphia: New Society Publishers, 1987); and Gene Sharp, *The Politics of Non-Violent Action* (Boston: P. Sargent, 1973).

14. Daniel Yankelovich, "How the Public Learns the Public's Business," *The Kettering Review* (Winter, 1985).

15. Everett Rogers, *The Diffusion of Innovation* (New York: Free Press, 1983). Also see Rogers, "Diffusion of the Idea of Beyond War," in Gromyko and Hellman, eds., *Breakthrough*, 240–48.

16. See especially Daniel Yankelovich and Sidney Harman, *Starting with the People* (New York: Houghton Mifflin, 1988); and Daniel Yankelovich and Richard Smoke, "America's 'New Thinking'." *Foreign Affairs* (Fall 1988):1–17.

17. Fisher and Ury, *Getting to Yes.*

18. M. Scott Peck, *The Road Less Traveled* (New York: Harper, Touchstone, 1980).

19. Tom Peters, *Thriving on Chaos: Handbook for a Management Revolution* (New York: Alfred A. Knopf, 1987).

Selected Bibliography

Allison, Graham T., Albert Carnesale, and Joseph Nye, Jr., eds. *Hawks, Doves, and Owls: An Agenda for Avoiding Nuclear War*. New York: W. W. Norton & Co., 1985.
———. *Fateful Visions*. Cambridge, Mass.: Ballinger, 1988.
Amin, Samir, et al. *Dynamics of Global Crisis*, New York: Monthly Review Press, 1982.
Arendt, Hannah. *On Violence*. New York: Harcourt Brace Jovanovich, 1969.
———. "Thinking and Moral Considerations: A Lecture." *Social Research* (October 1971):417–46.
Axelrod, Robert. *The Evolution of Cooperation*. New York: Basic Books, 1984.
Bahro, Rudolf. *The Alternative in Eastern Europe*. London: Times Books, 1978.
Baines, James. "The Peace Paradigm," in *The Whole Earth Papers*. 1, no. 1, reprinted 1983 and published by Patricia Mische, Global Education Associates, 522 Park Ave., East Orange, NJ 07017.
Beer, Francis A. *Peace Against War*. San Francisco: W. H. Freeman & Co., 1981.
Bercovitch, Jacob. *Social Conflicts and Third Parties: Strategies for Conflict Resolution*. Boulder, Colo.: Westview Press, 1984.
Beyond War. *Beyond War: A New Way of Thinking*. Palo Alto, Calif., 1985.
Birn, Donald. *The League of Nations Union 1918–1945*. New York: Oxford University Press, 1981.
Boulding, Elise. *The Underside of History: A View of Women Through Time*. Boulder, Colo.: Westview Press, 1976.
Braudel, Fernand. *Le Mediterranee et le monde mediterraneen a l'epoque de Philippe II*. 2d rev. and aug. ed. 2 vols. (Paris, 1966); trans. by S. Reynolds

as *The Mediterranean and the Mediterranean World in the Age of Philip II*. 2 vols. (London: 1972–1973).

Brock-Utne, Birgit. *Educating for Peace: A Feminist Perspective*. New York: Pergamon Press, 1985.

Caldicott, Helen. *Missile Envy: The Arms Race and Nuclear War*. Toronto: Bantam Books, 1986.

Camus, Albert. *The Myth of Sisyphus*. New York: Vintage, 1955.

Capra, Fritjof. *The Turning Point*. New York: Bantam, New Age, 1983.

Carr, Edward Hallett. *What Is History?* New York: Alfred A. Knopf, 1962.

Carter, Jimmy. *Keeping Faith*. New York: Bantam Books, 1982.

Chodorow, Nancy. *The Reproduction of Mothering: Psychoanalysis and the Sociology of Gender*. Berkeley: University of California Press, 1978.

Dinnerstein, Dorothy. *The Mermaid and the Minotaur: Sexual Arrangements and Human Malaise*. New York: Harper & Row, 1976.

Dougherty, James E. and Robert L. Pfaltzgraff. *Contending Theories of International Relations*. New York: Harper & Row, 1981.

Dyson, Freeman. *Weapons and Hope*. New York: Harper & Row, 1984.

Easlea, Brian. *Fathering the Unthinkable: Masculinity, Scientists and the Nuclear Arms Race*. London: Pluto Press, 1983.

Elbow, Peter. *Embracing Contraries*. New York: Oxford University Press, 1986.

Enloe, Cynthia. *Does Khaki Become You? The Militarization of Women's Lives*. London: South End Press, 1983.

Falk, Richard A. *A Study of Future Worlds*. New York: Free Press, 1975.

—— and Samuel S. Kim. *The War System: An Interdisciplinary Approach*. Boulder, Colo.: Westview Press, 1980.

Fisher, Roger and William Ury. *Getting To Yes: Negotiating Agreement without Giving In*. Boston: Houghton Mifflin, 1981.

—— and Scott Brown. *Getting Together: Building a Relationship that Gets to Yes*. New York: Houghton Mifflin, 1988.

Forcey, Linda R. *Mothers of Sons: Toward an Understanding of Responsibility*. New York: Praeger, 1987.

Freire, Paulo. *Pedagogy of the Oppressed*. New York: Herder and Herder, 1970.

Galtung, Johan, "Violence, Peace, and Peace Research," *Journal of Peace Research, 6 (1961):167–191*.

Garcia, Celina. "Androgyny and Peace Education." *Bulletin of Peace Proposals* 2 (1981) 163–178.

Gilligan, Carol. *In a Different Voice*. Cambridge, Mass.: Harvard University Press, 1982.

Gilpin, Robert. *War and Change in International Politics*. New York: Cambridge University Press, 1981.

Gleick, James. *Chaos: Making a New Science*. New York: Viking, 1987.

Glossop, Ronald J. *Confronting War: An Examination of Humanity's Most Pressing Problems*. Jefferson, N.C.: McFarland, 1983.

Gordon, Haim and Leonard Grob, eds. *Education for Peace: Testimonies from World Religions*. Maryknoll, N.Y.: Orbis Books, 1988.

Greene, Maxine. *The Dialectic of Freedom*. New York: Teachers College Press, 1988.

Greenwald, David S. and Steven J. Zeitlin. *No Reason to Talk About It: Families Confront the Nuclear Taboo*. New York: W. W. Norton, 1987.

Gregory, Donna, ed. *The Nuclear Predicament: A Sourcebook*. New York: St. Martin's, 1986.

Gromyko, Anatoly and Martin Hellman. *Breakthrough: Emerging New Thinking: Soviet and Western Scholars Issue a Challenge to Build a World Beyond War*. New York: Walker; Moscow: Novosti, 1987.

Harding, Sandra. *The Science Question in Feminism*. Ithaca, N.Y.: Cornell University Press, 1986.

Harris, Ian M. *Peace Education*. Jefferson, N.C.: McFarland, 1988.

Hartsock, Nancy. *Money, Sex, and Power: Toward a Feminist Historical Materialism*. New York: Longman, 1983.

Howard, Michael. *War in European History*. New York: Oxford University Press, 1976.

Isaak, Robert A. and Ralph P. Hummel. *Politics for Human Beings*. North Scituate, Mass.: Duxbury Press, 1975.

Jagger, Alison. *Feminist Politics and Human Nature*. Totowa, N.J.: Roman & Allenheld, 1983.

James, William. *Pragmatism: A New Name for Some Old Ways of Thinking*. New York: Longmans, Green and Co., 1947.

Janis, Irving L. *Victims of Groupthink*. Boston: Houghton Mifflin, 1972.

Kaplan, Fred. *The Wizards of Armageddon*. New York: Simon & Schuster, 1983.

Kaplan, Morton A. *System and Process in International Politics*. New York: John Wiley and Sons, 1957.

Keen, Sam. *Faces of the Enemy: Reflections of the Hostile Imagination*. San Francisco: Harper & Row, 1986.

Kennan, George F. *American Diplomacy 1900–1950*. Chicago: University of Chicago Press, 1951.

Kennedy, Paul. *The Rise and Fall of the Great Powers: Economic Change and Military Conflict from 1500 to 2000*. New York: Random House, 1988.

Kriesberg, Louis. *Social Conflicts*. 2d Ed. Englewood Cliffs, N.J.: Prentice Hall, 1982.

Krupat, Edward. *Psychology Is Social*. Glenview, Ill.: Scott, Foresman and Company, 1982.

Kuhn, Thomas S. *The Structure of Scientific Revolutions*. Chicago: University of Chicago Press, 1962.

Laing, R. D. *The Politics of Experience*. New York: Ballentine, 1967.

Lakey, George. *Positive Peace-Making*. Philadelphia: New Society Publishers, 1987.

Lebow, R. N., R. Jervis, and J. G. Stein, *Psychology and Deterrence*. Baltimore: Johns Hopkins University Press, 1984.

Macy, Joanna. *Despair and Personal Power in the Nuclear Age*. Philadelphia: New Society Publishers, 1983.

Mendlovitz, Saul H. *On the Creation of a Just World Order*. New York: Free Press, 1975.

Morenthau, Hans J. *Politics Among Nations: The Struggle for Power and Peace*. 2d ed. New York: Alfred A. Knopf, 1954.

Nisbet, Robert. *The Present Age: Progress and Anarchy in Modern America*. New York: Harper & Row, 1988.

Peck, M. Scott. *The Road Less Traveled*. New York: Harper, Touchstone, 1980.

Peters, Tom. *Thriving on Chaos: Handbook for a Management Revolution*. New York: Alfred A. Knopf, 1987.

Polak, Fred. *Image of the Future*. Trans. from the Dutch by Elise Boulding, one v. abr. San Francisco: Jossey-Bass, Elsevier, 1972.

Pruitt, D. G. and J. Z. Rubin. *Social Conflict: Escalation: Stalemate and Settlement*. New York: Random House, 1986.

—— and R. C. Snyder, eds. *Theory and Research on the Causes of War*. Englewood Cliffs, N.J.: Prentice-Hall, 1969.

Reardon, Betty. *Sexism and the War System*. New York: Teachers College Press, 1985.

——. *Comprehensive Peace Education*. New York: Teachers College Press, 1988.

Rifkin, Jeremy. *Declaration of a Heretic*. Boston: Routledge & Kegan Paul, 1985.

Rogers, Everett. *The Diffusion of Innovation*. New York: Free Press, 1983.

Schell, Jonathan. *The Fate of the Earth*. New York: Alfred A. Knopf, 1982.

Schwartz, Barry. *The Battle for Human Nature*. New York: W. W. Norton, 1986.

Sharp, Gene. *Making Europe Unconquerable*. Cambridge, Mass.: Ballinger, 1985.

——. *The Politics of Non-Violent Action*. Boston: P. Sargent, 1973.

Skinner, Quentin, ed. *The Return of Grand Theory in the Human Sciences*. New York: Cambridge University Press, 1985.

Sloan, Douglas. *Insights-Imagination: The Emancipation of Thought and the Modern World*. Westport, Conn.: Greenwood Press, 1983.

Smoke, Richard with Willis Harman. *Paths to Peace: Exploring the Feasibility of Sustainable Peace*. Boulder, Colo.: Westview Press, 1987.

Spender, Dale. *Women of Ideas and What Men Have Done to Them*. London: Routledge & Kegan Paul, 1982.

Teilhard de Chardin, Pierre. *The Future of Man*. Tr. by Norman Deumy. New York: Harper & Row, 1964.

Thomas, Daniel C. *Guide to Careers and Graduate Education in Peace Studies*. Amherst, Mass.: The Five College Program in Peace and World Security Studies, 1987.

Thorne, Barrie, Cheris Kramarae, and Nancy Henley, eds. *Language, Gender and Society*. Rowley, Mass.: Newbury Publishing House, 1983.

Toynbee, Arnold J. *A Study of History*. New York: Oxford University Press, 1934–1961.

UNESCO. *Thinking Ahead: UNESCO and the Challenges of Today and Tomorrow*. Paris: UNESCO, 1977.

Von Laue, Theodore H. *The Global City*. New York: Lippincott, 1969.

Wagar, W. Warren. *Building the City of Man: Outlines of a World Civilization*. New York: Grossman-Viking, 1971.

——. "Peace by Revolution: Civilian-Based Offense," in Howard F. Didsbury,

Jr., ed. *Challenge and Opportunities: From Now to 2001*. Bethesda, Md.: World Future Society, 1986.

Wallerstein, Immanuel. *The Capitalist World-Economy*. New York: Cambridge University Press, 1979.

———. *The Modern World-System*. New York: Academic Press, 1974–1980.

Waltz, Kenneth. *Man, the State and War*. New York: Columbia University Press, 1954.

———. *Theory of International Politics*. Reading, Penn.: Addison-Wesley, 1979.

Wein, Barbara, ed. *Peace and World Order Studies: A Curriculum Guide*. New York: World Policy Institute, 1984.

Wells, H. G. *The Open Conspiracy: Blue Prints for a World Revolution*. New York: Doubleday, Doran, 1928.

———. *Washington and the Riddle of Peace*. New York, 1922.

White, Ralph K. *Fearful Warriors: A Psychological Profile of U.S.-Soviet Relations*. New York: Free Press, 1984.

Woolf, Virginia. *Three Guineas*. London: The Hogarth Press, 1938; Repr. New York: Harcourt, Brace, Jovanovich, 1966.

Wright, Quincy. *A Study of War*. 2 vols. Chicago: University of Chicago Press, 1965.

Yankelovich, Daniel and Sidney Harman. *Starting with the People*. Boston: Houghton Mifflin, 1988.

Ziegler, Warren. *A Mindbook of Exercises for Futures Inventors*. Denver, Colo.: Futures Invention Associates, 1982.

Zinn, Howard. *A People's History of the United States*. New York: Harper & Row, 1980.

Zuckerman, Lord Solly. *Nuclear Illusions and Reality*. New York: Viking Press, 1982.

Index

nuclear strategic thinking, 33–36, 39–64; defense intellectuals and, 39–64

organic process of peace, 20–22
"An Orientation to a World Beyond War," 89
Osgood, Charles Egerton, 153

pacifism, 28
PAF study, 122, 128
Palmer, Glenn, 12, 177–88
paradigm(s), of peace, 8, 15–25
Parker, G., 115
patriarchy metaphors in nuclear discourse, 46–47
peace: conflict and, 177–88; conflict resolution strategies, 163–73; conflict spiral model, 153–54; cooperation and, 177–88; definitions of, 6–8; as dynamic organic process, 20–22; education and, 22–24; feminists and, 10–11; game theory and, 177–88; international conflicts and, 165–66; in international context, 169–70; interpersonal factors affecting, 163–73; Israeli-Egyptian conflict, 169; low-intensity conflict as threat to, 113–20; meanings of, 6–8; minimum deterence of war and, 7; negative peace, 6–8; nuclear policy and, 113–15; organic process of, 20–22; paradigm of, 8, 15–25; paradigms of, 15–25; patriarchal effects on, 99–105; peace imagery, 73–83; politics of, 8–11; positive peace, 6–8; problem solving and, 149–61; rational basis for hope and, 203–16; realist view, 7; strategies for studies of, 11–13; structural factors, 163–73; structuralism and, 197–202; studies of, 3–13; United Nations and international conflicts, 166–67; utopian imagery and, 73–75; women's attitudes toward, 97–110; World War I lessons, 189–94. See also peace studies

peacemaking, conflict resolution and, 170–73
peace studies, 3–13, 18–20; authentic inquiry as primary method of, 23; changing metaphors in, 24; curricula, 6–7; defined, 4–6; education as life enhancement, 22–24; essential impulse of, 28; language and, 18–20; objectives of, 5–6; practitioners of, 4–5; strategies for, 11–13. See also peace
perestroika, 9
personality factors. See interpersonal factors
phallic imagery. See sexual metaphors
Physicians for Social Responsibility, 89
Polak, F., 73, 76, 81
political changes related to personal changes, 18, 24–25
politics: definition of, 8; electoral, 3; of peace, 8–11; Politics Among Nations (Morgenthau), 31
positive peace, 6–8
power, women and, 99–101
Prisoner's Dilemma. See game theory
problem solving: conflict escalation and, 149–61; definition of, 157; outcomes of, 158–61
Pruitt, Dean G., 12, 21, 149–61
Public Agenda Foundation (PAF) study, 122, 128
public attitudes, ATS survey findings of, 122–32

Quader, Abdul, 165, 171
Quandt, William B., 169

Raiffa, Howard, 172
Reardon, Betty A., 6, 15–25
revisionist policies, 31
Rifkin, Jeremy, 21
Rousseau, Jean-Jacques, 178
Rubin, J. Z., 151, 160
Rummel, Rudolph, 171
Russett, Bruce, 168

Sackman, G. L., 9, 87
Sadat, Anwar, 169
St. Augustine, 17
Sarkesian, Sam, 118
Scarry, E., 62
Schell, Jonathan, 89
Schenitzki, D. P., 160
Schultz, George, 119
sexuality: division of labor and, 106–8; sexual harassment, 103–4
sexual metaphors, 42–47; and the arms race, 42–47; phallic imagery, 44–45; "virginity" as metaphor in nuclear discourse, 46–47
Shaffer, Harry G., 205
Shakespeare, William, 17
Sloan, Douglas, 21
Smoke, Richard, 9, 121–35
Smoker, Paul, 172
social interactions, rules regarding, 100–102
social psychological processes. See interpersonal factors
social violence, types of, 138–40
sociology of knowledge, 11
Socrates, 5
South Africa, women in, 97
Soviet Union: cold war with U.S., 150–54; Gorbachev's policies and, 125–30; INF agreement, 113–15; Prisoner's Dilemma and, 182–88; rational basis for hope and, 203–16; Third World and, 142–44; U.S. relations with, 121–22
Spencer, H., 74
spiral model, of conflicts, 153–54
Starr, Harvey, 168
State University of New York at Binghamton, 7
Stimson, Henry, 49
Strategic Defense Initiative, 93
strategies, for peace, 11–13
structural change model, of conflicts, 154
structural factors, peace and, 163, 168–73
structuralism, 197–202

structuralist perspective of peace studies, 11–12
subjective factors. See interpersonal factors
Sylvester, Christine, 10, 20
systematic perspective of peace studies, 11–12
systems analysis in peace studies, 11

Tacitus, 21
Teilhard de Chardin, P., 74
Teller, Edward, 49
Third World, peace movements in, 142–44
Thirty Years' War, 141
Thomas, Daniel C., 4, 14
Touval, Saadia, 169

UNITA, 119
United Nations, international conflicts and, 166–67
United Provinces, in nineteenth century, 140
United States: cold war with Soviet Union, 150–54; deterrence strategy, 116–19; INF agreement, 113–15; "new thinking of," 121–35; rational basis for hope and, 203–16; social violence in, 138–40; Soviet relations following World War II with, 142–44; Soviet relations with, 121–22; "Vietnam syndrome," 114
Ury, William, 172
Utne, B. B., 20
utopian imagery, 73–75

Valenti, JoAnn, 203
"Vietnam syndrome," 114

Wagar, Warren, 11, 20–21, 197–202
Wallace, Michael, 172
Wallerstein, Immanuel, 10, 137–45
war: the arms race, 33–36; bargaining power and, 29–30, 32–33; cold war, 150–54; conflict escalation and, 149–61; connection with maintaining peace, 27–37; conven-

About the Editor and Contributors

LINDA RENNIE FORCEY, Associate Professor at the State University of New York at Binghamton, is coordinator of the Peace Studies Concentration and director of the Peace Studies Education Center at Binghamton. She has written in the areas of women's and peace studies.

DONALD S. BIRN, Professor of History at the State University of New York at Albany, has written about the League of Nations Union, and is currently studying cultural propaganda. He has been active in peace studies programs for a number of years.

ELISE BOULDING, Professor Emerita of Dartmouth College, is a sociologist and peace activist, whose research includes numerous transnational and comparative cross-national studies on conflict and peace, development, family life, and women in society.

CAROL COHN is Senior Research Fellow at the Center for Psychological Studies in the Nuclear Age at the Harvard University Medical School. She is currently working on a discourse analysis of nuclear strategic thinking, and a critique of its role in political culture.

WILLIAM RICK FRY is a social psychologist at Youngstown University. He has published and done research in the field of negotiation studies.

CHARLES HAUSS is Professor of Political Science and Co-Chair of the Program in Soviet Studies at Colby College. His teaching and research areas of interest are in French politics and peace studies.

MICHAEL T. KLARE is Director and Associate Professor of the Five College Program in Peace and World Security Studies, based at Hampshire College in Amherst, Massachusetts, and defense correspondent for *The Nation*.

LOUIS KRIESBERG, Professor of Sociology at Syracuse University, is director of the program on the Analysis and Resolution of Conflicts. He has written numerous articles on social conflict, and is editor of an annual series entitled *Research in Social Movements, Conflicts, and Change*.

HAL NIEBURG is Professor of Political Science at the State University of New York at Binghamton. He is well known for his work on public opinion and popular culture in the United States.

GLENN PALMER, Assistant Professor of Political Science at the State University of New York at Binghamton, teaches and publishes in the international relations field.

DEAN G. PRUITT, Professor of Psychology at the State University of New York at Buffalo, is author of many books and articles on conflict resolution and negotiation. His current research is on the process of community mediation.

BETTY A. REARDON, Director of the Peace Education Program at Teachers College, Columbia University, also serves as director of Peacemaking in Education for Ecumenical Ministries in Education. She has been nationally and internationally involved in both the practical and theoretical aspects of peace education, and has published widely in the field.

GEORGE L. SACKMAN is Professor of Engineering at the State University of New York at Binghamton. He had previously taught at the Naval Postgraduate School, Monterey, California. His areas of research interest include signal processing, microwaves, and ultrasonic image systems. He has been active in the Beyond War movement since 1983.

RICHARD SMOKE is Research Director of the Center for Foreign Policy Development and Professor of Political Science, both at Brown University.

CHRISTINE SYLVESTER is Associate Professor of Political Science at Northern Arizona University. Her areas of research interest include the politics of southern Africa and women's studies.

W. WARREN WAGAR is Distinguished Teaching Professor of History at the State University of New York at Binghamton, where he teaches courses on World War II and the history of the future. He publishes widely in the field of intellectual history and future studies.

IMMANUEL WALLERSTEIN is an internationally known scholar, Distinguished Professor of Sociology, and Director of the Fernand Braudel Center for the Study of Economies, Historical Systems, and Civilizations at the State University of New York at Binghamton.

DANIEL YANKELOVICH is President of the Public Agenda Foundation and Chairman of The Daniel Yankelovich Group Inc.